# TERRORISM, GOVERNMENT, AND LAW

# TERRORISM, GOVERNMENT, AND LAW

## National Authority and Local Autonomy in the War on Terror

Edited by
**SUSAN N. HERMAN**
and
**PAUL FINKELMAN**

**PSI Reports**

PRAEGER SECURITY INTERNATIONAL
Westport, Connecticut • London

**Library of Congress Cataloging-in-Publication Data**

Terrorism, government, and law : national authority and local autonomy in the War on Terror / edited by Susan N. Herman and Paul Finkelman.
    p.  cm.
  Includes bibliographical references and index.
  ISBN 978–0–313–34733–7 (alk. paper)
  1. War and emergency powers—United States.  2. Terrorism—United States.  3. Executive power—United States.  4. Civil rights—United States.  5. War on Terrorism, 2001—Law and legislation—United States.  6. Federal government—United States.  7. Intergovernmental cooperation—United States.  I. Herman, Susan N.  II. Finkelman, Paul, 1949–
  KF5060.T47   2008
  345.73′02—dc22      2007048296

British Library Cataloguing in Publication Data is available.



Library of Congress Catalog Card Number: 2007048296
ISBN-13: 978–0–313–34733–7

First published in 2008

Praeger Security International, 88 Post Road West, Westport, CT 06881
An imprint of Greenwood Publishing Group, Inc.
www.praeger.com

Printed in the United States of America

The paper used in this book complies with the Permanent Paper Standard issued by the National Information Standards Organization (Z39.48–1984).

10 9 8 7 6 5 4 3 2 1

**Copyright Acknowledgments**

The following articles appeared, in earlier versions, in the *Brooklyn Law Review* in 2004 (David G. Trager Public Policy Symposium: "Our New Federalism? National Authority and Local Autonomy in the War on Terror," volume 69 pages 1201–1419) and are reprinted with permission: Ann Althouse, "The Vigor of Anti-Commandeering Doctrine in Times of Terror," *Brooklyn Law Review* 69 (2004): 1231–1275; Vikram Amar, "Converse 1983 Suits: An Idea Whose Time Has Arrived," *Brooklyn Law Review* 69 (2004): 1369–1398; Erwin Chemerinsky, "Empowering States Where It Matters: A Different Approach to Preemption," *Brooklyn Law Review* 69 (2004): 1313–1333; Ronald Chen, "State Incarceration of Federal Prisoners After September 11: Whose Jail Is It Anyway?" *Brooklyn Law Review* 69 (2004): 1335–1367; Paul Finkelman, "The Roots of *Printz*: Proslavery Constitutionalism, National Law Enforcement, Federalism, and Local Cooperation," *Brooklyn Law Review* 69 (2004): 1399–1419; Susan N. Herman, "Introduction," *Brooklyn Law Review* 69 (2004): 1201–1229; Ernest Young, "Welcome to the Dark Side: Liberals Rediscover Federalism in the Wake of the War on Terror," *Brooklyn Law Review* 69 (2004): 1277–1311.

An earlier version of Susan N. Herman, "Collapsing Spheres: Joint Terrorism Task Forces, Federalism, and the War on Terror," appeared in the *Willamette Law Review* in 2005 (volume 41, pages 941–969) and is reprinted with permission.

An earlier version of Jason Mazzone, "The Security Constitution," appeared in the *UCLA Law Review* in 2005 (volume 53, pages 29–151) and is reprinted with permission.

# Contents

# Introduction: National Authority and Local Autonomy in the War on Terror

Susan N. Herman

If the FBI asks local law enforcement agencies to interrogate Arab and Muslim men within their jurisdictions, may the Detroit Chief of Police decline to do so, or may the federal government require him to assist in nation-wide antiterrorism efforts? Would allowing the federal government to insist on local assistance be an example of undesirable federal overreaching or desirable national uniformity? If the FBI engages in a Joint Terrorism Task Force with local law enforcement officials in Portland, Oregon, may Portland police officers ignore surveillance-limiting Oregon state laws that apply to them but would not apply to the FBI? May those officers be bound to secrecy and prohibited from telling their employers if their colleagues have violated state law? If the city of Arcata, California, disapproves of powers the USA Patriot Act gives federal investigators, may it prohibit its law enforcement personnel from helping the FBI conduct investigations in Arcata, imposing a fine on them if they do so?

Questions about the ability of state and local governments to make their own policy choices form an important subset of questions in our national conversation about how far the federal government can or should go in its antiterrorism efforts. Clashes between claims of national authority and claims of local autonomy raise political questions, which play out within a framework of constitutional law.

The United States Constitution offers four potent strategies for preventing overreaching by the federal government. First, the Bill of Rights and subsequent amendments provide rights that individuals may claim in order to check the government. Rights are what most people think of when they think of the Constitution, but they are only one of a number of constitutional ideas about how to contain government and protect liberty. Second, in the body of the original Constitution, Articles I, II, and III create an elaborate system of checks and balances so that the power of the federal government will be shared by the executive, legislative, and judicial branches. Under this hydraulic system, the three branches must sometimes cooperate in order to take action, and sometimes compete to check one another's actions. This system of compelled cooperation and competition also provides a check on federal government actions by ensuring that no one branch wields too much unilateral power. Third, the Articles include particular structural provisions that complement individual rights by providing, for example, that trials must be by jury[1] or that the writ of habeas corpus cannot be suspended except in limited exceptional circumstances.[2] These provisions are part of a design that can prevent rights questions from even arising by imposing ex ante limitations on the choices various branches of the federal government may make, even when all branches concur. Finally, the Articles and amendments combine to "split the atom of sovereignty"[3] between the federal and state governments, creating a vertical check on the federal government that complements the horizontal check on each branch.

The shock waves generated on September 11, 2001, have profoundly challenged our previous understandings about the meaning of our Constitution in each one of these areas. There has been considerable discussion about the shape of our post-9/11 Constitution in the first three areas: (1) Should we as a nation be willing to recalibrate what we thought was the proper balance between our civil liberties and our security?[4] (2) Should we as a nation be willing to allow the President to make unilateral decisions regarding issues such as whether "enemy combatants" may be tried before military tribunals rather than the civil courts?[5] and (3) Do particular constitutional provisions, like the Suspension Clause of Article I prohibiting Congress from suspending the writ of habeas corpus except in cases of invasion or rebellion, limit the ability of Congress to strip the federal courts of jurisdiction to hear constitutional claims raised by Guantanamo detainees?[6] This book aims to start a broader conversation about the post-9/11 role of the fourth constitutional fail-safe, federalism, which is just as important as the first three but beneath the radar of most people who are not experts in constitutional law and even many who are.

There have been a few preliminary conversations about the manner in which the involvement of state and local governments in the war on terror may be challenging our received notions about the balance of power between the federal and state/local governments. In a *New York Times* article written in September 2001, Linda Greenhouse first observed that such issues might exist. Her article posed the question of whether recent Supreme Court decisions about the Constitution's balance of national and local power, which systematically tended to limit federal power and to channel decision-making authority to the states, might be questioned or modified to afford more authority to the federal government and less local choice in the wake of 9/11.[7] In November 2003, Brooklyn Law School held a symposium, the David G. Trager Public Policy Symposium, at which many of the authors represented in this volume began offering their own answers to some of the questions raised by Greenhouse, and posed many new questions of their own.[8]

To what extent might the increased preeminence of the federal government and its particular activities in connection with the war on terror affect our understanding of the proper relationship between the federal and state or local governments? The boundaries of federalism are critical to the war on terror because the Supreme Court's case law currently imposes some limits on how far the federal government may go in enlisting state and local law enforcement officials in their terrorism investigations. Unless the Court were to create an exception to current doctrine for antiterrorism investigations, for example, state and local law enforcement officials may decide for themselves whether they wish to question suspects designated by the FBI, because they are protected against federal "commandeering" of their officials.[9] Future decisions might or might not impose additional limitations on federal attempts to enlist state or local law enforcement officials. Some argue, for example, that the Constitution should be interpreted to prohibit state and local officials from enforcing immigration law, even on a voluntary basis.[10] How such limitations might apply to antiterrorism efforts is a question that has not yet been confronted by the courts. Conversely, the Supreme Court's constitutional interpretations also limit how far state and local governments can go in refusing to cooperate with federal investigative efforts. This body of law could also affect antiterrorism investigations if, for example, local law enforcement officials were prohibited from refusing to disclose the immigration status of their local residents to federal officials. Even if local law enforcement personnel may not themselves be commandeered, may they refuse to provide federal investigators access to their local databanks?

Some of the authors in this volume also observe that our structures of federalism have the potential to serve as an alternative check on federal overreaching if, as some believe likely, the courts prove to be unduly reluctant to find that various federal antiterrorism actions violate rights or other provisions of the Constitution. State and local governments may, to the extent that constitutional doctrine allows them to do so, reflect their own residents' views by creating oases of different approaches in individual states or localities. People around the country may also speak to the national government through the mediation of their state and local governments, rather than directly through election or lobbying of federal officials, or through judicial rights-based challenges. Grassroots movements, begun in narrow pockets of dissent, could ultimately spread and generate a different national consensus. The essence of federalism is to allow the states to act as "laboratories"[11] that can develop new approaches to challenge preexisting national hegemony.

The key question is to what extent states and localities will be empowered to make their own choices. Pre-9/11 constitutional law regarding the relationship between national authority and local autonomy tended to be dominated by justices and scholars at the conservative end of the political spectrum, who tended to disfavor big centralized government and to champion local choice.[12] Their judicially crafted limitations on federal government authority were generally opposed by those at the other end of the political spectrum, who have tended to favor a strong federal role in areas like civil rights enforcement and environmental regulation, and to be skeptical of states' rights arguments.[13] The Supreme Court applied the federalism-based limitations it developed during the 1990s to prevent Congress from enacting gun control laws,[14] remedies for violence against women,[15] and particular remedies for civil rights violations.[16] Now that the federal government may be perceived by those toward the left of the political spectrum as a greater threat to individual liberty, the potential antidote of local autonomy may seem more attractive to that constituency than it did during periods when "states' rights" arguments were associated with arch segregationists. And now that the federal government's agenda is to promote national security, centralized federal authority may seem more essential to those who believed that individual states should be allowed to opt out of federal schemes for civil rights or labor law enforcement. To what extent will judges and scholars who had identified themselves with a position on the law of federalism rethink their commitments and take up the structural arguments of the other side? Might judges who categorically declared that the federal government may never "commandeer" state or local officials change their minds and create an exception for antiterrorism investigations, or will they adhere to what they had described as an absolute neutral principle? Will the Supreme Court's law of federalism affect the war on terror, or will the war on terror affect our law or structures of federalism?

This book is designed to foster an important national conversation on the subject of federalism and the war on terror. To provide a context for readers, I will begin by providing some background on the constitutional law of federalism pre-9/11.

## THE CURRENT LAW OF FEDERALISM: OF *PRINTZ* AND PREEMPTION

Questions about when state and local governments may autonomously create and enforce their own laws and when they can be required to accede to and even cooperate with federal law have been central throughout the history of our country. One impetus for the drafting of the Constitution was to enhance the role the federal government had played under the Articles of Confederation, which had allowed the states to exercise considerable sovereignty.[17] The Constitution itself is fairly cryptic about the nature of the relationship between the federal and state governments. The Supremacy Clause of Article VI is clear in stating that laws consonant with the Constitution will be supreme, regardless of whether some states disagree with those laws.[18] Other provisions set some parameters for allocating decision-making authority. Article I, section 8, provides an affirmative list of powers granted to Congress, ranging from the power to regulate interstate commerce to the power to coin money and to declare war,[19] on the theory that the federal government may wield only those powers enumerated in the Constitution. Article I, section 9, negatively lists a number of things Congress may not do, like suspend habeas corpus, grant titles of nobility, or privilege the ports of one state over another. Article I, section 10, then prohibits the states from exercising power in certain areas (like coining money and declaring war) where federal choices are intended to be exclusive. Despite this general attempt to define the allocation of powers, it is not always easy to determine when a specific piece of legislation is appropriately considered to be on Congress's list.[20] It can be equally difficult to decide the extent to which the Tenth Amendment, which reserves to "the states respectively or the people thereof" the powers not conferred on the federal government,[21] limits the federal government's choices, or guarantees the states spheres of autonomy the federal government may not invade. The Supreme Court, fondly describing the balance of power the Constitution attempted to strike as "Our Federalism,"[22] has taken different positions over the years in calibrating how that balance is to be attained.

## FEDERALISM PRE-9/11

When the Constitution was young, foundational Supreme Court opinions written by Justices John Marshall and Joseph Story nurtured the newborn federal government and protected it against defiant claims of autonomy raised by powerful states. Maryland wanted to tax the Bank of the United States as a business within its state lines, but in 1819, in *McCulloch v. Maryland*,[23] Justice Marshall held that this claim of state prerogative unduly threatened federal interests as determined by Congress. The Supremacy Clause, as interpreted by Marshall, prevented citizens or individual states from impeding a federal enterprise. Marshall deemed Maryland's action a threat to federal interests because the power to tax is the power to destroy. Marshall also expressed concern about the fairness of Maryland's action, seeing another version of the detested taxation without representation in a tax that would be paid by those beyond Maryland's borders but benefit only those within Maryland. In that same case, Marshall concluded that Congress had sufficient power under Article I, section 8, of the Constitution to create the Bank of the United States, by generously interpreting the "Necessary and Proper" Clause as an enhancement rather than a constriction of Congress's powers.[24] Congress was afforded ample discretion to decide how to interpret the powers listed in Article I, section 8.

*Martin v. Hunter's Lessee*,[25] decided in 1816, also championed national authority at the expense of local decision-making. The Supreme Court ruled against Virginia's claim that its courts should be allowed to decide a dispute about the ownership of Virginia real estate without Supreme Court interference, on the ground that interpretation of a federal treaty was involved. The Court held that the United States Supreme Court must have the final authority to interpret a federal treaty even if that meant overruling the highest court in Virginia. In both of these cases, the Articles of the Constitution, which predated the Bill of Rights, were interpreted as allowing the federal government to subordinate local interests to its own national interests not because any individual had a right that Maryland or

Virginia had violated, but because of the structures of government the Constitution had created. The need for national uniformity in both of these cases trumped any claim of local autonomy.

The profoundly divisive issue of slavery pitted national authority against state autonomy in surprising ways. Congress and the Supreme Court set out to enforce the Constitution's uneasy compromise, which allowed states to decide for themselves whether or not to permit slavery, by limiting the prerogatives of the free states with respect to fugitive slaves. Pennsylvania, for example, recognized that even as a free state it was required to comply with the federal Fugitive Slave Law, but decided to implement its own antislavery policies by requiring meaningful process and proof before allowing an alleged fugitive slave to be seized in Pennsylvania and extradited to a slave state. The Supreme Court held that the federal law preempted even Pennsylvania's procedural modifications.[26] Even more notoriously, the Court held that the federal Constitution prevented Congress from making Dred Scott a free man when he moved to a free territory, on the ground that Scott's owner had a federal constitutional right to the "property" another state had given him the legal right to own.[27] These fundamental clashes over slavery and states' rights ultimately could not successfully be contained or resolved within the structure the Constitution had provided, and so they erupted into war.

Following the Civil War, the Reconstruction Era Amendments to the Constitution fundamentally rearranged the relationship between the federal and the state governments.[28] With newly minted constitutional limitations imposed on the states, the federal government was empowered to take the lead in promoting a newly expanded national agenda, with respect to matters like racial equality, even over the most adamant resistance of some state and local governments. Areas where the federal government could preempt local law, and where the states' own choices could be overruled grew exponentially. The United States Supreme Court invalidated, for example, a West Virginia statute mandating racist jury selection,[29] while Congress enacted statutes affording individuals civil rights enforceable by the Department of Justice in federal court.[30]

During the twentieth century, a long series of Supreme Court cases known to all first-year Constitutional Law students reacted to increasing federal regulation by first resisting and eventually approving Congress's power to enact federal labor laws and other legislation reflecting a desire for uniform national policies under the Commerce Clause.[31] By mid-century, it appeared that the courts, following the lead of John Marshall in *McCulloch*, would not second-guess Congress's political decisions about what to regulate on a national level. But in another historic series of decisions beginning in 1995, the Supreme Court, under the leadership of Chief Justice William Rehnquist, revived judicially enforced limitations on federal power, setting out constitutional rules that circumscribed the relationship between the federal and state and local governments and limited Congress's power both under the Commerce Clause[32] and the Fourteenth Amendment.[33]

## Local Autonomy: The *Printz* Principle

The current law of federalism empowers state and local governments, but only within limits. On the one hand, the Rehnquist Court derived from the Tenth Amendment a rule that the federal government is prohibited from "commandeering" local law enforcement officials.[34] In the main case elucidating this principle, *Printz v. United States*,[35] the Court found unconstitutional a provision of the federal Brady Act that would have required local law enforcement officials to assist in conducting background checks before issuance of a gun permit. The Court reasoned that the states, as discrete sovereigns, must have the right to choose whether or not to participate in a federal enforcement program. State employees are paid with state resources and therefore, according to Justice Antonin Scalia, author of the majority opinion in *Printz*, must always have the right to decline to implement a federal program. This decision split the Court, five Justices to four. In a dissenting opinion written on behalf of four members of the Court, Justice John Paul Stevens argued that if the federal interest were sufficiently grave, both logic and history argued for allowing the federal government to enlist local law enforcement agents in implementing a program representing the political will of the nation as a whole.[36] Uncannily, Stevens anticipated in 1997 that a battle against international terrorism might provide an occasion for the federal government to seek the assistance of local law enforcement officials.[37] Justice Scalia's majority opinion, however, took the position that there could be no balancing and no exceptions to the anti-commandeering principle because the structures of the Constitution are fixed and inviolate and cannot be altered depending on the nature of the federal interest at stake.[38]

## Federal Supremacy: The *Olmstead* Principle

On the one hand, *Printz* says that state and local governments should be allowed to choose when to lend their assistance to a federal investigation. But, on the other hand, state and local governments may not prohibit federal investigators from operating within their jurisdictions, even when the federal agents' actions would violate state law. The Supreme Court has held that, because of the Supremacy Clause,[39] the federal government may preempt state or local laws that thwart national interests.[40] In the classic case of *Olmstead v. United States*,[41] for example, the Court ruled that the federal government could with impunity ignore a Washington state statute that prohibited wiretapping. The federal agents were permitted to use evidence of bootlegging, which they had obtained by wiretapping Olmstead's telephone in disregard of the state law because the Supremacy Clause entitled them to override local laws in promoting their national agenda. Federal agents could use evidence obtained within the state of Washington by wiretapping telephones even though state agents would not have been permitted to do so. In light of *Olmstead*, the federal government unquestionably has the power to send its own FBI agents into Detroit or to Portland, Oregon, to conduct interrogations in any manner that is consistent with federal law, regardless of the wishes of the Detroit Chief of Police or the restrictions of Oregon state law. *Printz* prohibits commandeering local law enforcement officials; it does not prohibit circumventing or ignoring them.

## FEDERALISM POST-9/11

The examples described below, each involving a local challenge to federal policy in antiterrorism investigations, pose interesting and important questions about when state/local or federal policy will prevail.

### Local Autonomy? Police Chiefs' Refusal to Participate in FBI Interviews

In the fall of 2001, federalism first challenged federal hegemony in combating terrorism when the FBI requested the assistance of local law enforcement officials in questioning some 5,000 Arab and Muslim men around the country. In November, 2001, as briefly described above, Attorney General John Ashcroft requested the assistance of local police departments in interviewing, on the basis of a list compiled by the FBI, foreign men of Middle Eastern origin living within their communities in order to determine whether any of these men presented a terrorist threat or had useful information about potential terrorists. While many police departments agreed to the Attorney General's request, some refused and others expressed concerns, either normative concerns about the fairness of the interrogation program or practical concerns about whether acting as de facto federal agents would impede their ability to do their own jobs, or cause hostile reactions in communities that might react adversely to the interrogation program. Andrew Kirkland, Acting Chief of Police in Portland, Oregon, expressed concern that his officers could not interview individuals who were named on the FBI's list but not suspected of any specific crime because state law required a showing of probable cause prior to conducting such interviews.[42] In Detroit, Police Chief Charles Wilson, citing constitutional concerns and limited resources, refused to deploy his officers to "go out and treat people like criminals."[43] In Tucson, Captain John Leavitt agreed to cooperate with the Attorney General's request only if it did not violate local guidelines prohibiting racial profiling.[44] Chicago police, fearful of souring relationships with local immigrant communities, initially refused to conduct interviews but later worked out a plan with the FBI to provide assistance after the U.S. Attorney's Office first sent an informational letter to the interview subjects.[45]

Because *Printz* had held that local officers could not be "commandeered" to help enforce federal gun control laws, federal and local officials alike assumed that the local law enforcement agents could choose whether or not to cooperate with the FBI interrogation program and could not be forced to do so. If the FBI wished to have Muslim and Arab men interrogated in those cities therefore, agents would either have to negotiate with local law enforcement officials to gain their cooperation, or go to Detroit and Portland to conduct the interrogations themselves. In the fall of 2001, legal authority was not needed to compel the cooperation of most local law enforcement officials throughout the nation. As a result of public outrage in response to his reference to state law, Kirkland negotiated with the FBI to develop a script of questions he felt could be asked consistently with state law; state and county law authorities also opined that the state law should not be interpreted to preclude the FBI's desired interrogations.[46] So the question of whether the Court might reject Justice Scalia's absolutist view of state prerogatives over their own employees became moot. By the same token, there was no need for federal agents to seek to preempt Oregon's state law prohibiting state or local agents from conducting such interrogations without probable cause. Politics solved what could have become a thorny legal problem.

## Local Resistance to the Patriot Act: Bill of Rights Defense Committee Resolutions

The facet of federalism that limits the impact of local autonomy has also come into play in the war on terror as state and local governments have sought to make their own diverse decisions about whether federal antiterrorism legislation goes too far in infringing privacy, liberty, free speech, or freedom of association. Between 2002 and 2007, over 400 cities, towns, and villages, beginning with Ann Arbor, Michigan, plus eight states (Alaska, California, Colorado, Hawaii, Idaho, Maine, Montana, and Vermont) enacted variations on an ACLU-inspired Bill of Rights Defense Committee (BORDC) resolution expressing disagreement with various Patriot Act provisions and sometimes prohibiting local officials from assisting in federal enforcement efforts in various ways.[47]

The state resolutions call on the United States Congress to repeal provisions of the Patriot Act that allegedly infringe constitutional rights and sometimes seek to curtail local cooperation with the Act's provisions. The Hawaii resolution, for example, prohibited the use of state resources for activities under the Patriot Act that would infringe individuals' constitutional rights, including monitoring by law enforcement of political and religious gatherings and eavesdropping on communications between lawyers and their clients.[48] The Alaska resolution prohibited the state's law enforcement and other agencies from investigating individuals and organizations in the absence of a reasonable suspicion of criminal activity, from using state resources to implement federal immigration law, and from using racial profiling except to locate a specific suspect described with reference to the suspect's race.[49] The Vermont resolution, responding to the provision of the Patriot Act allowing federal officials to obtain an individual's library records, requested that the office of the Vermont Attorney General provide legal support to any local library refusing to turn over a patron's records.[50]

The city and town resolutions contain an even greater variety of provisions expressing local opposition to the Patriot Act and limiting the participation of local officials in the Act's enforcement. The Detroit resolution, passed on December 6, 2002, for example, expressed concern that the Patriot Act undermined the liberties of local residents of Arab, Muslim, or South Asian descent and affirmed the city's strong support for civil liberties; requested local libraries to warn their patrons that federal officers might obtain their library records; and directed the Detroit City Clerk to generate every six months a summary of all information provided to the federal government under the Patriot Act.[51] The Portland, Oregon, resolution of October 29, 2003 also affirmed that city's support for civil liberties; directed the city's police to refrain from enforcing federal immigration law and from investigating individuals and groups without particularized suspicion of criminal activity; and directed the City Attorney to disclose to the public every three months information about individuals detained on suspicion of terrorist activity and any sharing of information with federal officials.[52] Many communities objected to their law enforcement officers assisting in enforcement of federal immigration laws, on the theory that even illegal immigrants should be encouraged to use city or state services without fear if they wish to report a crime, provide information, or use public health services. Most controversially, an Arcata, California law imposed a fine of $57 on any city official who assists in Patriot Act enforcement.[53]

To the extent that these resolutions are expressions of local opinion about national policy questions, history provides precedents for believing that such expressions are not only permissible but also essential to our structures of government. Americans have organized on the local level from the time of the Committees of Correspondence, which were instrumental in fomenting the Revolution. Local declarations of independence provided a model for the national Declaration of Independence. One of the first discussions of the BORDC resolutions to have been published, by author Vikram Amar,[54] observed that the tradition of local governments weighing in on national policy, dating back to the eighteenth century, offers parallels to the BORDC campaign. State and local governments served as "the point of organization" against the Alien and Sedition Acts. Resolutions written by Thomas Jefferson and James Madison and adopted by the legislatures of Kentucky and Virginia, respectively, argued forcefully that these controversial federal enactments were unconstitutional for various reasons, including that the Sedition Act violated the First Amendment. During the pre-Civil War era, abolitionists used their local governmental bodies to criticize state and federal laws supporting slavery.[55] The expressive and hortatory portions of these resolutions allow state and local governments to serve as mediators between individuals who oppose federal policy and the federal government itself, as well as seedbeds with the potential to challenge and change federal law.[56]

To the extent the BORDC resolutions go beyond expression of disagreement with federal policy, however, additional questions are raised. The federal government may not be permitted to preempt local laws that govern only the conduct of state or local law enforcement officials in doing their own jobs. But, although the lines drawn by *Olmstead* and *Printz* are sharp in theory, they quickly begin to blur when applied to particular sets of facts. As a factual matter, at what point does the federal right to override local limitations on federal investigations, as sanctioned by *Olmstead*, become the illicit commandeering of local officials prohibited by *Printz*? Must a local law enforcement agency, for example, provide federal agents conducting an antiterrorism investigation access to their databanks, desk space, or copiers? Provisions of the BORDC resolutions that prohibit local law enforcement personnel from assisting in certain federal enforcement efforts, sometimes even sanctioning them for doing so, like the Arcata resolution, raise challenging questions about the nature of our federalism. May the federal government preempt a law like Arcata's on the ground that prohibiting an individual from assisting federal law enforcement agents in a federal investigation interferes with federal interests, as in *Olmstead*? Or under the principle of *Printz*, might a state successfully argue that the federal government may not interfere in a state's own internal organization by encouraging state or local employees to defy their legislature's or their agency's policy? If the legislature of Arcata, California, wishes to impose a uniform policy on its own city employees, may the federal government preempt that uniform policy by demanding that individual city employees be allowed to decide as individuals whether to cooperate with a federal investigation?[57] The role and effect of these resolutions is discussed in this volume, from opposite political vantage points, by Ann Althouse ("The Vigor of Anti-Commandeering Doctrine in Times of Terror") and Ernest Young ("Welcome to the Dark Side: Liberals Rediscover Federalism in the Wake of the War on Terror").

Some of the resolutions invite or allow local governments to draw their own conclusions about whether or not federal agents acting under Patriot Act provisions, for example, would be in violation of federal constitutional law. Vikram Amar, in his contribution to this book ("Converse 1983 Suits In Which States Police Federal Agents: An Idea Whose Time Has Arrived"), argues that this too is an appropriate role for state and local governments to play, and that federal officials should be liable in state courts for unconstitutional actions performed within the state. Allowing state and local governments to provide such additional protection for federal constitutional norms would be a dramatic development in the law of federalism, empowering state and local governments, while imposing tighter constraints on federal officials.

Federalism, at bottom, is about political accountability. The constitutional law of federalism tries to ensure that the appropriate majority can review the policy decisions and actions of its own government officials. A state or local legislature expresses the viewpoints of its constituents precisely because it is politically accountable to those constituents. Law enforcement officials are generally not directly politically accountable because they are usually hired by elected officials.

Their policy decisions and actions are often invisible to the people who pay their salaries and elect their supervisors.

Another example of this conflict between local and federal policy interests has already arisen and been litigated in the area of immigration enforcement.

## Local "Cooperation" with Immigration Enforcement and Federal Preemption

In 1989, New York City Mayor, Ed Koch, issued an Executive Order providing that no New York City officer or employee should transmit information respecting any alien to federal immigration authorities unless the disclosure was either required by law, authorized by the alien, or respecting an alien suspected by the agency of criminal activity. In 1996, Congress, in Section 642 of the federal Illegal Immigration Reform and Immigrant Responsibility Act [IIRIRA], provided that no person or agency may prohibit, or in any way restrict, a federal, state, or local government entity from sending information regarding an individual's immigration status to federal immigration officials, maintaining such information, or exchanging such information with any other Federal, State, or local government entity. New York City challenged this provision on the ground that it violates the Tenth Amendment and the prerogative of New York City to administer core functions of government, including provision of police protection and regulation of the City's own work forces. The City's concern was that undocumented aliens might fear to approach or cooperate with city agencies if they were afraid that the City would turn them over to the Immigration and Naturalization Service (INS) for deportation, and that the City would therefore be hampered in such functions as providing protection to crime victims and obtaining the cooperation of witnesses to crimes.

The District Judge rejected the City's Tenth Amendment claim that this local policy decision was among the "powers . . . reserved to the States respectively, or to the people" and ruled that the City policy was preempted.[58] The Second Circuit affirmed on a somewhat narrower ground, finding that the City's concern about protecting the confidentiality of undocumented aliens had not been expressed in a confidentiality policy of general applicability.[59]

On September 17, 2003, in response to this ruling vitiating city policy, Mayor Michael Bloomberg signed a new Executive Order governing acquisition and disclosure of a range of confidential information, including immigration status.[60] Under the new policy, a New York City officer or employee may inquire about immigration status only if (1) that status is necessary for a determination of eligibility for some program, service, or benefit, or (2) if the officer is required by law to make such inquiry. New York City law enforcement officers may not inquire about immigration status unless investigating criminal activity other than mere status as an undocumented alien, but police officers are not to inquire about the immigration status of crime victims, witnesses, or others seeking assistance. The new Executive Order also specifies under what circumstances such information may be disclosed. Immigration status generally may not be disclosed if the individual is not suspected of illegal activity other than "mere status as an undocumented alien," but may be disclosed if "such disclosure is necessary in furtherance of an investigation of potential terrorist activity."

Another clash between local and national policies regarding immigration was generated when on June 24, 2002, an internal Department of Justice (DOJ) memorandum reversed previous Department policy by asserting that state and local law enforcement officials possess at least some "inherent authority" to arrest and detain people for violations of immigration law, including civil violations.[61] DOJ requested local law enforcement cooperation as part of a "narrow anti-terrorism mission," to enhance enforcement of immigration laws by adding 650,000 state officers to the 20,000 federal border patrol agents, of whom only 1,947 have been employed for internal enforcement. Some critics question whether this devolution of federal power is constitutionally permissible.[62] Others conclude that state and local authorities lack inherent authority to arrest for civil violations of immigration law, but could enforce civil immigration laws if expressly authorized by federal and state law.[63]

As was the case with the fall 2001 interrogation program, many state and local agencies agreed to cooperate in these efforts voluntarily. Florida officials, for example, completed an agreement with the Justice Department authorizing thirty-five state troopers and other officers to arrest immigrants solely for over-staying a visa or entering the country illegally, even if they are not suspected of having committed any offense under state or local law.[64] When local officials cooperate voluntarily, Tenth Amendment issues do not arise, but other issues do. For example, would local officials enforcing federal immigration laws share the substantial immunity from prosecution that federal immigration officers enjoy?[65]

This issue continues to be a political hot potato. As one of his first actions on taking office, Governor Deval Patrick of Massachusetts rescinded the agreement the previous governor, Mitt Romney, had entered to offer state law enforcement personnel to enforce federal immigration law.[66]

Legislation introduced in the House of Representatives in November 2003 under the title Clear Law Enforcement for Criminal Alien Removal Act of 2003 (CLEAR) proposed to authorize local law enforcement officials to enforce immigration law.[67] The bill also proposed to use Congress's spending power to encourage state and local governments to participate in enforcement of immigration laws.[68] Under this proposal, two years after the date of enactment, any state or subdivision of a state that failed to have in effect a statute that expressly authorized state and local law enforcement officials "to enforce federal immigration laws in the course of carrying out the officer's law enforcement duties shall not receive any of the funds otherwise allocated to the states under 8 U.S.C. 1231(I) [Section 241(I) of the Immigration and Nationality Act]."[69] CLEAR also provided financial incentives by reallocating forfeited funds to compliant states, and sharing civil penalties collected due to state and local immigration enforcement with states and localities. Two years later, similar legislation was reintroduced as the Clear Law Enforcement for Criminal Alien Removal Act of 2005,[70] with the aim of authorizing state and local officers to enforce federal immigration law. As of the date of publication of this volume, the CLEAR Act had not been enacted.[71]

## Federal Preemption vs. State Disclosure Law: The New Jersey County Jails

Among those detained by federal authorities immediately in the aftermath of 9/11 were some 762 "special interest" aliens, primarily men from Arab or South Asian countries who were detained by the INS for varying numbers of months prior to their eventual deportation. Many of these detainees were housed in New Jersey state jails, including Hudson and Passaic County jails, pursuant to a voluntary agreement the federal government had previously entered with New Jersey state authorities to house federal detainees in New Jersey's excess jail space.

The Department of Justice refused to release the names of these special interest detainees, even when sued under the federal Freedom of Information Act.[72] A lawsuit brought in New Jersey state court by author Ronald Chen, now Public Advocate of New Jersey, took a different approach.[73] The plaintiffs sought to compel the sheriffs and wardens of the Hudson and Passaic jails to comply with a longstanding provision of New Jersey state law[74] mandating public disclosure of the identities of all jail inmates, a more explicit state counterpart to federal disclosure law. The trial court ordered the defendants to comply with the state law, staying that order for ten days at the request of the United States (which had been allowed to intervene in the litigation). The United States promptly filed an appeal and on the same day, April 17, 2002, Immigration and Naturalization (INS) Commissioner James Ziglar signed an emergency interim regulation superseding state law by prohibiting state jail officials from disclosing the identities of the detainees held on behalf of the INS, whether by contract or otherwise. The plaintiffs argued that the regulation exceeded the authority delegated to the Attorney General by Congress, violated the Administrative Procedure Act in that there had been no notice and comment period, and violated the Tenth Amendment. The New Jersey appellate court held that New Jersey law had been validly preempted and reversed the trial court's order of disclosure.[75] Chen's contribution to this book, "State Incarceration of Federal Prisoners After September 11: Whose Jail Is It Anyway?" discusses whether the appellate court had correctly found that the New Jersey disclosure law was preempted.[76] Author Erwin Chemerinsky, in "Empowering States When It Matters: A Different Approach to Preemption," argues for an approach to preemption under which an agency would not have been permitted to supersede state law in the absence of clear congressional approval.

## Preemption of Local Consent Decrees on Surveillance

In various locations around the country, consent decrees as well as local laws limit the ability of local police to monitor and infiltrate political or religious organizations. In New York City, in 1985, following litigation brought by political groups over police tactics in the 1960s and 1970s, the New York Police Department [NYPD] entered the *Handschu* Settlement.[77] Among other things, this settlement, approved by the district court judge and upheld by the Second Circuit, prohibited the police from investigating political organizations without first showing specific evidence of a pending crime by the group's members, limited the storage and dissemination of information gathered about political activities, and created procedures for citizen complaint and review.

In September 2002, New York City and the NYPD, citing changed circumstances after 9/11 and the department's need for greater freedom to investigate suspected terrorist organizations in order to prevent future attacks, asked the court to modify the consent decree. Over the opposition of the original *Handschu* plaintiffs, in early 2003 the District Court granted the city's motion, principally by rescinding the requirement that the police demonstrate evidence of pending criminal activity before investigating a group and its members.[78] On August 7, 2003, in response to the plaintiffs' complaint about police questioning of antiwar demonstrators arrested at a protest rally in Manhattan, the District Court incorporated as part of the modified decree the NYPD "Guidelines for Investigations Involving Political Activity" (which were based on FBI Guidelines).[79]

Meanwhile, a DOJ draft of proposed federal legislation dubbed "Patriot Act II," leaked to the public in early 2003, contained a provision that would have mandated discontinuance of all consent decrees that impeded terrorism investigations conducted by federal, state, or local officials. Had it been enacted, this legislation would have terminated all such decrees entered prior to September 11, 2001, including the *Handschu* Settlement.[80] This legislation had not been introduced in Congress at the time it garnered national publicity and was not introduced thereafter. In later rounds of the *Handschu* case, the District Court continued to monitor NYPD surveillance activities, modifying the order several times as circumstances changed.[81] Had the proposed "Patriot Act II" legislation been enacted, this continuing federal court involvement might not have been permissible.

## Joint Terrorism Task Forces

Additional federalism issues are presented by the Joint Terrorism Task Forces many local governments have joined, with agreements spelling out the nature of local cooperation with federal agents. Campus security guards, as well as police and sheriffs, have been deputized as federal agents. Even though these forms of cooperation are voluntary, they challenge our traditional "dual sovereignty" notions about the relationship between the federal and state/local governments. In my chapter, "Collapsing Spheres: Joint Terrorism Task Forces, Federalism, and the War on Terror," I describe the struggles over control and secrecy that culminated in Portland, Oregon, withdrawing from participation in a Joint Terrorism Task Force.

Finally, the crucial question of who will pay for post-9/11 enhanced security raises questions about unfunded federal mandates and the nature of the federal obligations on a constitutional as well as a political level, as described by author Jason Mazzone in "The Security Constitution."[82]

Will the war on terror have the unexpected consequence of breaking down barriers between levels of government, as it is breaking down barriers between branches of the federal government? Will the balance of federal/local power shift, as power has shifted among the branches of the federal government? As author Joseph Ellis noted in his recent book on the American founding,[83] part of the genius of our Constitution is that rather than attempting to provide definitive answers to all possible questions about structures, rights, and power, the Constitution provides a framework for a continuing debate and dialogue about these issues. The war on terror provides a new and important backdrop against which some key debates about the nature of the relationship between the federal and state/local governments will take place.


## SUMMARY OF CONTENTS

The contributors to this book all explore, from varying perspectives, how constitutional limitations apply to federal agents engaged in the war against terrorism and to local officials who are resisting what they believe to be federal government overreaching, often using the examples described above.

Ann Althouse (University of Wisconsin Law School), in a chapter entitled, "The Vigor of Anti-Commandeering Doctrine in Times of Terror," argues that the structures of federalism provide an attractive alternative to litigating the constitutionality of federal government actions in the war on terror. Her paper maintains that Justice Robert Jackson, concurring in the *Korematsu* decision,[84] was right in thinking that courts do not make sound decisions about the scope of civil liberties during times of war or national crisis, so that Patriot Act provisions that she might believe to be unconstitutional would be likely to be upheld by the courts. State and local opposition to Patriot Act policies, on the other hand, might actually cause the federal government to modify its policies. Althouse discusses the functions that state and local resistance might serve, comparing the current round of Bill of Rights Defense Committee resolutions to the opposition of Sheriff Printz, whose refusal to enforce a locally unpopular provision of federal law was upheld by the Supreme Court.

Ernest Young (University of Texas Law School), coming from the other end of the political spectrum, welcomes Althouse's born again-defense of the structures of federalism in his chapter, "Welcome to the Dark Side: Liberals Rediscover Federalism in the Wake of the War on Terror." While "states' rights" during the 1960s was often a code for supporters of racial segregation, Young ironically notes the current phenomenon of liberals coming over to "the dark side" and finally understanding that the structures of federalism might, as James Madison believed, provide a "double security" for liberty.[85] He describes this opportunistic attraction to the structures of federalism as a positive example of the flexibility of the structures themselves. State and local government can play an expressive role and can provide a potential rallying point against undesirable federal policy (although Young remains agnostic himself about whether the Patriot Act provisions some localities have protested are truly constitutionally problematic). As Young observes, the structures of federalism do not contain any fixed political valences.

My chapter, "Collapsing Spheres: Joint Terrorism Task Forces, Federalism, and the War on Terror," describes more fully what led Portland to withdraw from its Joint Terrorism Task Force and the implications of those events for antiterrorism efforts and our structures of federalism. The federal government, while not commandeering any assistance, would have disrupted Portland's internal checks and balances by conferring power on executive officials to make policy decisions without including the legislature.

The chapter by Ronald Chen (Public Advocate, State of New Jersey), "State Incarceration of Federal Prisoners After September 11: Whose Jail Is It Anyway?" provides background on the sequence of events and the federal and state actions at issue in the New Jersey jail case, described earlier, which provides a perfect petri dish for analyzing the scope of national authority and local autonomy.

Erwin Chemerinsky (Duke School of Law), in a piece called "Empowering States When It Matters: A Different Approach to Preemption," argues that the federal government should not be permitted to preempt state law unless Congress has clearly made the decision to do so. Requiring a clear expression of congressional will as a precondition to a finding of preemption would empower the states by allowing them more leeway to implement their own local policies and priorities. Under Chemerinsky's theory, for example, it would seem that the Bill of Rights Defense Committee provisions or Oregon state law probable cause requirements could not be preempted by unilateral action of the Department of Justice. The greater time and reflection required to enact federal legislation would position a thumb on the scale in favor of empowering state and local choice. Chemerinsky would also conclude that the New Jersey disclosure law discussed in Ronald Chen's article could not be preempted by a federal agency regulation, which is what the New Jersey court allowed to happen, unless Congress were to act to displace the state law requiring publication of the identities of the detainees in New Jersey jails.

Vikram Amar (University of California at Davis Law School) in "Converse 1983 Suits In Which States Police Federal Agents: An Idea Whose Time Has Arrived," argues that state courts and legislatures should be afforded authority to sanction federal officials who violate the federal Constitution within their states.

This would allow localities leeway to decide for themselves what conduct would violate federal constitutional norms, rather than ceding that issue to the federal courts or any other branch of the federal government, a right some of the BORDC resolutions claim. In an earlier essay,[86] Amar had discussed the role that state and local governments have played at various times during our history, as mediators between federal government actions and individual dissent from those actions. Like Chen and Chemerinsky, Amar seeks to empower state and local governments, in this case to develop more robust interpretations of constitutional law. This approach offers one provocative answer to the questions left open during the debates about the Virginia and Kentucky resolutions about the role of the states in formulating federal constitutional law.

Historian Paul Finkelman (Albany Law School) describes the surprising proslavery origins of our concept of national authority, as exemplified by the Supreme Court decision in *Prigg v. Pennsylvania*,[87] in which the Supreme Court ruled that federal law preempted a Pennsylvania state law providing procedural protections for fugitive slaves (or people mistakenly believed to be fugitive slaves) being extradited back into slavery. In "The Roots of *Printz*: Proslavery Constitutionalism, National Law Enforcement, Federalism, and Local Cooperation," Finkelman compares Pennsylvania's response to the prospect of enforcement of the locally detested Fugitive Slave Law with the refusal of local law enforcement officers to enforce the locally unpopular Brady Act provision invalidated in *Printz*, and the Bill of Rights Defense Committee resolutions reacting to locally unpopular provisions of the Patriot Act. He also discusses the Supreme Court's watershed treatment, in *Prigg*, of the question of the scope of local autonomy: although the Court held that federal law preempted Pennsylvania's attempt to add even process-based requirements to the Fugitive Slave Law, designed to impede the actions of federally sanctioned slave catchers, Justice Story's opinion suggests that state officials might not have been required to enforce the Fugitive Slave Law themselves.

Finally, legal historian and law professor Jason Mazzone (Brooklyn Law School) follows the money. In "The Security Constitution," Mazzone resurrects the "Protection Clause" of Article IV, section 4, which requires the federal government to "protect" each of the states "against Invasion, and on Application of the Legislature . . . against domestic Violence." He argues that this clause makes it a matter of constitutional obligation and not just politics for Congress to spend money at the level required for appropriate protection of each state, recalling Alexander Hamilton's amazingly apt commentary on the federal obligation to protect New York from sleeper cells and British invasion during the War of 1812— attacks Hamilton described as aimed not at New York, but at the nation. Mazzone, unlike some of the other authors, also concludes that the Constitution's preference for local action in the militia clauses[88] should mean that *Printz* should be distinguishable when protection is at issue, and so the federal government should indeed be permitted to commandeer state and local law enforcement officials in antiterrorism efforts, as long as Congress pays the bills.

With this book, we hope to spark a debate that, in the long run, may prove to be as significant as any of the other debates about the extent to which the events of 9/11 have challenged, or should challenge, our notions about the meaning of our Constitution.

## Notes

1. U.S. Constitution, Art. III, sec. 2, cl. 3.

2. Art. I, sec. 9 provides: "[t]he Privilege of the Writ of Habeas Corpus shall not be suspended, unless when in Cases of Rebellion or Invasion the public Safety may require it."

3. *United States Term Limits, Inc. v. Thornton*, 514 U.S. 779, 838 (1995) (J. Kennedy, concurring).

4. See, for e.g., Susan N. Herman, "The USA Patriot Act and the Submajoritarian Fourth Amendment," *Harvard Civil Rights-Civil Liberties Law Review* 41 (2006): 67–132 (discussing the constitutionality of the enhanced surveillance authority provided by the USA Patriot Act); Christopher Edley, Jr., "The New American Dilemma: Racial Profiling Post-9/11," in Richard C. Leone & Greg Anrig, Jr., eds., *The War on Our Freedoms: Civil Liberties in an Age of Terrorism* (New York: Public Affairs, 2003), 170–192 (discussing the new tenor of discussions of racial profiling post-9/11); David Cole, *Enemy Aliens: Double Standards and Constitutional Freedoms in the War on Terrorism* (New York: New Press, 2003) (discussing the impact of post-9/11 investigations and detentions on the rights of noncitizens); Lawyers Committee for Human Rights, "A Year of Loss: Reexamining Civil Liberties since September 11," September 5, 2002, http://www.humanrightsfirst.org/pubs/descriptions/loss_report.pdf.

5. See, for e.g., Military Order of November 13, 2001: Detention, Treatment, and Trial of Certain Non-Citizens in the War Against Terrorism, *Federal Register* 66 (2001): 57833, found to violate separation of powers norms in *Hamdan v. Rumsfeld*, 126 S. Ct. 2749 (2006). See Susan N. Herman, "The USA Patriot Act and the USA Department of Justice: Losing Our Balances?" *The Jurist*, December 4, 2001, http://jurist.law.pitt.edu/forum/forumnew40.htm (commenting on the impact of post-9/11 legislation and administrative actions on the checks and balances among the three branches of the federal government).

6. At the time this book went to press, the Supreme Court had heard argument in *Boumediene v. Bush* (Docket Number 06-1195), reviewing 476 F.3d 981 (D.C. Cir. 2007) (finding that the Military Commissions Act of 2006 did not unconstitutionally suspend habeas corpus protections), but had not yet issued a decision. For discussion of this issue, see, for e.g., Association of the Bar of the City of New York, "Letter to Congress Urging Opposition to Administration's Proposed Military Commissions Act of 2006," September 15, 2006, http://nycbar.org/pdf/report/CommissionsActLetterSenatorsSept15.pdf; Alison Nathan, "History Starts Today: The Perils of Habeas Stripping," *The Jurist*, September 26, 2006, http://jurist.law.pitt.edu/forumy/2006/09/history-starts-today-perils-of-habeas.php.

7. Linda Greenhouse, "Will the Court Reassert National Authority?" *New York Times*, September 30, 2001, D14. For contemporary responses, see Ernest Young, "The Balance of Federalism in Unbalanced Times: Should the Supreme Court Reconsider Its Federalism Precedents in Light of the War on Terrorism?" *Find Law's Writ*, October 10, 2001, http://writ.findlaw.com/commentary/20011010_young.html; Marci Hamilton, "Federalism and

September 11: Why the Tragedy Should Convince Congress to Focus on Truly National Topics," *Find Law's Writ*, October 25, 2001, http://writ.findlaw.com/hamilton/20011025.html.

8. The participants included Ann Althouse (University of Wisconsin Law School), Vikram Amar (University of California at Hastings Law School), Erwin Chemerinsky (University of Southern California Law School), Paul Finkelman (now at Albany Law School), Lucas Guttentag (ACLU Immigrants Rights Project), Arnold M. Howitt (Taubman Center for State and Local Government, John F. Kennedy School of Government, Harvard University), Vicki C. Jackson (Georgetown Law School), Jason Mazzone (Brooklyn Law School), Burt Neuborne (New York University School of Law), Elizabeth Rindskopf Parker (Dean, University of the Pacific, McGeorge School of Law), Judith Resnik (Yale Law School), Hon. David G. Trager (United States District Judge, Eastern District of New York, former Dean, Brooklyn Law School), Ernest A. Young (University of Texas Law School), and myself as convenor and moderator. A videotape of the symposium is available for viewing at http://www.brooklaw.edu/news/newsarchive/2003-11-21trager_symposium.php. Papers from the symposium were published in volume 69 of the *Brooklyn Law Review*.

9. See *Printz v. United States*, 521 U.S. 898 (1997).

10. Michael Wishnie, "State and Local Police Enforcement of Immigration Laws," *University of Pennsylvania Journal of Constitutional Law* 6 (2004): 1084–1115.

11. See *New State Ice Co. v. Liebmann*, 285 U.S. 262, 311 (1932) (J. Brandeis, dissenting).

12. Erwin Chemerinsky's chapter in this book, "Empowering States When It Matters: A Different Approach to Preemption," notes this tendency.

13. See, for e.g., Edward L. Rubin & Malcolm Feeley, "Federalism: Some Notes on a National Neurosis," *UCLA Law Review* 41 (1994): 903–952.

14. *United States v. Lopez*, 514 U.S. 549 (1995); *Printz v. United States*.

15. *United States v. Morrison*, 529 U.S. 598 (2000).

16. *Kimel v. Florida Board of Regents*, 528 U.S. 62 (2000) (Congress may not enforce damages provision of the Age Discrimination in Employment Act against state employers); *Board of Trustees of the University of Alabama v. Garrett*, 531 U.S. 356 (2000) (Congress may not enforce damages provision of the Americans with Disabilities Act against state employers); but see *Nevada Department of Human Resources v. Hibbs*, 538 U.S. 938 (2003) (damages provision of Family and Medical Leave Act may be enforced against state employers).

17. See *Federalist No. 10* (1787) (Madison); *Federalist No. 15* and *27* (Hamilton); Andrew C. McLaughlin, *A Constitutional History of the United States* (New York and London: D. Appleton-Century Company, 1935), 137–147.

18. U.S. Constitution, Art. VI, sec. 2 ("This Constitution, and the laws of the United States which shall be made in pursuance thereof; and all treaties made, or which shall be made, under the authority of the United States, shall be the supreme law of the land. . . . ").

19. See U.S. Constitution, Art. I, sec. 8, 10.

20. See, for e.g., *Gonzales v. Raich*, 545 U.S. 1 (2005), where the Court split five to four on the question of whether marijuana grown and sold within the state of California was sufficiently connected with "interstate commerce" to be subject to regulation under federal law.

21. U.S. Constitution, amend. X ("The powers not delegated to the United States by the Constitution, nor prohibited by it to the States, are reserved to the States respectively, or to the people.").

22. *Younger v. Harris*, 401 U.S. 37, 44 (1971).

23. *McCulloch v. Maryland*, 17 U.S. (4 Wheat.) 316 (1819).

24. U.S. Constitution, Art. I, sec. 8 ("[The Congress shall have power to] make all Laws which shall be necessary and proper for carrying into Execution the foregoing powers and all other powers vested in the Government of the United States, or in any Department or Officer thereof").

25. *Martin v. Hunter's Lessee*, 14 U.S. 304 (1816).

26. *Prigg v. Pennsylvania*, 41 U.S. 539 (1842), discussed at greater length by Paul Finkelman in this book.

27. *Dred Scott v. Sandford*, 60 U.S. 393 (1857).

28. U.S. Constitution, amends. XIII, XIV, and XV.

29. *Strauder v. West Virginia*, 100 U.S. 303 (1880).

30. See for e.g., *18 U. S. Code 18* (1996), sec. 241 (providing for federal criminal prosecution of civil rights violations).

31. See, for e.g., *A.L.A. Schechter Poultry Corp. v. United States*, 295 U.S. 495 (1935) (invalidating federal regulation of poultry market); *Carter v. Carter Coal Co.*, 298 U.S. 238 (1936) (invalidating federal regulation of coal industry); *United States v. Darby*, 312 U.S. 100 (1941) (allowing federal wage and hour requirements); *Wickard v. Filburn*, 317 U.S. 111 (1942) (allowing federal regulation of wheat consumed by the farmer who grew it).

32. See *United States v. Lopez* (invalidating federal law criminalizing possession of a firearm in a school zone); *United States v. Morrison* (finding Commerce Clause not an adequate basis for *Violence against Women Act*).

33. *United States v. Morrison* (finding Congress's enforcement power under the Fourteenth Amendment not an adequate basis for Violence against Women Act); *City of Boerne v. Flores*, 521 U.S. 507 (1997) (finding Fourteenth Amendment insufficient basis for Congress's enactment of Religious Freedom Restoration Act).

34. See *New York v. United States*, 505 U.S. 144 (1992) (Congress may not compel state legislature to enact legislation).

35. *Printz v. United States*.

36. Ibid., 939.

37. Ibid., 940 ("Matters such as the enlistment of air raid wardens, the administration of a military draft, the mass inoculation of children to forestall an epidemic, or perhaps the threat of an international terrorist, may require a national response before federal personnel can be made available.").

38. Ibid., 932 ("[W]here, as here, it is the whole *object* of the law to direct the functioning of the state executive, and hence to compromise the structural framework of dual sovereignty, such a 'balancing' analysis is inapplicable. It is the very *principle* of separate state sovereignty that such a law offends, and no comparative assessment of the various interests can overcome that fundamental defect. . . . We . . . conclude categorically, as we concluded categorically in *New York*: 'The Federal Government may not compel the States to enact or administer a federal regulatory program.' ").

39. U.S. Constitution, Art. VI, sec. 2.

40. See, for e.g., *American Insurance Association v. Garamendi*, 539 U.S. 396 (2003) (federal law preempts California remedies for Holocaust survivors); *Crosby v. National Foreign Trade Council*, 530 U.S. 363 (2000) (federal law preempts Massachusetts policy with respect to trade with Myanmar).

41. *Olmstead v. United States*, 277 U.S. 438 (1928).

42.  See Fox Butterfield, "Some Police Chiefs Object to Interviews," A Nation Challenged: The Interviews, *New York Times*, November 22, 2001 (final edition); Fox Butterfield, "Police Are Split on Questioning of Mideast Men," A Nation Challenged: The Interviews, *New York Times*, November 22, 2001 (final edition) (hereinafter as "Police Are Split on Questioning of Mideast Men"). Because there were only about two dozen Portland men on the FBI list, federal authorities noted that they could interview the men themselves, perhaps with some assistance from the Attorney General, and thus accept the Portland police position, see Sam Howe Verhovek, "Federal Effort Does Not Violate Law, Oregon Attorney General Says," A Nation Challenged: The Interviews, *New York Times*, November 28, 2001 (final edition).

43.  Fox Butterfield, "Police Are Split on Questioning of Mideast Men."

44.  Ibid.

45.  For a fascinating discussion of the impact of the war on terror on local law enforcement generally, see William J. Stuntz, "Local Policing After the Terror," *Yale Law Journal 111* (2002): 2137–2194.

46.  The Oregon Attorney General, Hardy Myers, responded to Kirkland's announcement and the controversy it generated by issuing an opinion that the questioning would not violate state law. See Sam Howe Verhovek, "Federal Effort Does Not Violate Law, Oregon Attorney General Says," A Nation Challenged: The Interviews, *New York Times*, November 28, 2001 (final edition).

47.  Bill of Rights Defense Committee, http://www.bordc.org.

48.  See *Senate Concurrent Resolution No. 18*, Hawaii, http://www.capitol.hawaii. gov/session2003/bills/SCR18_.htm.

49.  *Alaska House Joint Resolution 22*, May 17, 2003, http://www.legis.state.ak.us/ basis/get_bill_text.asp?hsid=HJR022A&session=23.

50.  Act of The General Assembly 2003–2004, No. R-203. *Joint Resolution Strongly Urging the President to Revise Executive Orders and Policies, and for Congress to Amend Provisions of the USA Patriot Act, which Seriously Erode Fundamental Civil Liberties*, http://www.leg.state.vt.us/docs/legdoc.cfm?URL=/docs/2004/acts/actr203.htm (Vermont).

51.  Detroit City Council, *Local Resolution to Protect Civil Liberties*, December 6, 2002, http://www.bordc.org/detail.php?id=245.

52.  *City of Portland Resolution*, October 29, 2003, http://www.bordc.org/detail.php? id=86.

53.  See Evelyn Nieves, "Local Officials Rise Up to Defy the Patriot Act," *Washington Post*, April 21, 2003 (final edition).

54.  Vikram David Amar, "Is it Appropriate, Under the Constitution, for State and Local Governments to Weigh In on the War on Terror and a Possible War In Iraq?" (hereinafter as "Is it Appropriate") *Find Law's Writ*, March 7, 2003, http://writ.news. findlaw.com/amar/20030307.html.

55.  Ibid.

56.  The resolutions are distinguishable from two state antifederal policy actions the Supreme Court recently found preempted by a need for national uniformity in a pair of recent cases, *American Insurance Association v. Garamendi*, 426–427 (federal law preempts California provision of remedies for Holocaust survivors supplemental to federal government agreements); *Crosby v. National Foreign Trade Council*, 530 U.S. 363 (2000) (federal law preempts Massachusetts policy governing state's trade with Myanmar).

57.  See Susan N. Herman & Jason Mazzone, Letter to New York City Council Speaker, Gifford Miller, December 9, 2003 (letter on file with author) (arguing that the New York City

resolution subsequently passed is an example of "federalism at its best." "Our structures of federalism are supposed to work by allowing parts of the country to preserve their distinct voices and to serve their distinct interests. As a city with a large immigrant population, New York may legitimately dissent from a national consensus that we should seek security even at the price of targeting immigrants generally and Arab and Muslim men in particular. We cannot, of course, prevent federal law enforcement officials from enforcing federal legislation like the Patriot Act. But we can certainly instruct our congressional delegation to seek to modify that legislation, and we can decline to further jeopardize members of our community by calling upon the New York Police Department and other city law enforcement agencies not to infiltrate mosques without some particular reason, and not to frighten immigrants into avoiding the police by questioning their immigration status when they wish to report a crime.")

58.  *City of New York v. United States*, 971 F. Suppl. 789 (S.D.N.Y. 1997), *aff'd*, 179 F.3d 29 (2d Cir. 1999).

59.  Ibid., 179 F.3d 29 (2d Cir. 1999).

60.  *Executive Order No. 41*, New York City, September 17, 2003.

61.  The memo was not released.

62.  See, for e.g., Michael J. Wishnie, "Laboratories of Bigotry? Devolution of the Immigration Power, Equal Protection and Federalism," *New York University Law Review* 76 (2001): 493, 527–528; Symposium, "Migration Regulation Goes Local: The Role of the States in U.S. Immigration Policy," *New York Annual Survey of American Law* 58 (2002): 283–446.

63.  See, for e.g., Jeff Lewis, et al., "Authority of State and Local Officers to Arrest Aliens Suspected of Civil Infractions of Federal Immigration Law," *Migration Policy Institute*, June 11, 2002, http://www.migrationpolicy.org/files/authority.pdf. For a relevant case, see *DeCanas v. Bica*, 424 U.S. 351 (1976) (unanimous opinion by J. Brennan) (federal immigration law does not preempt California statute imposing penalties on employers for hiring undocumented workers).

64.  See Susan Sachs, "Long Resistant, Police Now Start Embracing Immigration Duties," A Nation Challenged: The Interviews, *New York Times*, March 15, 2002 (final edition).

65.  Federal courts have ruled that absent federal authorization, a state law discriminating against legal permanent residents, is subject to strict scrutiny as alienage discrimination. If the law were *mandated* by federal statute, it would be subject to the lenient rational basis test applicable to federal immigration authorities. A more difficult question is whether a permissive federal statute diminishes the level of federal equal protection to which a state statute is subject. See *Aliessa v. Novello*, 754 N.E.2d 1085, 1098–99 (N.Y. 2001) (applying strict scrutiny in invalidating state discrimination against immigrants in welfare program, despite federal authorization).

66.  Jonathan Saltzman, "Governor Rescinds Immigration Order Frees State Police from Arrest Pact," *Boston Globe*, January 12, 2007 (third edition).

67.  *Clear Law Enforcement for Criminal Alien Removal (CLEAR) Act of 2003*, House Resolution 2671, sec. 101.

68.  Ibid., sec. 102.

69.  This section would provide for the federal government to reimburse states for the costs they incur in incarcerating undocumented criminal aliens.

70.  *Clear Law Enforcement for Criminal Alien Removal Act of 2005*, H.R. 3137, 109th Congress, http://www.govtrack.us/congress/bill.xpd?bill=h109-3137.

71. See Daniel Booth, "Federalism on ICE: State and Local Enforcement of Federal Immigration Law," *Harvard Journal of Law and Public Policy* 29 (2006): 1063–1083 for a discussion of the CLEAR legislation and its constitutionality. On the desirability of CLEAR, see Julia Malone, "Lawmakers Split on Immigration Act," *Atlanta Journal-Constitution*, October 2, 2003 (home edition).

72. The DOJ was sued in federal court under the Freedom of Information Act (FOIA), see *Center for National Security Studies v. Department of Justice*, 331 F.3d 918 (D.C. Cir. 2003), *cert. denied*, 540 U.S. Lexis 1104 (2004) (unsuccessful FOIA request for identities and information about fall 2001 detainees).

73. *ACLU of New Jersey, Inc. v. County of Hudson*, 352 N.J. Super. 44, 799 A.2d 629 (App. Div. 2002), *cert. denied*, 174 N.J. 190, 803 A.2d 1162 (2002).

74. *New Jersey Statutes Annotated* 30: 8–16 (West 1997).

75. *ACLU of New Jersey, Inc. v. County of Hudson*.

76. Under the theory of preemption advanced by Erwin Chemerinsky in his chapter in this book, a court could not properly have found preemption because Congress had not acted.

77. For a full description of the history of this litigation, see Jerrold L. Steigman, "Reversing Reform: The *Handschu* Settlement in Post-September 11 New York City," *Brooklyn Journal of Law & Policy* 11 (2003): 745–799.

78. *Handschu v. Special Services Division*, 273 F. Suppl. 2d 327 (S.D.N.Y. 2003).

79. *Handschu v. Special Services Division*, 288 F. Suppl. 2d 411 (S.D.N.Y. 2003).

80. *Domestic Security Enhancement Act: Section by Section Analysis*, sec. 312, January 9, 2003, http://www-tc.pbs.org/now/politics/patriot2-hi.pdf?mii=1.

81. See *Handschu v. Special Services Division*, 475 F. Suppl. 2d 331 (S.D.N.Y. 2007); 2007 U.S. Dist. LEXIS 43176 (S.D.N.Y. June 13, 2007).

82. See Jason Mazzone, "What Congress Owes New York," *New York Times*, April 24, 2003 (final edition).

83. Joseph J. Ellis, *Founding Brothers: The Revolutionary Generation* (New York: Knopf, 2003), 3–19.

84. *Korematsu v. United States*, 323 U.S. 214 (1944).

85. *Federalist 51*.

86. Vikram David Amar, "Is it Appropriate."

87. *Prigg v. Pennsylvania*.

88. U.S. Constitution, Art. I, sec. 8, cls. 15–16.

# The Vigor of Anti-Commandeering Doctrine in Times of Terror

Ann Althouse

## INTRODUCTION

Although the Rehnquist Court acquired a reputation for enforcing federalism,[1] in reality its efforts were not very robust. It crafted doctrine to show some deference to state and local government, but it did not threaten federal power where it is seriously needed. To a great extent, the Rehnquist Court *enhanced* federal power. It removed some unnecessary cases from the federal courts and deprived Congress of some power to posture for political effect,[2] but constraints of this kind increase the likelihood that Congress will attend to matters that genuinely require national coordination. Surely, the war on terrorism demands federal attention: Local efforts tailored to local preferences are obviously not enough to deal with an international network of terrorists that threatens national security. Yet, in carrying out the massive federal effort needed to deal with terrorism after September 11, 2001, the national government inevitably looks to the vast number of police, health workers, and other personnel employed at the state and local government levels.[3] Local officials are likely to contribute willingly to many of these efforts, especially in times of the greatest emergency or when federal money accompanies federal mandates. Nevertheless, at least some of the time, some local authorities will find reason to oppose the federal agenda.

Will the federalism doctrine developed by the Supreme Court in its pre-9/11 days protect the autonomy of state and local government officials who decide to resist the demands of federal authorities for assistance in the fight against terrorism? Let us consider the doctrine that developed prior to 9/11 and the motivations and aspirations behind it and then focus on what appears to be the most important component of federalism doctrine in this context, the "anti-commandeering" doctrine announced in *Printz v. United States*,[4] which bars Congress from imposing duties on state and local government officials. The majority of the Court took this position despite a warning by Justice Stevens that the Court ought to worry about the way its new doctrine would work "in times of national emergency":

> Matters such as the enlistment of air raid wardens, the administration of a military draft, the mass inoculation of children to forestall an epidemic, or perhaps the threat of an international terrorist, may require a national response before federal personnel can be made available to respond. If the Constitution empowers Congress and the President to make an appropriate response, is there anything in the Tenth Amendment, "in historical understanding and practice, in the structure of the Constitution, [or] in the jurisprudence of this Court," that forbids the enlistment of state officers to make that response effective?[5]

Justice Stevens was prescient. It is easy now to envision emergencies that would cry out for the full cooperation of the vast numbers of police, health workers, and other personnel of state and local government. Did the Court really mean to preserve the niceties of federalism in the face of events of this kind? Could local officials form their own views about the importance of, for example, smallpox inoculations after a bioterrorism attack and accordingly decline to help?

In the aftermath of the 9/11 attacks various municipalities, as well as a few states, passed resolutions directing their officials to refuse to participate in the antiterrorism efforts of the federal government. These resolutions did not oppose the fight against terrorism in general; rather, they took issue with some aspects of enforcement, particularly the heightened powers of surveillance authorized by the USA PATRIOT Act.[6] These local laws acknowledged federal supremacy in the form of the Constitution, but expressed independence in articulating the content and extent of constitutional rights and asserted that the current federal antiterrorism efforts violated these rights. Thus, these laws created the potential for multiple interpretations of the Constitution, a multiplicity that the autonomy recognized in *Printz* could—as we shall see—shield from review.

Ideas about the normative value of federalism have been expressed from the time of the founding to the present-day Supreme Court. For example, before the Bill of Rights was appended to the Constitution, James Madison attempted to convince people that the structure of federalism would protect them from the abuses of power. He wrote in *Federalist No. 51*:

> In a single republic, all the power surrendered by the people is submitted to the administration of a single government; and the usurpations are guarded against by a division of the government into distinct and separate departments. In the compound republic of America, the power surrendered by the people is first divided between two distinct governments, and then the portion allotted to each subdivided among distinct and separate departments. Hence a double security arises to the rights of the people. The different governments will control each other, at the same time that each will be controlled by itself.[7]

Americans have become accustomed over the years to thinking about constitutional rights as their protection from government abuse and about the states as potential *violators* of rights that require the supervision of federal courts enforcing federal rights against them. Assertions about federalism, particularly coming from the Rehnquist Court, which many perceive as lacking sufficient interest in the enforcement of rights, have struck some commentators as working only to shield the abuses of state and local government.[8] But what happens when federal authorities begin to overreach? Those who disparage federalism doctrine may think that constitutional rights offer the best hope for controlling abuses of the federal government. Yet that hope has its limits, because it depends on the willingness of the federal courts to interpret and enforce constitutional rights vigorously.[9] Yet when it comes to national security, judges are tempted to constrain rights and to defer to the political branches of the federal government.[10]

But does the autonomy of state and local government recognized in *Printz* have any greater potential to protect Americans from the abuse of their rights by the federal government? At the very least, the mechanisms of federalism work differently from the use of federal courts to enforce federal rights, and in that difference there is some potential for state and local government to work as "a double security . . . to the rights of the people."[11] So let us look at the *Printz* case and then focus on the relationship between the anti-commandeering doctrine and the protection of individual rights. I will argue that the war on terrorism should not lead to the creation of an "emergency" exception to the anti-commandeering doctrine and that courts ought to preserve the anti-commandeering doctrine in its absolute form not only *in spite of* the war on terrorism, but precisely because it can also protect individual rights that the war may lead courts to narrowly construe.

## THE *PRINTZ* ANTI-COMMANDEERING DOCTRINE

In *Printz v. United States* (1997), the Supreme Court held that it is "fundamentally incompatible with our constitutional system of dual sovereignty" for the federal government to commandeer state or local government officials to "administer or enforce a federal regulatory program."[12] At issue was the Brady Handgun Violence Prevention Act,[13] which required state and local law enforcement officials to perform background checks on persons who attempt to buy handguns. Rather than delaying until a federal system could be put into effect, Congress relied temporarily on the existing institutions of local government. The Act demanded that local "chief law enforcement officers" ("CLEOs") receive paperwork from gun sellers and make a "reasonable effort," within five days, to determine whether their customers fell into any of the categories forbidden by federal law to purchase guns.

Justice Scalia, writing for a majority of the Court, could not begin his analysis with the text of the Constitution, because it lacked a specific clause upon which to premise the anti-commandeering doctrine. Calling attention to this deficiency,

Justice Stevens proclaimed in dissent: "There is not a clause, sentence, or paragraph in the entire text of the Constitution of the United States that supports the proposition that a local police officer can ignore a command contained in a statute enacted by Congress pursuant to an express delegation of power enumerated in Article I."[14] In the dissenters' view, the Commerce Clause authorized Congress to regulate gun sales, and the Necessary and Proper Clause encompassed the means of forcing state and local government officials to administer the regulation. With no explicit text to support its doctrine and needing to rely on the entire text of the Constitution and the Tenth Amendment, the majority consulted the historical materials for inferences about the meaning of constitutional federalism. Justice Scalia's opinion stressed the early history of the use of congressional power, on the theory that Congress's failure to use such a "highly attractive power" in its earliest years implied a belief that the Constitution forbade the assignment of compulsory tasks to state and local government. Efforts to show that Congress had in fact used this power failed to impress the Court. It discounted the Extradition Act of 1793, which required the "executive authority" of a state to arrest fugitives at the request of other state executives, because that Act rested directly on the Constitution's Extradition Clause.[15] Since there were no early statutes compelling the state executive in the absence of such a "particularized constitutional authorization," the Extradition Act, in the majority's view, contributed to the inference that Congress received no implied power authorizing compulsion. Congress *requested* state help with the imprisonment of federal convicts. By offering compensation and making alternate provisions when a state refused, Congress—according to the majority—revealed its understanding that compulsion would overreach its constitutional power.

There were a few early instances of Congress requiring state *courts* to perform various tasks, but these did not count, in the majority's view, because courts differ from the other institutions of state and local government. The Supremacy Clause (in Article VI of the Constitution) explicitly requires state courts to apply federal law, and Article III implicitly requires the same by making the creation of the lower federal courts optional. Moreover, quite aside from these constitutional provisions, it is the ordinary role of courts to enforce whatever law applies in the cases that fall within their jurisdiction. State courts are courts, and as such they must follow the law according to a judicial method. For a state court to apply the law of another sovereign is not to be "commandeered" by an outside power, but to follow the requirements of the rule of law itself. There is no subordination except to the rule of law.

*Printz* did not rely merely on historical interpretation; its federalism had normative appeal in its present-day applications. "This separation of the two spheres is one of the Constitution's structural protections of liberty," Justice Scalia wrote.[16] He repeated language from Justice O'Connor's opinion in *Gregory v. Ashcroft*: "Just as the separation and independence of the coordinate branches of the Federal Government serve to prevent the accumulation of excessive power in any one branch, a healthy balance of power between the States and the Federal

Government will reduce the risk of tyranny and abuse from either front."[17] Justice Scalia also quoted the language from *Federalist No. 51*, characterizing federalism as "a double security...to the rights of the people."[18] He concluded with an important warning: "The power of the Federal Government would be augmented immeasurably if it were able to impress into its service—and at no cost to itself— the police officers of the 50 States."

Dissenting, Justice Breyer asserted that there is simply no across-the-board liberty-enhancing effect in protecting state and local governmental autonomy when Congress has seen fit to use the states in service of ends that fall within its constitutional powers. He noted that "[m]odern commerce and the technology upon which it rests" necessitate regulation at the national level, thus diminishing what will be done at the local level and undermining, over time, the participatory democracy that occurs within the smaller, decentralized institutions of local government.[19] He criticized federalism doctrines that constrained Congress's use of state and local government. The modern economy needs "government large enough to secure trading rules that permit industry to compete in the global market place, to prevent pollution that crosses borders, and to assure adequate protection of health and safety by discouraging a regulatory 'race to the bottom.'"[20] Because it must regulate, if Congress cannot commandeer state and local government officials as it sees fit, it must create a huge, overweening federal government. Justice Breyer wrote this before the 9/11 attacks, which have exerted even more pressure on constitutional doctrine, increasing the likelihood that courts will acknowledge greater national power and permit actions that will not only change the role of state and local government but that will also threaten individual liberties. This presents a new occasion to reconsider federalism in light of history. If Justice Breyer could be so concerned by the way modern-day commerce might produce a dangerously aggrandized national government, shouldn't we be even more concerned about enlarging the national government to meet the needs of the war on terrorism?

In the end of his opinion in *Printz*, Justice Scalia made short work of what he dismissed as "a cluster of arguments that can be grouped under the heading: 'The Brady Act serves very important purposes, is most efficiently administered by CLEOs during the interim period, and places a minimal and only temporary burden upon state officers.'"[21] This is just the sort of argument that will likely be offered in support of relying on state and local government to help in an emergency with the fight against terrorism, so it is helpful to pause and note just how little regard the *Printz* Court had for arguments of this kind. The formal, structural principle mattered, according to the *Printz* Court, and would be enforced despite compelling, counterbalancing exigencies.[22] Justice Scalia wrote: "[W]here...it is the whole *object* of the law to direct the functioning of the state executive, and hence to compromise the structural framework of dual sovereignty, such a 'balancing' analysis is inappropriate. It is the very *principle* of separate state sovereignty that such a law offends, and no comparative assessment of the various interests can overcome that fundamental defect."[23]

To the majority, constitutional federalism is worth enforcing even though it seems "'formalistic' . . . to partisans of the measure at issue," who tend to see the value of a law recently adopted to serve a "perceived necessity" of the time.[24] By "resist[ing] the temptation" to approve of "an expedient solution to the crisis of the day," the Court claimed to be serving the long-term interest in avoiding the concentration of power,[25] so that decentralized government would still be in place to provide a "double security" for the rights of the people.[26]

In the post-9/11 period, clearly the federal government has offered and is likely to continue to offer "expedient solution[s] to the crisis of the day." The question now is whether courts will continue to "resist the temptation" and see the value of deterring the concentration of power in the federal government. Similarly, one might wonder whether some of those who criticized *Printz* for its hard-nosed inflexibility in the face of a gun-control policy they favored will see good use for it in resisting what they may now perceive as overreaching federal authority in the fight against terrorism. The tables have now been turned with respect to policy preferences, which will test the principles of both sides of the Court and the commentators who aligned with them after *Printz*.

## THE RELATIONSHIP BETWEEN ANTI-COMMANDEERING DOCTRINE AND PROTECTING INDIVIDUAL LIBERTY

Let us consider the relationship between the anti-commandeering doctrine announced in *Printz* and the protection of individual rights. Madison, writing in *Federalist No. 51*, associated the structures of federalism with the protection of individual liberty. Similarly, ideas about constitutional rights lay in the background of the *Printz* litigation. To a large extent, ideas about constitutional rights will provide the motivation for invoking the anti-commandeering doctrine in the context of the war on terrorism. Indeed, local resistance to participating in federal antiterrorism efforts has already resulted from beliefs that these efforts infringe on constitutional rights. Although there are the limitations inherent in relying on structural constitutional doctrine rather than constitutional rights, the anti-commandeering doctrine has some potential for preserving a robust understanding of individual rights, perhaps beyond any version of rights that any of the branches of the federal government, including the federal courts, would be willing to endorse directly.

*Printz* analyzed constitutional federalism, the scope of Congress's affirmative powers, and the force of the Tenth Amendment, but the controversy also entailed concerns about the right to bear arms.[27] Only Justice Thomas's concurring opinion considered this aspect of the case. Noting the long lapse of time since the Court had addressed the scope of the Second Amendment[28] and the vivid recent scholarly attention to the question of whether it describes a personal right,[29] he saw a "colorable argument" that the Brady Act violated not only constitutional federalism but also the right to bear arms. And, in fact, the litigants in *Printz* were concerned about gun rights. The National Rifle Association ("NRA") financed four of the cases attacking the Brady Act, including the two consolidated in *Printz*.[30] The lawyer who handled the cases, Stephen P. Halbrook, specialized in Second Amendment cases.[31] The petitioners, Richard Mack[32] and Jay Printz,[33] cared about gun rights as well as their increased workload. The decision to rely on the federalism ground did not reflect a lack of interest in Second Amendment rights. As the plaintiffs' lawyer, Halbrook told the press: "From the point of view of litigation strategy, the court understands 10th amendment issues[.] They don't understand the Second Amendment so much."[34]

Thus, to some extent, the *Printz* case did involve resistance to federal power based on a conception of individual constitutional rights. Protecting federalism in *Printz* allowed a broad conception of Second Amendment rights to survive without contradiction.[35] Local government officials could continue to nurture their belief in an interpretation of gun rights far more vigorous than anything the Court has ever shown a willingness to embrace. Quite apart from the fact that the Court has never said that the Fourteenth Amendment incorporates the Second Amendment,[36] and even if the Court were willing to read the amendment as guaranteeing a personal right to bear arms, it would still require an expansive reading of that right to see it as barring the fairly reasonable limitations imposed by the Brady Act. By litigating about federalism, Printz, Mack, Halbrook, and the NRA did not have to expose their robust vision of gun rights to judicial scrutiny. Gun rights may very well have been the motivating force behind their litigation effort, but they won precisely because they relied on a constitutional theory that did not require the Court to engage them in the debate about the meaning of constitutional rights. If they had, it is likely that they would have lost; and if so, they would have not only lost the case but provoked an authoritative judicial opinion puncturing the vision of expansive rights that they so treasured.

The fight against terrorism has raised concerns that the federal government has overreached its legitimate power. Concerns about racial profiling, invasions of privacy, unreasonable searches, and infringement on free speech fueled a political movement, led by groups such as the American Civil Liberties Union and the Bill of Rights Defense Committee, urging state and local government to adopt resolutions directing their officials not to participate in at least some aspects of the antiterrorism effort.[37]

My own city of Madison, Wisconsin, was one of the many cities that adopted resolutions purporting to resist the impositions of the federal government. The relevant portion of its resolution, illustrative of the sort of resolutions adopted in many places,[38] announces the city's policy to forbid the following activities "in the absence of probable cause of criminal activity:"

1. any initiation of, participation in, assistance or cooperation with any inquiry, investigation, surveillance or detention; and
2. the recording, filing, and sharing of any intelligence information concerning any person or organization, even if authorized by federal law

enforcement, acting under new powers granted by the USA PATRIOT Act or Executive Orders. This includes collection and review of library lending and research records, as well as book and video store sales and/or rental records; and

3. the retention of intelligence information. Information that is currently held shall be thoroughly and carefully reviewed by the City Attorney or other appropriate City official to be designated by the Mayor, for its legality and appropriateness, using the United States and Wisconsin Constitutions. Any information that was collected is permanently disposed of if there is no probable cause of criminal activity; and

4. enforcement of immigration matters, which are entirely the responsibility of the Immigration and Naturalization Service. No city service will be denied on the basis of citizenship; and

5. profiling based on race, ethnicity, citizenship, religion, or political values.[39]

The Madison resolution, like others adopted around the country, begins with an acknowledgment of the authority of the United States Constitution and its superiority to all other law, including subconstitutional federal law. It proclaims the city's "long and proud tradition" of respecting constitutional rights, its regard for its own "highly diverse population," and its concern that the fight against terrorism "not be waged at the expense of essential civil rights and liberties." The Madison resolution refrains from declaring that the Act is unconstitutional, but it does express concern that the USA PATRIOT Act "threatens civil rights and liberties guaranteed under the United States Constitution."

A former assistant attorney general for the Office of Legal Policy at the Justice Department, Viet Dinh, who drafted much of the USA PATRIOT Act,[40] has minimized these local resolutions as "merely statements of principle of saying that the Constitution . . . is sacred and that the states and locals will not do anything in abridgement of the Constitution."[41] According to Dinh's characterization, no one should violate the Constitution, but since at that time no courts had found that any provisions of the PATRIOT Act violate constitutional rights, the resolutions meant little. Yet the resolutions implicitly take the position that some of the activities authorized by the PATRIOT Act are unconstitutional. Then Attorney General, John Ashcroft, summarized the purpose of the PATRIOT Act as "t[aking] down the wall between intelligence and enforcement."[42] In distinct contrast, the state and local government resolutions specifically limit their participation to law enforcement, responding only to "probable cause of criminal activity" instead of any lower standard, and withhold participation in intelligence efforts altogether. The limitation asserted in the resolution is scarcely a boilerplate acknowledgment of constitutional rights: It is a robust interpretation of the meaning of constitutional rights that implicitly denounces the central purpose of the PATRIOT Act. Confining participation in federal antiterrorism efforts to this extent is therefore true resistance to the federal program, not merely a bland statement of a truism about the superiority of the Constitution over other federal law. The resolutions embody a policy of resisting the version of federal rights propounded by the Bush administration, a policy that has the potential to survive a United States Supreme Court interpretation of the meaning of those rights that agrees with the administration. Moreover, the resolutions may also invoke state constitutions, which, although they do not bind federal officials, do limit state officials. As long as no federal law preempts the provisions of a state's constitution, state constitutional law may offer far more expansive rights than those found in the federal Constitution, rights interpreted by state courts without supervision by the United States Supreme Court.[43] By relying on the anti-commandeering doctrine, local officials can, if they choose, find the power to uphold a far more expansive view of individual rights than they could defend in court directly.

As written, the resolutions depict state and local government stepping up to the job of providing "a double security . . . to the rights of the people," the vision of *Federalist No. 51*. Surely, state and local government officials may lack the nerve to persist in following the announced policy. It is one thing to pass these resolutions in the atmosphere of a city council meeting, amid idealistic expressions about rights—but it is quite another to follow through when federal officials make real requests and where resistance to these requests may allow a terrorist attack to occur. Yet, this structural safeguard for rights can work independently of federal interpretation of federal constitutional rights if the anti-commandeering doctrine survives in its absolute form and if state and local government officials have the courage to invoke it.

Litigation strategy prompted Printz and Mack to rely on federalism doctrine instead of directly asserting constitutional rights. Resistance to federal antiterrorism efforts is also taking a form that could be vindicated through reliance on federalism. The war on terrorism might move the courts to erode or abolish the anti-commandeering doctrine, but for now let us assume the courts will be willing to adhere to the anti-commandeering doctrine, in its absolute form, so that state and local government officials, if they have the nerve, will be able to decline to carry out the antiterrorism tasks Congress or the President attempts to assign to them. What is lost and what is gained by using federalism doctrine to resolve the controversy rather than analyzing whether constitutional rights are violated?

It should be noted that constitutional rights do not drop out of the picture simply because federalism doctrine is used for litigation purposes. Constitutional rights continue to motivate and justify decisions to invoke state and local autonomy. Without the ability to frame their resistance in the language of rights, state and local government officials might not be able to win public support for their resistance, which would otherwise resemble the federalism-based resistance to the civil rights movement that still merges federalism and hostility to rights in the public mind. Moreover, public demand for resistance to the federal commandeering of state and local government officials arises out of deep beliefs about the meaning and importance of rights and the special need for vigilance in the face of strong claims about national security.

Ideas about constitutional rights are not the only basis for state and local government officials to resist federal demands. They also have political disagreements with the federal government. They may question the need for those efforts, care about maintaining good relations with an immigrant community,[44] or believe they have superior techniques for dealing with security matters. They may want to satisfy preferences of their own constituents, who may be suspicious of or hostile to federal policy. Of course, political and policy interests also underlie decisions to bring lawsuits even when the claims asserted are claims of constitutional right. There is never a necessary link between the claim one chooses to rely on in court and the motivation for seeking a particular outcome from that court. What is important here is that when one chooses to base one's claim on a constitutional right, the court deciding the case will need to say what the scope of the claimed right is. Rights claimants expose their expansive, idealistic visions to courts that might very well deflate them.

If Printz and Mack had presented a Second Amendment right to the courts in attacking the Brady Act, their case would have produced an interpretation of that right that might very well have disappointed them. Indeed, that is exactly what their lawyer expected and why he relied on the federalism ground. If they had relied on the Second Amendment and succeeded, they would have procured a decision about rights that not only would have endorsed a vision of liberty that they treasured, but also would have obligated every government actor to respect that right, including the many officials who were voluntarily following the requirements of the Brady Act and who would not invoke their power to refuse commandeering. It would have prevented the federal government as well from using its own personnel to perform the background checks on gun buyers. Printz and Mack won their case by relying on the federalism ground: the Court recognized their autonomy to opt out of the gun control enforcement. If they had relied on the Second Amendment they probably would have lost, however, and if that had happened, there would be a decision in U.S. Reports denying the existence of a right they believed they had. The anti-commandeering doctrine thus deprived us of *information* about the meaning of a right.

Would it be better to force litigants like Printz and Mack to rely on claims of constitutional rights in order to increase the likelihood that courts will produce opinions telling us what our rights are? If there are rights, one may feel tempted to argue, they should be proclaimed so that government actors would know what they need to do and could be sanctioned if they fail. The main problem with this attitude is that frequently the answer courts will give is that the claimed right does not exist, thereby putting the judicial stamp of approval on power that government was already inclined to exercise. Leaving a pall of doubt over the claimed right might have caused government actors to act with extra precaution, cutting a broad swath around known rights, unless exigent circumstances push them to take actions challenging the constitutional limit. Since a decision based on rights will constrain Congress and all other state and local government actors who may favor the measure in question, courts feel pressure not to overexpand interpretations of constitutional rights. Because of this restraint that limits the judicial interpretation of rights, protecting the autonomy of state and local government offers an important alternative, preserving an expansive conception of rights in localities that place a high value on the particular liberty in question.

This alternative highlights the way structures of federalism can account for variation in conditions and preferences from place to place.[45] There are varying local preferences about the balance between individual liberties and actions government might take to increase the physical security of its citizens. There is also variation in how much local citizens desire to exercise a particular liberty and how serious the threat to physical safety in their area is. The *Printz* case clearly illustrated this kind of difference. It is well known that persons in rural localities in the West tend to value their own access to guns and are relatively less concerned with the danger created when felons acquire guns than are citizens living in urban areas in the Northeast. By avoiding a decision based on the Second Amendment in *Printz*, the Court was able to satisfy the widest array of preferences, as local CLEOs were able to respond to what their own citizens wanted. Printz and Mack could opt out, but the regulations and enforcement structure of the Brady Act could survive in places where people had different values.

Yet, if rights are important, should they not trump these local preferences? A powerful lesson learned in the civil rights era was that the local majoritarian preference might be quite reprehensible. The law speaks in terms of rights precisely to deny the preference of the majority, and there has long been a particular worry about the parochial preferences of small, localized majorities.[46] But what if the local majoritarian preference is to *increase* individual liberty, if it is to take a very expansive view of rights, beyond what courts would be willing to carve in stone as constitutional law? The autonomy of local governments can preserve a vigorous culture of rights, as the resolutions described above indicate. It was at the local level, in particular cities, with a specific set of citizens, where the resistance to the PATRIOT Act gained a foothold. Is this not the "double security . . . to the rights of the people" to which Madison referred in *Federalist No. 51*?

Should we regret that the anti-commandeering doctrine relieves pressure that might otherwise push state and local government officials to challenge the constitutionality of actions taken by the federal government? By giving the state and local government officials a less judgmental way to disengage from a federal program, the *Printz* doctrine discourages some vigorous debate about the meaning of constitutional rights: Instead of fighting over the meaning of constitutional rights, the different governmental institutions can go about their own business, performing their separate functions in their separate ways. Yet nothing prevents state and local government from deciding when to invoke their *Printz*-given right to be left alone based on their own ideas about what rights are and when to assert rights directly. The anti-commandeering doctrine thus functions to preserve an idealistic view of rights, at a time when courts, motivated by the strongly urged needs of the federal government to protect security, would tend not to take the idealistic view of rights. Moreover, the ability of state and local government to resist being commandeered creates pressure on the federal government not to go too far, not to put too low a value on individual liberty, so that it can inspire voluntary participation even in the places that have a strong tradition of valuing individual rights.

## FEDERAL POWER IN THE EVENT OF EMERGENCY

Will the anti-commandeering doctrine retain vigor in the context of the war on terrorism? The *Printz* Court stated its doctrine in absolute terms, warning of the importance of "resist[ing] the temptation" to accept "an expedient solution to the crisis of the day."[47] But the war against terrorism may give rise to irresistible temptation, pushing judges to reframe or explain away the doctrine. To what extent should emergency affect the *Printz* anti-commandeering doctrine? The *Printz* majority, professing strict adherence to the concept of dual sovereignty, brushed off an entire "cluster" of arguments for weighing the importance of the power against the burden on state and local government.

Taking the opposite tack, Justice Stevens was not only willing to balance federal and state interests; he was also ready to assign a heavy weight to federal interests and to minimize the burdens imposed on the state. After warning of the important needs that might arise in the case of an emergency, such as a terrorist attack, Justice Stevens proceeded to accept the problem of gun violence as an emergency, citing 12,489 murders around the country over the course of one year.

Although the number of deaths per year from gun violence is considerable, exceeding the number of deaths from the 9/11 attacks by more than a factor of four, the deaths result from disconnected incidents of localized violence. Unlike the international network of terrorism, disconnected criminal acts, even if frequent and widespread, do not require a nationally coordinated response. State and local government has traditionally handled problems of violent crime, which are susceptible to decentralized treatment. In fact, decentralized treatment of crime problems can be superior, as it is tailored to local conditions and preferences. Moreover, it can be more protective of individual rights. For example, if Congress were to attempt to federalize the crime of murder, in all likelihood, it would make the death penalty available. That law would then supersede the choices of many states that have embraced a more robust vision of the right against cruel and unusual punishment in their own law than the United States Supreme Court has adopted as a matter of federal constitutional law.

In *Printz*, what was more important to Justice Stevens than his own view that gun violence constituted an emergency was that Congress had made a "policy judgment" that it amounted to an emergency, and that it would therefore supposedly usurp the legislative function for the Court to substitute its own assessment. Justice Stevens not only wanted to use a balancing test to analyze whether state and local government could claim autonomy as a matter of constitutional law; he wanted to preclude the Court from deciding the weight of the interests in the balance. At the opposite extreme, the majority thought it was especially important to resist the temptation to balance at all and seemed to scoff at assertions of emergency. Justice Scalia observed that every generation thinks whatever it cares about is a "crisis" justifying an exception to constitutional structures, which it is only too ready to characterize as empty formality. It is hard to criticize the formality or inflexibility of the majority's dual sovereignty analysis, however, if the alternative is a balance of interests that the judge is forbidden to weigh. The supposed balancing process becomes in essence complete judicial restraint, leaving Congress as the judge of the scope of its own power.

This resort to judicial restraint has characterized the discussion of the broad range of federalism issues in the opinions of Justice Stevens, along with those of Justices Souter, Ginsburg, and Breyer. These Justices consistently defer to congressional decision making about the proper balance between federal power on the one hand and state and local power on the other. For them, judicial restraint completely subsumes federalism, so that whatever efforts Congress thinks ought to be undertaken as a matter of national policy become ipso facto constitutional (as long as individual rights are not violated). One ought to realize then that for these Justices, it is not really the case that emergency justifies national power, but that the congressional decision to act itself creates the power.

Arguably, this restraint should not extend to unilateral actions taken by the President, the sort of actions likely to be taken in the most extreme emergencies. If the reason for deference is genuinely the belief (frequently endorsed by the *Printz* dissenters)[48] that Congress is structured to take account of the interests of state and local government, then decisions by the President alone do not deserve the same deference. If the real reason these Justices do not favor the enforcement of federalism is, however, the low valuation of state interests compared with federal interests, one might expect them to favor deference to decisions of the President as well (at least unless they see those decisions as detrimental to individual liberty).

One doubts whether emergency mattered at all to the dissenters, other than to critique the majority's absolute position. Would they have argued for the narrow construction of individual rights to ensure that government would be in a position to deal with hypothetical emergencies? If not, it would seem that the rejection of judicially enforceable federalism is the motivating force behind their position. Congress is trusted not because of anxiety about emergencies, but because state and local government autonomy is not a significant enough value to matter in the equation. What is missing from the *Printz* case, then, is a serious confrontation with the problem of emergency from the perspective of someone who thinks that constitutional federalism is important and deserving of judicial preservation.

In looking for a way to supply the analysis about emergency that is missing in *Printz*, I found myself drawn to Justice Jackson's dissenting opinion in *Korematsu v. United States*,[49] perhaps the most thoughtful meditation on the role of the judiciary in times of emergency to be found in the Supreme Court's cases. The *Korematsu* majority upheld a conviction for the violation of a military order excluding persons of Japanese descent from the West Coast during World War II.

Despite the recognition that "all legal restrictions which curtail the civil rights of a single racial group are immediately suspect,"[50] the majority took the position that "under circumstances of direst emergency and peril . . . the power to protect must be commensurate with the threatened danger."[51] Extrapolating to the anti-commandeering doctrine, one might speculate that it will collapse in a truly dire situation that demands the assistance of local authorities.

Consider, then, Justice Jackson's response. He admitted that "[i]t would be impracticable and dangerous idealism to expect or insist that each specific military command in an area of probable operations will conform to conventional tests of constitutionality" and that "[t]he very essence of the military job is to marshal physical force, to remove every obstacle to its effectiveness, [and] to give it every strategic advantage."[52] However, he also thought that courts should stand apart from such operations rather than to distort the meaning of constitutional law to uphold them. He assumed that the period of emergency would end soon enough, and that it would be better to preserve the law in a form untainted by considerations of military exigency. The executive could achieve its goals, but could not call upon the courts to aid it in its extraconstitutional efforts.

Justice Jackson also wrote that courts were not capable of framing doctrine that would account for the emergency, because "[i]n the very nature of things, military decisions are not susceptible of intelligent judicial appraisal."[53] Here, Justice Jackson expressed an idea about judicial incompetence somewhat similar to Justice Stevens's, yet surely the two positions differ. Jackson was writing about what the majority had called "circumstances of direst emergency and peril." Stevens simply accepted Congress's characterization of unconnected murders widely dispersed over time and space as an emergency. The scope of judicial incapacity recognized by Justice Stevens was thus far greater.

The present-day conditions of the war on terrorism are quite different from the emergency Justice Jackson needed to reconcile with judicial power. This war could continue indefinitely, with perhaps many years passing before there is another visible attack[54] or with no further attack ever occurring. Jackson could justify judicial inaction because he could trust that the military emergency would end: "A military order, however unconstitutional, is not apt to last longer than the military emergency . . . But once a judicial opinion rationalizes such an order to show that it conforms to the Constitution, or rather rationalizes the Constitution to show that the Constitution sanctions such an order, the Court for all time has validated the principle."[55]

But let us assume for the sake of argument that at least some aspects of the war on terrorism do constitute an emergency comparable to the one Justice Jackson considered. And again, let us accept that the anti-commandeering doctrine is in place and deserves to be respected as a matter of constitutional law.[56] Courts might attempt to follow the advice of Justice Jackson and leave the absolute doctrine untouched, while still looking for a way to defer to the choices of the national government out of deference to the exigencies of war. Adopting this stance, courts would not opine about whether the anti-commandeering doctrine absolved state and local government officials from the obligation to perform assigned tasks, nor would they provide a forum for adjudicating any sort of penalty that federal law might attempt to impose on them. The benefit of this approach, under Jackson's theory, is that it avoids creating a new emergency principle of constitutional law that would "then lie[] about like a loaded weapon ready for the hand of any authority that can bring forward a plausible claim of an urgent need."[57] We do better to tolerate a mere "incident" of unremedied constitutional violation than to find a way to incorporate it into constitutional doctrine, in Jackson's view, where it will have "a generative power of its own," affecting everything that follows.[58] To respond to the current emergency by abolishing the anti-commandeering doctrine or reframing it to include an exception for the "direst emergency and peril" to make national power "commensurate with the threatened danger" would be to take a position corresponding to that of the *Korematsu* majority. The *Korematsu* majority constrained individual rights; the proposal to build an emergency exception into the *Printz* doctrine constrains the autonomy of state and local government.

Strikingly, Justice Jackson's solution in *Korematsu* seems quite a bit like the refusal of state and local government officials to contribute to the efforts of the federal government: "I should hold that a civil court cannot be made to enforce an order which violates constitutional limitations even if it is a reasonable exercise of military authority. The courts can exercise only the judicial power, can apply only law, and must abide by the Constitution, or they cease to be civil courts and become instruments of military policy."[59]

As we noted above, state courts were treated differently from state legislatures and state executive officials in the anti-commandeering cases, because courts are bound by the rule of law, and state courts must enforce federal as well as state law, because it is part of the applicable law that binds them. By the same token, federal courts, including the Supreme Court, are bound to the rule of law, including constitutional law, with its principle of supremacy over other federal law. Normally, we would understand that to mean that judges must strike down the unconstitutional acts of government in cases in which they have jurisdiction. Under Jackson's *Korematsu* approach, constitutional law, in the case of dire, military emergency, simply becomes a justification for judicial passivity. The courts themselves resist being commandeered into the enforcement of military commands, on the theory that these commands fall outside of the regime of law that binds courts.

Should courts today respond with Jacksonian passivity to emergency measures taken in the war on terrorism? Jackson's idea was palatable precisely because the peril of World War II would end soon enough. Should a modern day court, however, stand back and allow the federal government to transgress rules of constitutional law because of the war on terrorism, which is potentially endless? Those who already disapprove of the anti-commandeering doctrine, like the *Printz* dissenters, might favor placing the doctrine on indefinite hold. Yet, surely, they would not treat individual rights similarly, the way Justice Jackson was willing to condone what he thought was unconstitutional race discrimination.

Even if much of the war on terrorism does not rise to the level of the "direst emergency and peril" faced by Justice Jackson, some incidents in the future could. Consider, for example, a serious bioterrorism attack, unleashing anthrax simultaneously in numerous cities around the United States.[60] The national government would surely need to rely on the work of the large numbers of local police and other government personnel in place around the country; we can expect that it would act immediately, commandeering local personnel to carry out severe procedures to contain and eradicate the disease. One response to this scenario is that the anti-commandeering doctrine simply would not matter: Everyone would comply. The situation itself would motivate public officials to join together and accept direction from the authority that is in a position to coordinate efforts. If we can predict this response, we should not worry about what courts ought to do about the anti-commandeering doctrine in the case of the "direst emergency and peril." Indeed, the test of whether such a condition exists is whether it inspires this unquestioning compliance.

Yet it is not beyond comprehension that some local officials would think that the threat of the disease in their locality does not justify some extreme measures they are commanded to enforce. Some local government workers might think they know better about the risks of the disease weighed against the dangers of the vaccine or might feel sympathetic to local individuals with exaggerated fears about vaccinations. Still, would anyone seek the courts' opinion about the validity of commandeering? The federal government might simply substitute military personnel wherever there were pockets of noncompliance. The real prospect of the use of military personnel would prompt many would-be resisters to go along. Funding can also help secure voluntary compliance. The entire problem of resistance could be averted in advance with plans for emergency that include consent, for example, as a condition on spending money to put various antiterrorism safeguards in place.[61]

The circumstances would be very different from the *Korematsu* problem that Justice Jackson confronted, where the federal government imposed harsh restrictions on private individuals who had every reason to feel deeply wronged, entitled to disobey in secret, and convinced that their disobedience would harm no one. Here, the federal government would be trying to *use* local officials to perform services in an emergency. These officials themselves would not be regarded as the problem, but as a means for dealing with the problem. Most of these officials as public servants would want to comply. Those who did not, presumably only a few if the emergency is *genuinely dire*, would be conspicuous dissidents from national policy. They would be in a position to give voice to the arguments against government policy, unlike, say, Korematsu, who tried to avoid detection. In fact, they would need to explain themselves because they would be exposed to public criticism for their failure to help. The pressure to comply with federal orders would increase in proportion to the severity of the emergency, but it would also decrease in proportion to the strength of their argument that the federal government was abusing its power and infringing on individual rights. At the same time, however, the prospect of noncompliance would exert pressure on federal policymakers to inspire compliance by providing adequate funding and by proposing measures that are not perceived as abusive.

Would the resisting local officials be charged with crimes or subjected to sanctions? Perhaps only then would the matter arrive in court, at which point there would be no need to adopt the Jacksonian device to avoid penalizing them: Adhering to the absolute anti-commandeering doctrine would produce the same result. Clearly, respecting the anti-commandeering doctrine is different from enforcing constitutional rights. Jackson sought a way to avoid interfering with the efforts of the national government and still allow Korematsu to go free. But that dichotomy already exists in the anti-commandeering doctrine: the national government is free to take the steps it wants to take with its own personnel and state and local government is able to refuse to contribute to those efforts.

This resolution of the problem has an advantage to those who are concerned with individual rights, which the courts would probably slight if they were asked to enforce them at the expense of strong national security considerations. Imagine individuals attempting to procure injunctions from courts so that they could avoid inoculations or quarantines after a severe bioterrorist attack. They would surely fail. Yet the sensitivity of some local officials to their concerns could lead those officials to resist taking orders from the federal government, and that potential for resistance might generate more careful decision making at the federal level, taking account of individual liberties to some extent. Officials resisting commandeering would raise the objection that the federal effort violated the constitutional rights of individuals, the very rights that courts would avoid enforcing in "circumstances of the direst emergency and peril." Indeed, if a court ever did face the anti-commandeering question in these circumstances, it would undoubtedly respond to the actual context: The more intrusive on individual rights particular measures are, the more appealing noncompliance would look. By denying the means of commandeering to the federal government, the courts have created an incentive to adopt policies that inspire compliance, thus preserving a beneficial structural safeguard for individual rights.

Preserving the *Printz* doctrine in its absolute form, instead of trying to design an exception based on emergency, also eliminates the problem of asking a court to identify what constitutes a genuinely dire emergency. The willingness of Justice Stevens in *Printz* to view murder as a national emergency should serve as a warning against creating a doctrinal exception. Even if courts endeavored to keep the emergency exception under control, claims about the war on terrorism will tend to look strong. Reexamine the list of matters that the current local resolutions resist: Which ones could not be justified as part of the emergency of the war on terrorism? More importantly, putting an absolute power to resist in the hands of state and local government creates pressure that works in favor of protecting individual rights. There is good reason to think that opposition at the local political level has moderated the behavior of the federal government and that this method of controlling the national government is more effective than lawsuits based on individual rights. This is precisely the vision of federalism found in *Federalist No. 51.*

## CONCLUSION

Over the course of U.S. history, conditions have changed, causing people to look more and more to the national government for solutions to modern-day problems. It would seem that the war on terrorism could only increase the demand for the national government to extend its reach into more and more aspects of American life. One might well predict, then, that the war on terrorism will finish off the Rehnquist Court's federalism revival: Federalism neurotics[62] will need to snap out of their nostalgia and face the hard realities of a brutally changed world. What can survive of the Madisonian "double security . . . to the rights of the people"? How can the states play an important role in controlling abuse by the federal government when we are forced to look to the federal government to deal with such monumental threats?

It is well recognized, however, that the federal government might go too far in prosecuting its war on terrorism. It has not been my purpose here to express an opinion on whether or not it has, but the local resolutions I have discussed are part of the evidence that many people *believe* or *fear* that the federal government has gone very far wrong and has committed many serious violations of constitutional rights. Not surprisingly, those who worry about the violation of constitutional rights tend to assume that the rights themselves offer the best hope for a cure. Remembering how state and local government has in the past attempted to use federalism arguments to deflect claims of constitutional rights, those same governments tend not to look to federalism for the protection of rights.

I have sketched out my reasons for thinking that federalism, in particular the autonomy protected by the anti-commandeering doctrine, can protect constitutional rights better than the direct assertion of claims based on those rights. State and local government officials exert pressure on the federal government that works differently from constitutional rights. Claims of autonomy, justified by the Supreme Court's decision in *Printz*, can arise out of strong interpretations of constitutional rights. These interpretations may be drastically overstated or naively idealistic and, consequently, quite unlikely to move courts to rein in the federal government as it pursues national security. But state and local government autonomy can exert pressure on the federal government to moderate its efforts and take care not to offend constitutional rights, even rights that the courts would not now be willing to enforce. To carry out its programs, the national government will need to inspire the confidence of the vast numbers of police and other personnel employed at the state and, especially, local government level.

Because state and local government autonomy can work as a safeguard for the rights of the people, the anti-commandeering doctrine should remain in place, in full force, unmodified by any sort of emergency exception. Courts, if they are given the opportunity to rethink the anti-commandeering doctrine, should continue to "resist the temptation" to adopt "an expedient solution to the crisis of the day." It is true that this autonomy deprives the national government of a means to carry out programs that may be vitally important. But in cases of the "direst emergency and peril," the great majority of persons employed at the state and local level of government can be expected to respond without objection. Where there are pockets of noncompliance, the federal government can send in its own personnel, including the military. The different levels of government will exert pressure on each other. State and local government will tend to resist only when the emergency is not dire and when the actions of the federal government offend local beliefs, often idealistic beliefs about constitutional rights. The federal government will want to win compliance and will take steps to inspire cooperation, such as offering ample funding and framing demands that take account of ideas about individual rights. Remove the anti-commandeering doctrine, or temper it with an emergency exception, and this beneficial interaction is lost.

## Notes

1.  See, for e.g., Linda Greenhouse, "For a Supreme Court Graybeard, States' Rights Can Do No Wrong," The Nation; Long Term, *New York Times*, March 16, 2003 (final edition) (referring to "a stunning series of federalism decisions that have curbed the power of Congress to bind the states to the full reach of federal law," and that represent a "federalism revolution," "ignited" by Chief Justice Rehnquist and "likely to define his place in Supreme Court history").

2.  Thus, it resisted the federalization of crimes and torts traditionally handled at the state level by placing a limit of the exercise of the commerce power. *United States v. Morrison*, 529 U.S. 598 (2000) (finding insufficient power to create a tort cause of action for gender-motivated acts of violence); *United States v. Lopez*, 514 U.S. 549 (1995) (finding insufficient power to make gun possession in a school zone a crime).

3.  See William J. Stuntz, "Local Policing After the Terror," *Yale Law Journal* 111 (2002): 2137–2194 (describing the huge disproportion in personnel of police nationwide employed at the local level).

4.  *Printz v. United States*, 521 U.S. 898 (1997).

5.  Ibid., 940.

6.  *Uniting and Strengthening America by Providing Appropriate Tools Required to Intercept and Obstruct Terrorism Act of 2001 ("USA PATRIOT Act")*, Public Law No. 107–156, *U.S. Statutes at Large* 115 (2001): 272.

7.  *The Federalist No. 51* (James Madison).

8.  See, for e.g., Jack M. Balkin & Sanford Levinson, "Understanding the Constitutional Revolution," *Virginia Law Review* 87 (2001): 1045–1110.

9.  The usual ability of state courts to enforce federal law, see U.S. Constitution Art. VI (Supremacy Clause), disappears when it is asserted against federal officials. See *U.S. Code 28* (2000), sec. 1442 (providing for removal to federal court when federal officials are sued or prosecuted in state court). See also *Tarble's Case*, 80 U.S. 397 (1871) (precluding state courts from issuing habeas relief for persons held in federal custody).

10. See *Korematsu v. United States*, 323 U.S. 214, 244 (1944) (J. Jackson, dissenting).

11. *Printz v. United States*, 922.

12. Ibid., 935.

13. *Gun Control Act of 1968*, Public Law No. 90-618, *U.S. Statutes at Large* 82 (1968): 1213 (codified as amended in scattered sections of *U.S. Code 18*) (hereinafter "GCA"), amended by *Brady Handgun Violence Prevention Act*, Public Law No. 103–159, *U.S. Statutes at Large* 107 (1993): 1536 (codified as amended in scattered sections of *U.S. Code 18*) (hereinafter "Brady Act"). This body of law regulated the purchase of handguns in various ways, such as imposing age and residency requirements and prohibiting sale to convicted felons, unlawful aliens, and others.

14. *Printz v. United States*, 944.

15. *Act of February 12, 1793*, 2d Cong., 2d sess., ch. 7, *U.S. Statutes at Large* 1 (1793): 302.

16. *Printz v. United States*, 921.

17. *Gregory v. Ashcroft*, 501 U.S. 452, 458 (1991), quoted in *Printz v. United States*, 921).

18. *Federalist No. 51* quoted in *Printz v. United States*, 922.

19. *Printz v. United States*, 977 (J. Breyer, dissenting) quoted in *College Savings Bank v. Florida Prepaid Postsecondary Education Expense Board*, 527 U.S. 666, 703–704.

20. *College Savings Bank v. Florida Prepaid Postsecondary Education Expense Board*, 703.

21. Ibid., 931–932.

22. Importantly, he set to one side "laws of general applicability." *Printz v. United States*, 932. See also *Reno v. Condon*, 528 U.S. 141 (2000) (upholding *The Driver's Privacy Protection Act of 1994, U.S. Code 18* (1994), sec. 2721–2725 (1994 ed. and Suppl. III), which regulated the disclosure and sale of information acquired by states in the process of licensing drivers).

23. *Printz v. United States*, 932. Here, Justice Scalia invoked the strict separation of powers cases: *Bowsher v. Synar*, 478 U.S 714, 736 (1986) (declining to subject principle of separation of powers to a balancing test); *INS v. Chadha*, 462 U.S 919, 944–946 (1983) (same); *Plaut v. Spendthrift Farm*, 514 U.S. 211, 239–240 (1995) (holding legislated invalidation of final judgments to be categorically unconstitutional).

24. *New York v. United States*, 505 U.S. 144, 187 (1992) quoted in *Printz v. United States*, 933. By contrast, Justice Breyer, in dissent, criticized the "inflexibility" of the majority's "absolute principle . . . , which poses a surprising and technical obstacle to the enactment of a law that Congress believed necessary to solve an important national problem." *Printz v. United States*, 978 (J. Breyer, dissenting).

25. *New York v. United States*, 187, quoted in *Printz v. United States*, 933.

26. *Federalist No. 51*, quoted in *Printz v. United States*, 922.

27. The *Printz* majority did observe that statutes in the petitioners' states directed them not to interfere with gun rights. See *Printz v. United States*, 934 n.18 (citing *Montana Code Annotated*, sec. 45-8-351(1) (West 1995); *Arizona Revised Statutes Annotated*, sec. 13-3108(B) (West 1989), and declining to decide whether they prohibited the actions required by the Brady Act).

28. *Printz v. United States*, 937–938 and n.1 (J. Thomas, concurring) (citing *United States v. Miller*, 307 U.S. 174, 178 (1939) (limiting second amendment right to "ordinary military equipment" that is capable of serving the purpose of "common defense")). Justice Thomas would constrain commerce clause doctrine to the point where it would not reach

"wholly *intra*state, point-of-sale transactions." Ibid., 937 (J. Thomas, concurring) (citing *United States v. Lopez*, 514 U.S. 549, 584 (1995) (concurring opinion)).

29. *Printz v. United States*, 938 n.2 (citing many scholarly writings, including the following, which was written by counsel for the petitioners: Stephen P. Halbrook, *That Every Man Be Armed, The Evolution of a Constitutional Right* (Albuquerque, NM: University of New Mexico Press, 1984)).

30. Sam Howe Verhovek, "5 Rural Sheriffs Are Taking the Brady Law to Court," *New York Times*, April 25, 1994 (final edition) (noting that four of five lawsuits were "financed by the National Rifle Association").

31. See Stephen P. Halbrook, *Freedmen, the Fourteenth Amendment, and the Right to Bear Arms, 1866–1876* (Westport, CT: Praeger Publishers, 1998); Halbrook, *That Every Man Be Armed: The Evolution of a Constitutional Right* (Albuquerque, NM: University of New Mexico Press, 1984); Halbrook, *Right to Bear Arms: State and Federal Bills of Rights and Constitutional Guarantees* (Westport, CT: Greenwood Press, 1989); Halbrook, *Firearms Law Deskbook: Federal and State Criminal Practice* (St. Paul, MN: Clark Boardman Callaghan/West Group, 1995); "Testimony of Stephen P. Halbrook," Senate Committee on the Judiciary, Subcommittee on Constitution, Federalism and Property, Hearings on the Enforcement of the Second Amendment by Congress the Intent of the Fourteenth Amendment, *Federal News Service*, September 23, 1998, http://www.fnsg.com/transcripta.htm?id=19980923t0462&query=halbrook (arguing in favor of federal legislation extending the right to bear arms to actions by the states, using Section 5 of the Fourteenth Amendment).

32. See Tom Diemer, "Gun Law Records Check Worries Local Officials; High Court to Determine Whether Measure Complies with 10th Amendment," *Plain Dealer (Cleveland, OH)*, April 21, 1996 (final edition).

33. Howard Berkes, "Sheriffs Sue Government Over Brady Bill," morning edition, National Public Radio broadcast, May 25, 1994 (describing Printz as "a card-carrying member of the National Rifle Association," who "called the NRA when he heard how much work he'd have to do to enforce the Brady law").

34. See Tom Diemer, "Gun Law Records Check Worries Local Officials; High Court to Determine Whether Measure Complies with 10th Amendment," *Plain Dealer (Cleveland, OH)*, April 21, 1996 (final edition).

35. For the classic article arguing that the judiciary will "underenforce" some aspects of the Constitution and that therefore other institutions should participate in the articulation of "constitutional norms," see Lawrence Gene Sager, "Fair Measure: The Legal Status of Underenforced Constitutional Norms," *Harvard Law Review* 91 (1978): 1212, 1224–1226. For a recent article analyzing the Second Amendment in light of Sager's thesis and arguing that the amendment has been made "a constitutional pariah, barred from associating with other 'high caste' civil liberties our judges have labored to protect," see, Brannon P. Denning, "Gun Shy: The Second Amendment as an 'Underenforced Constitutional Norm,'" *Harvard Journal of Law & Public Policy* 21 (1998): 719–792.

36. See *Presser v. Illinois*, 116 U.S. 252 (1886); *United States v. Cruikshank*, 92 U.S. 542 (1875).

37. See Carol Rose, "Ashcroft Bars the Doors to Democracy," op-ed, *Boston Globe*, September 16, 2003 (third edition) (op-ed by executive director of the ACLU in Massachusetts, criticizing USA PATRIOT Act for authorizing excessive surveillance of citizens and political organizations and praising the resolutions passed in "more than 160 towns and cities... in support of the Bill of Rights and against the unconstitutional

provisions of the USA PATRIOT Act"); John W. Dean, "Grassroots Opposition to Rights-Infringing Antiterrorism Tactics," FindLaw/CNN.com, September 15, 2003, http://www.cnn.com/2003/LAW/09/15/findlaw.analysis.dean.patriot/index.html.

38. See Susan Schmidt, "PATRIOT Act Misunderstood, Senators Say; Complaints about Civil Liberties Go Beyond Legislation's Reach, Some Insist," *Washington Post*, October 22, 2003 (final edition) (noting "nearly 200 cities and three states have passed resolutions contending that the PATRIOT Act . . . tramples on civil liberties"). See also Bill of Rights Defense Committee, "Resolutions Passsed, and Efforts Underway, by State," http://www.bordc.org/list.php.

39. Bill of Rights Defense Committee, Madison Area Peace Coalition, "Resolution to defend the Bill of Rights and Civil Liberties," http://www.bordc.org/detail.php?id=60. The resolution also calls upon "any state or federal law enforcement agencies working within the City of Madison [to] comply with the policies and procedures of the Madison Police Department, and regularly report to the Mayor the extent and manner in which they have acted under the USA PATRIOT Act or new Executive Orders. This includes the names of any detainees held in the Madison area, or any Madison residents detained elsewhere. The Mayor will then publicly report to the Common Council." Ibid.

40. See Amy Goldstein, "Fierce Fight Over Secrecy, Scope of Law; Amid Rights Debate, Law Cloaks Data on Its Impact," *Washington Post*, September 8, 2003 (final edition).

41. See "Deadly Attack; Too Tough," *News Hour* with Jim Lehrer PBS television broadcast, August 19, 2003, http://www.pbs.org/newshour/bb/terrorism/july-dec03/patriot_8-19.html (statement of Viet Dinh, noting that as of that date "not a single provision of the USA PATRIOT Act has been overturned by a court" and that "the ACLU's challenge . . . two weeks ago was the first time that any provision was actually challenged").

42. Mark Hollis, "Ashcroft Defends PATRIOT Act; 'Our Strategy Is Succeeding,' He Tells Floridians," *Sun-Sentinel (Fort Lauderdale, FL)*, September 25, 2003 (Broward metro edition).

43. See *PruneYard Shopping Center v. Robins*, 447 U.S. 74, 81 (1980) (recognizing independent power to articulate the meaning of rights in state constitutional law). The United States Supreme Court recognizes state court authority over the interpretation of state constitutional law, but it is unlikely to remain passive when strong federal interests are at stake, as the litigation over the 2000 presidential election made eminently clear. See Ann Althouse, "The Authoritative Lawsaying Power of the State Supreme Court and the United States Supreme Court: Conflicts of Judicial Orthodoxy in the Bush-Gore Litigation," *Maryland Law Review* 61 (2002): 508–575.

44. See, for e.g., Jodi Wilgoren, "University of Michigan Won't Cooperate in Federal Canvass," A Nation Challenged: The Interviews, *New York Times*, December 1, 2001 (final edition) (reporting complaints by "Arab-American leaders, immigration lawyers and others . . . about the Justice Department's plan to question around 5,000 men ages 18 to 33 who have arrived here since January 1, 2000, from countries suspected of links to terrorism," objections by "police departments in Detroit; Oregon; Austin and Richardson, Tex.; San Francisco and San Jose, Calif.," and refusal by the University of Michigan to help with the interviews).

45. See Steven G. Calabresi, "A Government of Limited and Enumerated Powers": In Defense of *United States v. Lopez*," *Michigan Law Review* 94 (1995): 752–831; Michael W. McConnell, "Federalism: Evaluating the Founders' Design," *University of Chicago*

*Law Review* 54 (1987): 1484–1512 (reviewing Raoul Berger's *Federalism: The Founders' Design*).

46. *The Federalist No. 10* (Madison) (noting that smaller democratic constituencies find it easier to "concert and execute their plans of oppression").

47. *New York v. United States*, 505 U.S. 144, 187 (1992), quoted in *Printz v. United States*, 933 (1997).

48. See, for e.g., *United States v. Morrison*, 529 U.S. 598, 649–650 (2000) (J. Souter, dissenting) (citing the thesis detailed in *Garcia v. San Antonio Metropolitan Transit Authority*, 469 U.S. 528 (1985)); *Alden v. Maine*, 527 U.S. 706, 805–806 (1999) (J. Souter, dissenting) (same); *Printz v. United States*, 956–957 (J. Stevens, dissenting) (same).

49. *Korematsu v. United States*, 244 (J. Jackson, dissenting).

50. *Korematsu v. United States*, 216.

51. Ibid., 220.

52. Ibid., 244 (J. Jackson, dissenting).

53. Ibid., 245 (J. Jackson, dissenting).

54. The eight-year period between the first World Trade Center bombing in 1993 and the September 11 attack in 2001 illustrates the long time frame used by Al Qaeda. Moreover, the "area of probable operations" might be the entire country.

55. *Korematsu v. United States*, 246 (J. Jackson, dissenting).

56. Four members of the Supreme Court rejected the doctrine in its entirety, and many commentators agree. It may be that that the uses of the anti-commandeering doctrine I have discussed will convince some *Printz* opponents to rethink their position. But, obviously, one solution to the obstacles discussed in the text would be simply to overrule *Printz* and abolish the doctrine altogether. My view is that *Printz* raised a close question as a matter of original intent, but was justified on pragmatic and normative grounds. My purpose is to examine those grounds in light of the new circumstances of the war on terror.

57. *Korematsu v. United States*, 246 (J. Jackson, dissenting).

58. Ibid., 245.

59. Ibid., 247.

60. See Judith Miller, "U.S. Has New Concerns about Anthrax Readiness," *New York Times*, December 28, 2003, sec. 1, 20 (noting "concerns about the nation's vulnerability to terrorist attacks with" anthrax spores after fresh intelligence that an attack of this kind is "a top Al Qaeda objective").

61. Efforts are being made to create advance plans for dealing with many of the potential emergencies, including bioterrorism attacks. See "National Press Club Luncheon Address by Homeland Security Department Secretary Tom Ridge," *Federal News Service*, April 29, 2003 (noting commitment of federal government to fund state and local government because of their crucial role in protecting against terrorism, with $1.6 billion provided as of March 2003 and plans for an additional $1.5 billion). One reason for supporting the continuation of the anti-commandeering doctrine in its absolute form is precisely because it creates an incentive for adequate funding and for advance planning.

62. See Edward L. Rubin & Malcolm Feeley, "Federalism: Some Notes on A National Neurosis," *UCLA Law Review* 41 (1994): 903–952.

# Welcome to the Dark Side: Liberals Rediscover Federalism in the Wake of the War on Terror

Ernest A. Young

## INTRODUCTION

For several decades now, American liberals have not had much good to say about federalism. The reason is not far to seek: At many key points in our history, the banner of "states' rights" has been raised in order to defend fundamentally repugnant substantive policies—most obviously, slavery in the nineteenth century and Jim Crow segregation in the twentieth. Many have assumed that the story of state-based racial oppression reveals a fundamental truth about the dynamics of federalism, that is, that the States will always be less "progressive" than the national government. We have tended to forget other points in our history that reveal a different pattern, such as Virginia and Kentucky's protest against the Alien and Sedition Acts, or the abolitionist northern states' resistance to the federal Fugitive Slave Law.

The worm may be turning, however, in the wake of the conservative Bush Administration's War on Terror. As Ann Althouse's thoughtful chapter in this book discusses, several states and dozens of local governments have taken stands against perceived excesses in the federal USA PATRIOT Act,[1] either simply by expressing their disapproval or, in some cases, by ordering their officers not to cooperate in the administration of the national law.[2] Vikram Amar's contribution urges (in response to similar concerns about federal overreaching) that state legislatures and/or courts should create state-law causes of action against federal officials for violations of federal constitutional rights.[3] More generally, on a range of issues, liberals may be starting to wake up to the fact that they can no longer count on control of the national government.[4]

The substantial expansion of federal legislative power after 1937 coincided with a period of relatively stable Democratic control of the national legislature. But the Republican takeover of Congress in 1994, not to mention what many liberals considered a radical Republican executive after 2000, may well have shaken liberals' faith that federal power could be counted upon to solve the nation's problems or even that policy initiatives emanating from Washington would always be benign. On issues ranging from gay marriage to physician-assisted suicide to environmental protection, individual states have staked out "progressive" positions that have then come under attack from the Republican administration in Washington, DC. As a result,[5] at least some liberals have taken up the cause of state autonomy.

This chapter seeks to place the role of state and local governments in the war on terror in the context of broader debates about federalism.[6] The beginning of the chapter follows Professor Althouse's lead in focusing on the question of the national government's ability to require state and local cooperation with federal antiterrorism initiatives. This issue is evocative for several reasons: It illustrates the several different ways in which federalism promotes and protects individual freedom, resonating with a long, if mostly forgotten, history of state governmental resistance to national measures thought to encroach on civil liberties. The strong concern of nationalists about state and local noncooperation on antiterrorism measures, moreover, gives the lie to nationalist assurances that "political safeguards" will always be sufficient to protect the federal balance. Finally, state and local resistance to national antiterrorism measures demonstrates the expressive function of state and local governments as a voice for the People, thereby raising complex questions about first amendment limits on the federal government's ability to stifle state-centered dissent.

I then step back to assess more general questions raised by recent liberal support for state autonomy. I argue that liberals are right to embrace federalism, because state autonomy has no intrinsic correlation to politically conservative outcomes; moreover, in an era when conservatives may control at least important parts of the national government for some time, some states will offer liberals their best source of institutional support. I also address the question of opportunism, concluding that the Framers designed our system of horizontal and vertical separation of powers around the expectation that individuals and groups would support one institution or the other at any given time for politically opportunistic reasons. I suggest, however, that the liberal embrace of federalism now is more likely to be credible to the unpersuaded if it is coupled with a more principled and long-term acceptance of state autonomy.

Two caveats are in order. The first is that I am personally skeptical of—and at best agnostic about—claims that the War on Terror in general or the USA PATRIOT Act in particular actually represent a major threat to civil liberties.[7] There is no doubt, however, that many on both the political Left and Right perceive such a threat, and I do not believe their concerns to be trivial. The War on Terror thus provides a good laboratory for assessing the ability of state and local governments to resist perceived threats to civil liberties.

Second, I have long insisted that the political labels of "liberal" and "conservative" are subject to a variety of interpretations. In this chapter, I use those terms in their general political senses, as opposed to situational or institutional meanings of those terms.[8] One can make a "conservative" case for gay rights or environmental protection, for example, but that would be counterintuitive to the sense in which I will generally use the term here. Likewise, one can argue that federalism is a creature of Enlightenment Liberalism's rationalistic institutional design, or that it facilitates incremental social change congenial to Burkean conservatives. What I want to insist upon here, however, is that federalism has no dependable liberal or conservative valence as those terms are understood today in an intuitively political sense. As the War on Terror vividly illustrates, political liberals ought to be open to the possibility that state autonomy may become their new best friend.

## COMMANDEERING, LIBERTY, AND THE WAR ON TERROR

Criminal law enforcement has traditionally been a state and (primarily) local responsibility in this country. The distribution of law enforcement manpower reflects this history: A 2000 census of state and local law enforcement agencies counted over one million full-time law enforcement personnel,[9] while a 2002 survey of federal law enforcement found approximately 93,000 full-time personnel.[10] As William Stuntz recently observed, "the federal government has never employed a sizable fraction of the nation's law enforcement officers or prosecutors, nor housed a large portion of its prisoners."[11] September 11 may have changed the general perception that states and localities should take the lead in assuring domestic safety; we have, after all, just created a massive new federal Department of Homeland Security. The practical reality of enforcement resources seems likely to change more slowly, however. At least in the short term, the FBI and other federal law enforcement institutions are unlikely to cover the many responsibilities that "homeland security" entails without substantial state and local assistance.

This federal need for assistance quite properly motivates Professor Althouse's focus on the anti-commandeering doctrine. That doctrine holds that "the Federal Government may neither issue directives requiring the States to address particular problems, nor command the States' officers, or those of their political subdivisions, to administer or enforce a federal regulatory program."[12] The Federal Government cannot, in other words, simply compel state and local cooperation in antiterrorism enforcement. This rule eschews "case-by-case weighing of the burdens or benefits" on the ground that "such commands are fundamentally incompatible with our constitutional system of dual sovereignty."[13] Absent a substantial modification of current doctrine, then, the anti-commandeering principle is unlikely to yield to strong national interests in antiterrorism enforcement. The federal government's ability to secure state and local assistance will thus depend on its ability to secure willing—or at least grudging—compliance.

In the overwhelming majority of cases, of course, we can expect such co-operation to be forthcoming. A vocal minority of state and local governments, however, have announced their opposition to many of the federal policies that comprise the War on Terror. The most common form of state or local action consists of resolutions that reaffirm support for civil liberties and diversity, express particular concerns about the PATRIOT Act and other national antiterror policies, and urge state or local officials to uphold the rights of their citizens.[14] Some jurisdictions have gone further and forbidden their officers to cooperate with federal officials in the enforcement of some aspects of the PATRIOT Act. The relevant prohibitions typically prohibit local officials from cooperating only in measures that violate federal constitutional rights.[15] That would not be exceptional in itself; after all, federal officials likewise lack power to act in contravention of such rights. The important point, however, is that these local jurisdictions seem to reserve for themselves the authority to determine what amounts to a violation of federal rights rather than deferring to federal officials (or federal courts) on that issue.[16] This reservation of interpretive authority is important, given that the scope of the federal rights in question—rights against the chilling of free expression, free association, search and seizure safeguards, and equality norms against "profiling" and the like, to name just a few examples—will often be deeply contested.

These assertions of interpretive autonomy by state legislatures and local city councils recall a similar challenge to federal supremacy two centuries ago in the Virginia and Kentucky Resolutions.[17] Those resolutions, authored by James Madison and Thomas Jefferson, respectively, protested Congress's adoption of the Alien Friends Law, which allowed the President to order deportation of aliens, and the Sedition Law, which made seditious libel a federal criminal offense.[18] Much like the PATRIOT Act, these laws were enacted to enhance national security in the face of foreign threats; like the anti-PATRIOT Act measures, the Virginia and Kentucky Resolutions insisted that the federal laws overstepped the bounds of national power and intruded too far on constitutional liberties. Indeed, the Resolutions may have raised the more specific issue of commandeering addressed by Professor Althouse; as Wayne Moore has pointed out that they were issued "at a time when the Union depended heavily on cooperation by state governments for enforcing federal laws," and at least Jefferson's version "apparently contemplated disregard by state officials of the Alien and Sedition Acts."[19]

As I have already said, I am somewhat skeptical as to whether the concerns voiced in the contemporary anti-PATRIOT resolutions have much validity on the merits. These state and local initiatives do, however, offer vivid evidence of how federalism protects individual liberties. Much as they did during the eighteenth century controversy over the Alien and Sedition Acts, state and local governments have become a rallying point for political opposition to national policy.

In focusing on that interaction between federalism, political opposition, and liberty, I will first catalog the various institutional and political mechanisms by which federalism protects liberty, each of which finds an illustration in debates over the War on Terror. I will then explore the relevance of the "political safeguards" of federalism, both as a force tending to moderate state and local departures from federal policy and as a possibly inadequate protection for government-centered dissent. Finally, I ask whether the ability of state and local governments to mobilize dissent ought not to be protected in the same way that we protect other expressive organizations—that is, by according them rights against governmental suppression under the First Amendment.

## Federalism and Liberty

It is worth remembering that the Framers' original design focused entirely on structure: Specific enumerations of human rights—probably the primary vehicle for talking about liberty today—were added as a political concession following ratification of the original document.[20] That original document built on the assumption that liberty was best secured through a rigorous commitment to federalism and separation of powers. As Madison argued in Federalist 51, these institutional arrangements provide "a double security . . . to the rights of the people. The different governments will controul each other; at the same time that each will be controuled by itself."[21]

Few would argue today that federalism and separation of powers are a sufficient condition for individual liberty. The Federalists probably deserved to lose the debate about the need for enumerated freedoms, and few would choose to repeal the Bill of Rights and take our chances with sole reliance on structure. But our modern preoccupation with rights provisions may have encouraged us to overlook the possibility that structure remains a necessary condition for liberty.[22] Especially in times of terror, rights provisions may become "parchment barriers"[23] to governmental oppression. Sometimes it takes a government to check a government.

State and local institutions secure liberty in a number of different ways. The first is by functioning as a rallying point for political opposition to national policy.[24] Individuals are often ineffective speakers when they act alone; that is why First Amendment doctrine has long protected the role of political associations in mobilizing political expression. The Court recognized a right of political association in *NAACP v. Alabama*, for example, and has defended free speech rights for corporations on the similar ground that they are effective organizations for disseminating messages that the public has a right to hear.[25] Yet, often the most effective organizations for organizing and transmitting dissent are themselves governmental institutions. This should hardly be surprising. Such institutions, unlike private organizations, generally are constitutionally required to be open to a variety of points of view and responsive to the political will of the People. By transmitting the political dissent of their constituents, state and local resolutions against the PATRIOT Act reflect the Founders' notion (embodied in the Virginia and

Kentucky Resolutions) that state and local governments should "act as intermediaries between the people and the federal government."[26] As Alexander Hamilton observed in *Federalist 26*, "the state Legislature . . . will constantly have their attention awake to the conduct of the national rulers and will be ready enough, if any thing improper appears, to sound the alarm to the people and not only to be the VOICE but if necessary the ARM of their discontent."[27]

A second and related mechanism operates where state and local politics serves as the seedbed for political change at the national level. Turnover in government may be an effective guarantee against tyranny; it assures that a particular faction cannot become entrenched and unaccountable in power. Such turnover may become more difficult where the political opposition has no opportunity to demonstrate its own competence to rule. As some observers of British politics have noted, for example, the present "out" party—the Tories—have no governmental subunits in which they can gain practical experience, try out new policies, and gain governing credibility because Britain remains largely a unitary state.[28] In America, by contrast, the party that is "out" in Washington will almost certainly be "in" in at least a couple of dozen states and literally thousands of localities, and the experience of practical governance at those levels often provides the springboard for successful political takeovers at the national level.[29] Four of our last five Presidents were successful state governors at a time when their party was out of power at the national level.[30] It should thus come as no surprise that in the early stages of the 2004 presidential race the candidate who voiced the most effective criticism of the Bush Administration's War on Terror was a former governor of Vermont. And even within a particular political party, the necessities of governing and the unique political cultures of individual states may spur state politicians to oppose the party orthodoxy in Washington.[31] In the current election cycle, mayors of large cities are playing a similar role.[32]

What is true of politicians is also often true of social movements. Both abolition and the civil rights movement started at the state and local levels before they "went national."[33] So did many of the reform currents that came together in the Progressive movement around the turn of the last century.[34] It should surprise no one that as civil libertarians seek to persuade their fellow citizens of the dangers they see lurking in the PATRIOT Act, most of their initial successes have come in city councils and, less frequently, in the state legislatures.

Professor Althouse notes a third mechanism: The ability of state institutions to articulate an alternative—and possibly broader—understanding of federal rights. As she explains, the inability of Congress to "commandeer" Sheriff Printz to enforce the Brady Act enabled him to act upon a broader view of Second Amendment rights than the federal courts would likely have been willing to recognize.[35] Similarly, states like Oregon that permit physician-assisted suicide may be influenced at least in part by a broader view of due process than that of the U.S. Supreme Court's; states like Massachusetts recognizing gay marriage may likewise seek to articulate a broad view of due process or equal protection not yet accepted in the federal courts.[36] Each of these visions has encountered opposition at the national level, and their survival may depend in part on the strength of federalism constraints on Congress's preemptive power over state law.[37]

We see the same dynamic in the context of the War on Terror. Constitutional concerns about the PATRIOT Act and other antiterrorism measures are widespread; they include, to name just two examples, concerns about the erosions of Fourth Amendment privacy and chilling effects on First Amendment expression. Despite these concerns, however, few courts have been willing thus far to invalidate any of the Act's provisions.[38] It is thus *Printz*'s anti-commandeering doctrine that creates the constitutional space for state and local governments to vindicate their own, possibly broader understandings of these rights by refusing to participate in federal enforcement efforts they consider suspect.

We might think of Professor Althouse's argument as a limited form of state-based interpretive departmentalism. At the federal level, the departmentalist position holds that the branches of the federal government each have authority to render final constitutional interpretations in certain instances.[39] The Supreme Court upheld the constitutionality of the Bank of the United States in *McCulloch v. Maryland*, for example, but it had no authority to stop President Andrew Jackson from vetoing efforts to recharter the Bank based on his own interpretive conclusion that the Bank was constitutionally illegitimate.[40] Wayne Moore has traced a state-based version of departmentalism to the Virginia and Kentucky Resolutions, suggesting that they "reflect an assumption that the states have authority to interpret and exercise their powers even in opposition to authoritative decisions by one or more federal officials."[41] It is doctrines like *Printz*—and *Lopez*—that make space for this sort of autonomy: Because Congress may not compel state and local officers to participate in federal law enforcement efforts, states and localities may decide whether to allow such participation based on their own views of whether those enforcement efforts transgress constitutional norms.[42]

The final, simpler point is that the national government's need for state and local cooperation may enhance liberty by forcing national authorities to moderate their positions. Requiring the consent of multiple actors before the government can act is a pervasive institutional strategy in the Constitution; it is most familiar, obviously, in separation of powers where two distinct legislative organs and the Executive Branch ordinarily must concur before a bill can become law.[43] The autonomy of state governmental institutions often functions in the same way. The War on Terror is only one of a wide range of governing activities that the national government lacks the resources to undertake on its own. Congress also depends on state implementation in areas ranging from environmental law to welfare provision. Although Washington possesses powerful levers by which to "persuade" states to cooperate—such as the conditional spending power[44]—at some level it must still persuade state authorities that federal policy is sufficiently legitimate, wise, and fair to warrant their participation. This need to rule by persuasion is likely to force compromise and moderation across a wide range of federal endeavors.

Again, the War on Terror illustrates the dynamic. State and local authorities are likely to be willing, even eager, to assist national antiterrorism efforts in the vast majority of cases. After all, the States' constituents are being protected, too. But the formal declarations of reservations about the PATRIOT Act discussed here are likely to be only the tip of the iceberg in terms of state and local reluctance to cooperate with measures that their citizens find extreme or unfair. On some points, federal authorities may feel strongly enough about a particular measure to devote scarce federal resources to it even without state and local cooperation. But resource constraints will almost inevitably dictate that this cannot be the norm, and the need for state cooperation seems likely to force national authorities to compromise and accommodate state objections into federal policy. In some instances, such objections may come to be seen as valuable feedback about a policy that all acknowledge is a work in progress. That is no doubt one reason why Viet Dinh, a former Justice Department lawyer and one of the authors of the Act, recently welcomed the spate of state and local resolutions as part of an ongoing intergovernmental dialogue about appropriate antiterrorism measures.[45]

Critics of federalism have often assumed that the libertarian argument for state autonomy must rely on apocalyptic scenarios in which the States somehow rise up and oppose national tyranny through force of arms.[46] The dynamics of the War on Terror, however, demonstrate the emptiness of that canard. Federalism best protects liberty over time, through the day-to-day operations of a government in which nothing much can get done without the cooperation of multiple actors at multiple levels. And potential dissenters will surely have more of an impact if they have their own governmental institutions around which to organize their efforts, as well as their own constitutional space in which to implement and demonstrate the effectiveness of alternative policies. In our history, these dynamics have often come to the fore in times of national stress, and the present tumult is no exception.

## The Political Safeguards of National Policy

One irony of the debate over state and local opposition to national antiterrorism policy arises out of the fear that such opposition will unduly jeopardize national security. Some critics of the commandeering doctrine have suggested that it may fatally undermine national antiterrorism efforts.[47] The irony stems from the tendency of such warnings to downplay the immense political pressures that states and localities will face to comply with federal initiatives. After all, proponents of national power are fond of arguing that state governments can protect themselves through the political process; these nationalists thus reject the need for hard constitutional rules requiring national authorities to respect their autonomy.[48] It seems fair to wonder why similar political dynamics suddenly become inadequate when we speak of protecting the national side of the federal balance.

Justice Stevens's prescient dissent in *Printz* is an example. There, Justice Stevens warned that the commandeering doctrine might cripple federal policy in "times of national emergency," when "matters such as the enlistment of air raid wardens, the administration of a military draft, the mass inoculation of children to forestall an epidemic, or perhaps the threat of an international terrorist, may require a national response before federal personnel can be made available to respond."[49] But in the same opinion, Justice Stevens emphasized "the political safeguards protecting Our Federalism."[50] "Given the fact that the Members of Congress are elected by the people of the several States," he argued, "it is quite unrealistic to assume that they will ignore the sovereignty concerns of their constituents."[51] The Justice never explained why, given pervasive bonds of political party and shared administration of existing programs that tie state, local, and national officials together, as well as their common accountability to the same constituents, state and local governments would ignore a request for support from national officials on a matter of imminent national emergency. Why do we presume that federal officials look on the institutions of state government with benign concern, but that state and local officials will be recalcitrant and uncooperative unless the national government can compel their obedience?

There are two obvious but contrasting explanations for inconsistency on this point. One is that some opponents of judicially enforced federalism are really just opponents of federalism per se. They do not really think "political safeguards" are ever an adequate substitute for hard constitutional rules providing or limiting power; rather, they advance the political checks argument as a cover for the true position that state autonomy is simply not worth protecting. I certainly would not attribute this view to Justice Stevens; as I have argued elsewhere, he has long been the most ardent defender of state autonomy on questions involving the federal preemption of state law.[52] But to the extent that many in the academy probably do feel this way, it would surely be preferable to simply debate the question whether federalism serves important values—and whether courts are free to disregard the state-protective principles embodied in the Constitution's text and history— straight up. The surprising political valence of state and local autonomy in the terrorism context may, of course, have an important influence on that debate.

The second plausible explanation is that some sincere advocates of the "political safeguards" thesis may sour on it when it comes to protecting national policy. That is only natural: One tends to examine arguments more critically when they threaten values one personally holds dear, and nationally oriented academics (most of whom teach at "national" law schools) may subject the notion of informal guarantees to more searching scrutiny when they are no longer simply protections for often benighted state policies. That scrutiny would be welcome, even if it raises the same sort of opportunism questions I consider in the next section of this chapter. It is likely to take us closer to what I suspect is the truth of the matter: that political safeguards are important in many instances, but unlikely to be a sufficient protection for either state autonomy or national power in all conceivable instances.[53]

A third possibility is that political safeguards actually do work better for states than for the national government. The particular political mechanisms involved in each case are different, and it is at least logically possible that the mechanisms protecting state autonomy are stronger than those protecting national power. But any realistic appraisal suggests that the opposite is more likely to be true. The classic "political safeguards" mechanisms protecting state autonomy posited by Herbert Wechsler and others—primarily, the representation of the States in Congress—have been dissected elsewhere and arguably rejected even by the nationalists on the Court.[54] In particular, federal representatives are at best unreliable partisans of state political institutions; in many instances, they may view state politicians as competitors for power.[55] More recent scholarship has suggested that states are instead protected by various intermediary institutions—primarily political parties and cooperative bureaucratic arrangements—that tie the fate of state and national politicians together.[56] But these institutions are two-way streets and most likely protect national authority as often as they protect states.[57] National power, however, also benefits from Congress's ability to withhold critical federal resources upon which states have become dependent, as well as the President's ability to rally national opinion against recalcitrant states. On balance, the political process would seem to protect national authority at least as well as it does states—and probably better.

The debate over commandeering and the War on Terror thus raises two salient points about the "political safeguards" of federalism. First, fears that state and local opposition will cripple national antiterrorism efforts are surely overblown. Most of the time, immense political pressure—as well as legitimate concern for public safety, of course—will cause states and localities to do whatever national authorities ask.[58] The second point, however, is that nationalist worries that political safeguards might fail in important instances ought to cause everyone to think twice about exclusive reliance on such safeguards in the reverse situation—that is, when the question is protecting state autonomy. I discuss one such situation in the next section.

## State and Local Dissent as Protected Expression

If one of the ways that state and local governments protect liberty is by mobilizing dissent against national policies, then maybe it's time we started taking these activities seriously as dissent. Dissenting political views held by private entities, of course, are protected from suppression through the First Amendment. I have already laid out the basic rationale for extending similar protection to state and local governments: They provide an institutional means, much like political associations and corporations, for mobilizing and organizing the expressive activities of individuals. Judge Richard Posner has thus observed that "to the extent . . . that a municipality is the voice of its residents—is, indeed, a megaphone amplifying voices that might not otherwise be audible—a curtailment of its right to speak might be thought a curtailment of the unquestioned first amendment rights of those residents."[59] But courts and commentators have generally been reluctant to extend such protection to state and local governments.[60] A definitive resolution of that issue would take far more space than I can give it here, but I do want to make a few preliminary observations suggesting that the question is worth pursuing.[61]

The text of the First Amendment itself is specific as to who may not restrict speech—"Congress shall make no law"—but not as to whose speech is protected. A plausible first cut at the text would be that no one's speech may be restricted, whether they are an individual, a corporation, or a political institution. Indeed, the Court's decisions upholding the free speech rights of corporations have insisted that "the identity of the speaker is not decisive in determining whether speech is protected. Corporations and other associations, like individuals, contribute to the 'discussion, debate, and the dissemination of information and ideas' that the First Amendment seeks to foster."[62] If "the identity of the speaker is not decisive," then it is hard to see why this reasoning should not be extended to state and local governments. And in fact, as the Virginia and Kentucky Resolutions demonstrated in the early Republic, those sorts of governmental institutions have played an important part in articulating political dissent. As Akhil Amar has noted, "state governments in 1798–99 played a role similar to that of the institutional press or the opposition party today: monitoring the conduct of officials in power, and coordinating opposition to central policies deemed undesirable."[63]

What seems to have happened is that, in the wake of the movement to incorporate the Bill of Rights against the States, state and local governments have come to be seen almost exclusively as potential censors rather than as right holders under the Free Speech Clause. But nothing logically precludes an entity from taking on either role, depending on the circumstances. Private actors may, for instance, be classified as state actors in certain circumstances and become bound not to restrict the speech of others;[64] few would argue, however, that such actors do not retain their own speech rights as well. Likewise, it is clear that government employees retain important free speech rights even though they are part of the government and therefore bound to respect the speech rights of others.[65]

One might argue that government employees have no right to freedom of expression when they speak on behalf of the government in their official capacity. Hence, the "official" political positions taken by state and local governments cannot be protected speech. A typical argument thus insists that "the common understanding of the First Amendment as a limit on government, rather than a license for it to speak, is natural given the language of the amendment. . . . To transform a restriction on government into a positive right vested in the state would do violence to the Amendment's language."[66] But the "government" is not a unitary entity in our system. The First Amendment's text refers specifically to "Congress" making "no law," and we know that some of the most important dissent from congressional measures in the early republic came from state governments. State and local governments are not speaking on behalf of the national government when they oppose national policy; the foundation of our system of dual sovereignty is that the national and state governments are separate entities, each accountable to the People through independent channels and not directly accountable to one another.[67] Nor does the incorporation of the First Amendment into the Fourteenth, so that it binds state and local governments as well as Congress, change this argument. The fact that private individuals now have speech rights against both the national and state governments does not logically entail that state governments do not retain similar rights against the center.

Another line of argument would assert that state and local institutions are not persons and thus should not bear the same rights as individuals. But we crossed that firebreak long ago when we accorded rights under the Fourteenth Amendment to associations and corporations.[68] The Court has long recognized the critical role that private associations like the NAACP (National Association for the Advancement of Colored People) play in organizing and amplifying divergent political views, as well as the individual interest in hearing the ideas that associations and corporations disseminate. Moreover, one of the principal objections to corporate speech rights— that corporations enjoy an unfair advantage in the political marketplace because of the accumulations of capital they represent—is probably less applicable to state and local governments. Not only are some states and many localities likely to be poorer than many corporations, governments can be held democratically accountable for their expressive activities in ways the corporations cannot.[69]

State and local governments do differ from individuals and private corporations to the extent that actions by governmental institutions may have the force of law. Often, however, this is not the case. Most of the resolutions adopted by state and local governments condemning the PATRIOT Act have no legal force; they simply express those governments' disapproval of what Congress has done. It is hard to see how any principled distinction could be drawn between such resolutions and similar political speech by a private actor. Any effort by Congress to ban these anti-PATRIOT Act resolutions would be instantly recognizable as censorship, and that is no doubt why Congress has made no effort to do so.

The more difficult questions arise when we move to governmental actions that have both expressive and regulatory components. A local measure might, for example, forbid federal agents operating within the city to conduct surveillance authorized by the PATRIOT Act. According First Amendment protection to such a measure would pose a serious threat to the supremacy of federal law. Any law that a state or locality enacts has an expressive component: It embodies a particular view on a question of public policy. (If nude dancing has a sufficient expressive component to be "speech,"[70] then surely an enacted law will always qualify.) But the Supremacy Clause clearly requires that state law must yield in the face of a conflict with a valid federal statute. A state might decide to make a political statement in favor of economic growth over environmental protection, for example, by enacting a law authorizing industry to pollute as much as it likes. No one doubts, however, that such a law would be preempted by federal environmental measures requiring stricter pollution controls—notwithstanding the fact that the state law could be properly viewed as a piece of political expression.

National supremacy means that state and local governments probably cannot enjoy the same free speech rights that private individuals, associations, and corporations enjoy. Contemporary First Amendment doctrine has generally been unwilling to draw a sharp distinction between speech and conduct. The relevant questions are generally whether the conduct in fact expresses a message and whether the government's regulation is directed at that message.[71] Where subnational governments are the speakers, we are likely to need something more like a line between actions that simply express the state or locality's own view and those that regulate or otherwise confer legal obligations on others. While these sorts of lines may not always be easy to draw, they are unlikely to be significantly more difficult than any number of other doctrinal distinctions in contemporary free speech law. The point is simply that that law will require significant doctrinal adaptations where governmental speakers are involved.

Another reason that state and local governments might enjoy comparatively less freedom of expression than individuals is that—unlike private parties—governmental bodies are also the objects of constitutional restrictions. Under the Fourteenth Amendment, for example, state actors are bound by an obligation not to discriminate that is of equal constitutional dignity as the First Amendment that creates rights of free expression. The Seventh Circuit has thus held that "even if municipalities do have First Amendment rights . . . we do not think they have the right to foment, whether through speech or otherwise, governmental discrimination on grounds of race."[72] One might similarly argue that a local government could not subsidize an exhibition of Andres Serrano's "Piss Christ," a photo depicting a crucifix immersed in the artist's urine, on the ground that the exhibition would constitute hate speech in violation of the government's constitutional obligation not to discriminate against religious groups.[73] Although the government's ability to restrict such exhibitions would present a more serious question, its ability to promote them would turn not only on the contours of the free speech right but also on the restrictions imposed by the Equal Protection Clause, as well as the First Amendment's religion clauses. That analysis would likely produce a considerably narrower right of governmental speech than a private individual would enjoy in the same situation.

Finally, we might worry that, even when state or local governments express views without any regulatory effect, those views might have uniquely harmful consequences arising from their source in a governmental body. Suppose, for example, a local city council announces to its citizens that the PATRIOT Act is unconstitutional and invalid, and further urges them not to cooperate with investigative requests from federal officials. Such an announcement might be intended simply as expression of an opinion with no regulatory effect, but because it comes from a governmental body its audience might misconstrue it as either an authoritative decision that the Act is invalid or, even worse, a binding governmental directive not to comply. Again, such possibilities show why the First Amendment rights of governmental entities might not be construed as broadly as those of individuals; we might want a lower standard for holding government speech to be unprotected incitement, for example.[74] But such hypotheticals do not, in my view, establish that state and local governments should enjoy no speech protections at all.

The anti-commandeering doctrine may serve as one workable accommodation of state and local expressive interests, despite the fact that the Court has never justified it in precisely those terms. Modern First Amendment doctrine recognizes a robust right against compelled speech; as Chief Justice Burger observed in *Wooley v. Maynard*, the Free Speech Clause protects "both the right to speak freely and the right to refrain from speaking at all."[75] Indeed, one of the few cases in which the Supreme Court has recognized that state governmental entities enjoy First Amendment interests involved precisely this right not to speak.[76] From this standpoint, it makes sense to say that national authorities cannot compel state or local officials to express support for federal policy by participating in the enforcement of measures with which they disagree. Commandeering thus distorts the political process—a central concern of both federalism and speech doctrine—not only by blurring lines of political accountability but also by undermining the ability of state and local governments to articulate a different point of view.[77]

I do not want to suggest that this is the only legitimate justification for the anti-commandeering doctrine, or that that doctrine exhausts the circumstances in which the First Amendment ought to protect state autonomy. Nonetheless, this way of thinking about commandeering may have the twin virtues of placing that doctrine on a firmer constitutional footing in some circumstances and of making it easier for liberals to swallow. Liberals have traditionally embraced speech rights, after all, while viewing "states' rights" with considerable suspicion. But the conjunction of federalism and rights concerns in the commandeering context is only one of a vast range of linkages that ought to lead liberals to embrace state autonomy in a much broader range of circumstances. I turn to that issue next.

## CONSERVATIVES, LIBERALS, AND STATE AUTONOMY

The readiness of some political liberals to embrace state autonomy as a means of opposing the War on Terror represents something of a shift in the traditional political valence of federalism disputes. Liberals have generally viewed state autonomy with profound suspicion. Many have agreed with a much-cited diatribe by Edward Rubin and Malcolm Feeley that "there is no normative principle involved [in federalism] that is worthy of protection."[78] I argue first that this suspicion is misplaced at this point in our history. Liberals are right to embrace federalism; the odd point is that it has taken them so long to do it.

Any such embrace does raise questions of opportunism, however. Some may see newfound support of state autonomy as hypocritical, given longstanding liberal opposition to state power in the past. I suggest below that there is nothing inherently wrong with such opportunism; in fact, the Founders anticipated that precisely this sort of political self-interest would play a crucial role in maintaining the balance of our constitutional structure. It does seem likely, however, that structural arguments either for or against state autonomy will be taken more seriously if they are advanced in a principled fashion—that is, if advocates of particular structural arrangements demonstrate their willingness to defend those arrangements even when they do not like the political consequences.

## It's About Time

The war on terror is not the only issue on which state autonomy may serve politically liberal goals. Particular states recently have staked out more progressive positions than the national government on issues ranging from global warming to gay marriage, and political liberals have begun to criticize the shifting of authority from the states to the nation on issues from education to health care. Although many liberals have begun to support state autonomy on a number of these issues, one often detects the same discomfort that one sees in commentary on the War on Terror. Referring to Democratic presidential candidates' criticism of the federalization of education policy, for example, one liberal advocate opined that "when you start to hear national Democrats talking as if they are keynote speakers at the Federalist Society, that should be a cause for concern."[79]

I think that instinct is profoundly mistaken. The first point is that, to someone of my own (post-Baby Boom) generation, liberal antipathy to federalism seems so "Sixties." Seth Kreimer, for instance, has said that "in my formative years as a lawyer and legal scholar, during the late 1960s and 1970s, federalism was regularly invoked as a bulwark against federal efforts to prevent racial oppression, political persecution, and police misconduct."[80] That sentiment is surely understandable, and it probably explains much liberal opposition to federalism in the academy. But while I would never claim that these wars—against racism, for instance—have been won, I do think it is fair to say that the battle to federalize those subjects is over.[81] We remain a society divided over race, but few would dispute today that the answers to most racial questions, such as affirmative action, must be sought in national terms. This may not be an entirely good thing from a liberal perspective: Because we have cast the rules governing school desegregation in federal terms, there is little room for state and local experimentation that departs from the Supreme Court's recent decisions restricting desegregation remedies.[82]

On many of the rights issues that retain a federalism dimension, by contrast, it is far from clear that liberal distrust of state autonomy makes sense. Some of the most recent controversies at the intersection of federalism and rights have involved physician-assisted suicide, gay marriage, and medical marijuana. Each of these questions has pitted particular states taking a progressive stance—Oregon's protection of the right to die, Massachusetts's and Vermont's moves to authorize gay marriage, and California's legalization of some medical marijuana use— against strong efforts at the national level to stifle those experiments. The best hope of defending these "liberal" state positions, moreover, may lie in arguing limitations on the scope of the national Commerce Power or restrained notions of federal preemption rather than in reliance on claims of individual right.[83]

Professor Finkelman's contribution to this book offers a case study in liberal suspicion of state and local institutions.[84] He argues that while Justice Stevens's *Printz* dissent was correct to predict that denying Congress the right to commandeer state and local law enforcement would lead to an expansion of the national police force, we should embrace this scenario because federal law enforcement is more respectful of rights. "The willingness of states to oppress religious and ethnic minorities is well known," he asserts.[85] But it is instructive to look at the sources Professor Finkelman cites for that proposition: *Meyer v. Nebraska*,[86] a case decided in 1923, and a book about "nativism" in education during the period 1917–1927.[87] More recent examples could no doubt be cited, although whether one could find enough to support Finkelman's on-balance judgment of state and local inferiority is far less clear. As William Stuntz has pointed out, two of the most important constraints on police misconduct are democratic accountability and resource limitations, and these restrict local law enforcement to a far greater extent than they do federal authorities.[88] What is more fascinating, however, is the willingness of many liberals simply to assume that if state and local officials were less respectful of liberty than their federal counterparts in the 1920s, the same must be true today.

Professor Chemerinsky's entry provides a useful corrective to this sort of assumption, identifying a different but related set of issues.[89] His chapter focuses on a large class of cases involving preemption of state law by federal statutes. Such cases, as I have pointed out elsewhere, implicate the core of the states' capacity to govern themselves; federal preemption, after all, displaces state law in favor of policies enacted at the national level.[90] Moreover, preemption cases generally involve a regulated entity—usually a business—challenging relatively rigorous state regulation on the ground that it conflicts with a more lenient regulatory regime adopted in Washington, DC. To the extent that liberals often favor more rigorous regulation of business and industry, then, they ought usually to take the pro-states side in preemption cases. And, in fact, the pattern that emerges in Supreme Court preemption opinions reflects this political tendency, while standing the Justices's usual positions about federalism on their head: The liberal/nationalists on the Court, such as Justice Stevens, tend to vote for the states and against preemption, while the conservative/states-righters interpret federal measures broadly to preempt state law.[91] I am not as ready as Professor Chemerinsky to explain this pattern purely in terms of political ideology; the pattern of results, in my view, is too complicated and there are too many crosscutting variables, such as judicial philosophies of statutory construction.[92] Nonetheless, the preemption cases offer a large class of contested federalism issues, in which the pro-states side has been more congenial to political progressives.[93]

One hopes that current controversy over the state and local anti-PATRIOT resolutions may encourage more liberal jurists and scholars to be open to federalism-based arguments in contexts beyond preemption of state regulation. I have already noted the example of Justice Stevens, who has been a champion of state autonomy in preemption cases but has little use for the anti-commandeering doctrine. But perhaps if we see that doctrine as fostering state and local dissent from potentially repressive national policies, and as shielding state authority to interpret the Constitution more generously than federal actors who claim interpretive supremacy, then *Printz* will look considerably more appealing to progressives. It may be too much to hope that the Court's nationalists will reconsider some of their prior dissents, but perhaps they might moderate their unusually adamant opposition—embodied in vows to disregard state decisions (the principle that the Court should be reluctant to overturn prior decisions) and continue dissenting indefinitely[94]—to the Court's federalism precedents.

It is hardly true, of course, that all states take a more progressive position than the national government on contemporary issues like environmental policy or gay marriage. But that is precisely the point. National authority can be an effective tool for imposing rights supported by a national consensus on outlier states that refuse to go along. As my colleague Scot Powe has argued, this is basically what happened on race and related issues during the 1960s as a national majority, persuaded of at least some basic commitment to racial equality, imposed its more progressive views on a recalcitrant South.[95] But where no such consensus has been achieved, resolution of a rights issue at the federal level may well stifle progressive change. That is certainly the intent behind at least some aspects of the federal *Defense of Marriage Act* and, more clearly, proposals for a federal constitutional amendment banning gay marriage.[96] It is only natural that people who fervently believe in an individual right or some other aspect of reform would want that reform implemented uniformly across the nation. But the hope that the national government will do the "right thing" right away in every case is utopian. In many instances, incremental change beginning at the state and local level will be the best hope for progressive reform.

The politics of the last decade ought to reinforce this point. For many decades it seemed like the Democratic Party's dominance of Congress would never end, and many liberals no doubt derived their preference for national power from that political fact. But it did end, and the Republican Party controlled all three branches of the national government between 2000 and 2006.[97] Riding public discontent with the war in Iraq, Democrats did recapture both Houses of Congress in 2006, and they stand an excellent chance of regaining the Presidency in 2008. But long-term demographic trends, as well as redistricting measures in several crucial states, render these developments insecure.[98] One cannot, of course, completely rule out a Democratic "restoration," but surely liberals would do well to hedge their bets on that score. In the meantime, their interests will often lie both in promoting progressive reform at the state level and in defending the structural principles that will make those local victories stick.

All this points to a truth that history well bears out: The political valences of national power and state autonomy constantly have shifted back and forth throughout our history. In the Progressive Era, liberals were often based in the states and distrusted federal (particularly federal judicial) power;[99] in the 1960s and 1970s, the opposite was more often true. Prior to the Civil War, slaveholders relied on federal authority to recover escaped slaves, while more enlightened state governments in the North sought to preserve some modicum of due process for accused escapees.[100] It is an ahistorical mistake to take the particular political patterns of the last third of a century for immutable structural truth. One simply cannot ascribe a reliable political tendency to federalism.[101]

## THE LEGITIMACY (AND PERILS) OF OPPORTUNISM

Perhaps one reason that political liberals have been reluctant to embrace federalism, even in situations like the War on Terror where state autonomy may promote their interests, is that they fear appearing opportunistic. Certainly the tone of much commentary in the popular press—accusing Republicans of hypocrisy for proposing national measures when they are supposed to be the party of "states' rights," for example—suggests something wrong with choosing structural principles based on short-term political advantage.[102] And, indeed, I want ultimately to suggest that such a short-term strategy is not a great idea. I do think, however, that the case for opportunism is somewhat stronger than some might think. In fact, such opportunism seems to be exactly what our Founders expected—and counted upon.

Consider, for instance, Madison's discussion of structural safeguards in *Federalist 51*.[103] One interesting aspect of that essay is that it treats the division of power among different institutions as both a safeguard of liberty in its own right and, on the other hand, as a somewhat fragile arrangement that must itself be protected against "a gradual concentration of the several powers in the same department."[104] Madison's answer to this danger is to rely on opportunism: We must give "to those who administer each department, the necessary constitutional means, and personal motives, to resist encroachments of the others." Hence, "ambition must be made to counteract ambition. The interest of the man must be connected with the constitutional rights of the place."[105] We do not hope for individuals to defend structural arrangements out of principled commitment; rather, the system operates by a "policy of supplying by opposite and rival interests, the defect of better motives."[106]

Just as we have misgivings about opportunism today, this sort of solution was not intrinsically appealing to a generation used to thinking in terms of republican virtue. Madison acknowledges that "it may be a reflection on human nature, that such devices should be necessary to controul the abuses of government."[107] He does not linger long over what cannot be helped, however. "But what is government but the greatest of all reflections on human nature?" he asks. "If men were angels, no government would be necessary."[108] We may praise republican virtue when we find it, then, but the system must be built in such a way as to hold together even when principled commitment is lacking.

If anything, the issue-based calculations that motivate political liberals and conservatives to embrace and discard federalism may be an improvement on the more venal, patronage-type motivations that Madison seemed to have most directly in mind. In any event, the main point is that there is nothing inherently surprising or wrong about political factions embracing state autonomy when that structural principle supports their preferred policy outcomes. The most reliable "political safeguard of federalism" in the Founders' scheme is not the hope that federal representatives will be mindful of the institutional interests of their state governmental counterparts back home; rather, it is that whenever a particular federal measure is proposed, the people opposed to that measure on its policy merits will have an incentive to argue that the matter should be left to the states.

At the same time, I do think that one can raise a pragmatic objection to too much opportunism in structural matters. Anytime a proponent or opponent of a particular measure bolsters the policy argument for that measure on the merits with an argument from structural principle, the reason must be that the advocate thinks this additional structural argument will make a difference with some members of his audience. In other words, the choice to engage in structural argument presupposes some subset of decision makers who do not feel sufficiently strongly about the policy merits to be persuaded on those grounds alone, but who do care about structure. I will confess that I myself fall into this camp: I remain relatively agnostic on the War on Terror, but I do feel strongly that Congress should not commandeer state and local officers. I suspect that decision makers and observers who fit this particular description do tend to care somewhat whether structural arguments directed to them seem overly opportunistic; they may wonder, for example, whether the advocate of a particular policy would be willing to accept a similar argument for state autonomy on a question where he might not like the policy outcome. There is, in other words, a measure of credibility to be gained by attempting to be at least somewhat principled on structural questions.

A second caveat has to do with the long-term implications of structural safeguards. The point of those safeguards, as I discussed at the beginning of this chapter, is to preserve space for the freedom to disagree by dividing power and governing competence. By arguing for state and local autonomy, then, political partisans not only may serve their short-term interests; they may also hedge their bets against defeat on a whole range of issues at the national level. In this sense, state and local autonomy may be in the long-term interests of any group that is not sure of victory at the national level for its entire political program.

The upshot of these musings is twofold: First, observers of political debate should be a little less quick to cry "hypocrisy" when political liberals embrace state autonomy, or when political conservatives opt for national power. That is simply the natural political dynamic that the Framers anticipated. But second, political partisans should—for the sake of their own credibility—be cautious about too much opportunism in these matters. By taking a little longer-term perspective on the need for balance in the federal system, moreover, they may preserve the necessary institutional space for future disagreement.


## CONCLUSION

The War on Terror has made for strange bedfellows in any number of respects. Libertarians on the far right have joined with civil liberties advocates on the left to oppose the expansion of law enforcement powers. The Labour Prime Minister of Great Britain has tied his political fortunes inextricably to the most conservative

Republican President in many, many years. And liberals have come to embrace "states' rights"—even if they often cannot bear to use the term—as a mechanism for fostering political resistance to the PATRIOT Act. Welcome to the Dark Side, indeed.

My primary point in this chapter has been to suggest that this is as it should be. Federalism is about dividing power; nothing much depends on what the power in question is being used for. It is also about providing institutional space for a diversity of political views. As such, it should surprise no one that a commitment to state and local autonomy would take on the hue of political opposition to the prevailing orthodoxy at the center, whatever that orthodoxy happens to be. Relatively few people are likely to embrace federalism for its own sake—that may, in fact, be primarily the office of law professors, who are well known to suffer from a somewhat tenuous connection to political reality. Rather, support for state autonomy vis-à-vis national power on both left and right has ebbed and flowed throughout our history, according to the dynamics of whatever political issue is most salient at any given time.

This observation does, of course, have a somewhat melancholy implication for those of us who do care more about structural issues than day-to-day politics. In suggesting that liberals are right to embrace federalism in the context of the War on Terror, we have not uncovered any fundamental new truth about state autonomy; there is no reason, in other words, to assume that liberals will—or should—take the States' side in whatever the next big political debate turns out to be. Partisans of state autonomy can nonetheless welcome these new allies while they last, even if we cannot be confident they will stay around for long.

## Notes

1. *Uniting and Strengthening America by Providing Appropriate Tools Required to Intercept and Obstruct Terrorism (USA PATRIOT Act)*, Public Law No. 107–156, *U.S. Statutes at Large* 115 (2001): 272. One cannot help but wonder how long it took some enterprising staffer to come up with that acronym. For a survey of the Act's provisions, see Michael T. McCarthy, "Recent Developments—USA PATRIOT Act," *Harvard Journal on Legislation* 39 (2002): 435–454.

2. See Ann Althouse, "The Vigor of Anti-Commandeering Doctrine in Times of Terror" (hereinafter as "The Vigor of Anti-Commandeering Doctrine"), in this book.

3. See Vikram David Amar, "Converse 1983 Suits in Which States Police Federal Agents: An Idea Whose Time Has Arrived," in this book.

4. This realization may be at the root of Erwin Chemerinsky's entry here, which mounts a general critique of the Rehnquist Court's preemption jurisprudence for broadly construing federal law to squelch progressive impulses at the state level on a number of issues. See Erwin Chemerinsky, "Empowering States When It Matters: A Different Approach to Preemption," in this book.

5. The correlation of political forces at the national level has changed significantly since the original version of this article appeared in the Brooklyn Law Review

in 2004, and it may change again before the present volume shows up on *anyone's* shelf. I have considerable confidence in predicting, however, that for the foreseeable future *neither* conservatives *nor* liberals can count on a stable, long-term control of national policy.

6. "War on Terror" is itself a contested term. See, for e.g., Philip B. Heymann, *Terrorism, Freedom, and Security: Winning without War* (Cambridge: The MIT Press, 2003), (hereinafter as *"Terrorism, Freedom, and Security"*) 19–33 (arguing that thinking about the struggle against terrorism in terms of "war" is counterproductive). I have no dog in that fight, and I use the term only as a common shorthand for a broad governmental effort to make American society more secure from terrorist attacks.

7. For arguments that the war on terror does threaten civil liberties, see, for example, Heymann, *Terrorism, Freedom, and Security*; David Cole, "The New McCarthyism: Repeating History in the War on Terrorism," *Harvard Civil Rights-Civil Liberties Law Review* 38 (2003): 1–30.

8. See generally Ernest A. Young, "Judicial Activism and Conservative Politics" (hereinafter as "Judicial Activism") *University of Colorado Law Review* 73 (2002): 1182–1203 (distinguishing between situational, political, and institutional forms of conservatism).

9. Brian A. Reaves & Matthew J. Hickman, "Census of State and Local Law Enforcement Agencies, 2000," *U.S. Department of Justice Bureau of Justice Statistics Bulletin* (October 2002): 1, http://www.ojp.usdoj.gov/bjs/pub/pdf/csllea00.pdf. Over 75 percent of these employees were local police. See ibid., at 2.

10. Brian A. Reaves & Lynn M. Bauer, "Federal Law Enforcement Officers, 2002," *U.S. Dept of Justice, Bureau of Justice Statistics Bulletin* (August 2003): 1, http://www.ojp.usdoj.gov/bjs/pub/pdf/fleo02.pdf. The later federal figure reflects a 6 percent increase over 2000 levels, concentrated largely in the Bureau of Alcohol, Tobacco, and Firearms, the Customs Service, and the Immigration and Naturalization Service. See ibid. Although the survey was conducted prior to enactment of the Department of Homeland Security Legislation, it seems likely that the increase in personnel reflects, at least to some extent, federal reaction to the September 11 attacks.

11. William J. Stuntz, "Terrorism, Federalism, and Police Misconduct," *Harvard J. of Law & Public Policy* 25 (2001): 665; see also Ronald K. Chen, "State Incarceration of Federal Prisoners After September 11: Whose Jail Is It Anyway?" (in this book), chronicling the national government's use of state facilities in New Jersey to detain aliens suspected of ties to terrorism.

12. *Printz v. United States*, 521 U.S. 898, 935 (1997).

13. Ibid.

14. For an example of a typical resolution, see City of Austin, Texas, Resolution No. 030807–37 (2003), http://www.bordc.org/detail.php?id=22.

15. The ordinance of the City of Arcata, California—which has received a great deal of national media attention—includes the following two provisions:

> SEC. 2191: No Unconstitutional Detentions or Profiling: "No management employee of the City shall officially engage in or permit unlawful detentions or profiling based on race, ethnicity, national origin, gender, sexual orientation, political or religious association that are in violation of individuals' civil rights or civil liberties as specified in the Bill of Rights and Fourteenth Amendment of the United States Constitution."

> SEC. 2192: No Unconstitutional Voluntary Cooperation: "No management employee of the City shall officially assist or voluntarily cooperate with investigations,

interrogations, or arrest procedures, public or clandestine, that are in violation of individuals' civil rights or civil liberties as specified in the Bill of Rights and Fourteenth Amendment of the United States Constitution."

City of Arcata, California, Ordinance No. 1339 (2003), http://www.arcatacityhall.org/Ordinance%201339.html.

16. The Arcata ordinance, for example, provides for a procedure whereby the city administration must notify the City Council if federal authorities make a request for cooperation that would violate the ordinance's requirements, and provides that the City shall provide legal defense for any city official prosecuted for actions in compliance with the ordinance. See ibid., secs. 2193, 2194.

17. See generally Wayne D. Moore, "Reconceiving Interpretive Autonomy: Insights from the Virginia and Kentucky Resolutions," (hereinafter as "Reconceiving Interpretive Autonomy") *Constitutional Commentary* 11 (1994): 315–354.

18. See generally James Morton Smith, *Freedom's Fetters: The Alien and Sedition Laws and American Civil Liberties* (Ithaca, NY: Cornell University Press, 1956); Moore, "Reconceiving Interpretive Autonomy;" *Constitutional Commentary*, 11 (1994): supra note 17: 341; Garry Wills, *A Necessary Evil: A History of American Distrust of Government* (New York: Simon & Schuster, 1999), 134–152. The resolutions themselves may be found at *Writings of Thomas Jefferson*, ed. Albert Ellery Bergh, (Washington DC: Thomas Jefferson Memorial Association of the United States, 1905), 7: 289–309, and 17 *James Madison, Papers*, eds., William T. Hutchinson & William M.E. Rachel (Chicago, IL: University of Chicago Press, 1962) (Virginia). In addition to their arguments that the federal statutes were unconstitutional, the resolutions also articulated various theories of state governmental authority over national law. See Moore, "Reconceiving Interpretive Autonomy," 318, distinguishing between "nullification, reversal, and interposition." These more extreme forms of governmental resistance are outside the scope of this essay.

19. Moore, "Reconceiving Interpretive Autonomy" 321. This noncooperation seems to have been sufficient to foreclose any actual prosecutions under the Alien and Sedition Acts in Kentucky.

20. The original Constitution did contain a few specific rights guarantees, such as the prohibition on bills of attainder and ex post facto laws. See U.S. Constitution, Art. I, sec. 9, cl. 3. But most contemporary discussion of rights focuses on provisions added by amendment later on.

21. James Madison, *The Federalist No. 51*, ed., Jacob E. Cooke (Hanover, NH: Wesleyan University Press, 1961), 351 (emphasis added). All subsequent references to *The Federalist* are to the Cooke edition.

22. Compare *Clinton v. New York, 524 U.S. 417, 450 (1998)* (J. Kennedy, concurring) ("It would be a grave mistake . . . to think a Bill of Rights in Madison's scheme then or in sound constitutional theory now renders separation of powers of lesser importance."). The same opinion emphasizes the importance of both horizontal and vertical separation of powers—that is, federalism. See ibid. (noting that the Framers "used the principles of separation of powers and federalism to secure liberty in the fundamental political sense of the term, quite in addition to the idea of freedom from intrusive governmental acts").

23. See James Madison, *The Federalist No. 48*, 333 ("Will it be sufficient to mark, with precision, the boundaries of these departments in the Constitution of the government,

and to trust to these parchment barriers against the encroaching spirit of power?") Madison is speaking here of formal demarcations of separated powers, without institutional checks and balances, but his observation is equally applicable to individual rights guarantees.

24. See, for e.g., Barry Friedman, "Valuing Federalism," *Minnesota Law Review* 82 (1997): 403 (observing that state governments "serve as an independent means of calling forth the voice of the people"); Adam B. Cox, "Expressivism in Federalism: A New Defense of the Anti-Commandeering Rule?" (hereinafter "Expressivism in Federalism"), *Loyola of Los Angeles Law Review* 33 (2000): 1324–1325.

25. *NAACP v. Alabama*, 357 U.S. 449, 460 (1958) (recognizing that "effective advocacy of both public and private points of view, particularly controversial ones, is undeniably enhanced by group association"); see *First Nat'l Bank of Boston v. Bellotti*, 435 U.S. 765, 776–786 (1978)

26. Moore, "Reconceiving Interpretive Autonomy," 335.

27. Alexander Hamilton, *The Federalist No. 25*, 169.

28. See "A Tale of Two Legacies—Learning from the Republicans and the Tories," *The Economist*, December 21, 2002 (U.S. edition) (arguing that the Tories "face problems in imitating Mr. Bush [by regaining power at the national level] not least because they lack a testing ground for their ideas"). The new Devolution Acts, devolving some legislative authority to Scotland, Wales, and Northern Ireland, may ultimately change this dynamic. See generally Colin B. Picker, " 'A Light unto the Nations'—The New British Federalism, the Scottish Parliament, and Constitutional Lessons for Multiethnic States," *Tulane Law Review* 77 (2002): 1–90; Adam Tomkins, *Public Law* (Oxford: Oxford University Press), 1–2 (arguing that the British constitution is less unitary than is often thought). But devolution is unlikely to help the Tories in the short term, since the devolved regions have traditionally not been hospitable to their party.

29. See Seth F. Kreimer, "Federalism and Freedom," *Annals of the American Academy of Political and Social Science* 574 (2001): 70–71 (hereinafter as "Federalism and Freedom") (noting historical examples in which "the existence of state-level alternatives to the nationally dominant political orthodoxy has made an electoral—if not a military—challenge to that orthodoxy more likely").

30. See E. J. Dionne, Jr., "Govs 4, Senators 0. Tough Odds," *Washington Post*, January 4, 2004 (final edition); David S. Broder, "Required Reading on Dean," *Washington Post*, January 14, 2004 (final edition); "One Cheer for the Democrats," *The Economist*, November 9, 2002 (U.S. edition), 34.

31. See, for e.g., "A Green in Wolf's Clothing," *The Economist*, December 20, 2003 (U.S. edition) (discussing Republican governor Arnold Schwarzenegger's support for environmental protection in California); "One Cheer for the Democrats," *The Economist*, November 9, 2002 (U.S. edition) (observing that "in the 1990s the Republicans almost split into two parties: a pragmatic one based in the governors' mansions, and an ideological one in Congress").

32. See, for e.g., "Leading by Example," *The Economist*, June 30, 2007 (U.S. edition).

33. See, for e.g., J. Morgan Kousser, " 'The Supremacy of Equal Rights:' The Struggle against Racial Discrimination in Antebellum Massachusetts and the Foundations of the Fourteenth Amendment," *Northwestern University Law Review* 82 (1988): 941–1010 (describing abolitionist efforts at the state level); Taylor Branch, *Parting the Waters: America in the King Years, 1954–63* (New York: Simon & Schuster, 1988), 128–205 (chronicling the Montgomery bus boycott).

34. See, for e.g., Harry N. Scheiber, "State Law and 'Industrial Policy' in American Development, 1790–1987," *California Law Review* 75 (1987): 432.

35. Althouse, "The Vigor of Anti-Commandeering Doctrine."

36. The Massachusetts recognition of gay marriage rested on state constitutional grounds. See *Goodridge v. Department of Public Health*, 798 N.E.2d 941, 948 (MA: 2003). But such state provisions often provide a vehicle for articulating—without fear of Supreme Court reversal—an alternative view of federal rights.

Efforts to amend the Massachusetts Constitution to reverse *Goodridge* recently failed in the state legislature after an extended battle. See Frank Philips, "Legislature Votes to Defeat Same-Sex Marriage Ban," *Boston Globe*, June 14, 2007, http://www.boston.com/news/globe/city_region/breaking_news/2007/06/legislators_vot_1.html.

37. Those constraints might take either of two forms. First, a narrow construction of the Commerce Clause might deny federal power over marriage or physician-assisted suicide. See, for e.g., Stephanie Hendricks, "Note, Pain Relief, Death with Dignity, and Commerce: The Constitutionality of Congressional Attempts to Regulate Physician-Assisted Suicide in Oregon via the Commerce Clause After Lopez and Morrison" (hereinafter "Death with Dignity"), *Willamette Law Review* 37 (2001): 691–716; Grant S. Nelson & Robert J. Pushaw, Jr., "Rethinking the Commerce Clause: Applying First Principles to Uphold Federal Commercial Regulations but Preserve State Control Over Social Issues" (hereinafter "Rethinking the Commerce Clause") *Iowa Law Review* 85 (1999): 170–172 (discussing same-sex marriage). More likely, a strong version of the presumption against preemption in statutory construction might raise the legislative costs and narrow the scope of preemptive federal legislation.

38. But see *Humanitarian Law Project v. Ashcroft*, 309 F. Supp. 2d 1185 (C.D. Cal. 2004), affirmed in part, *Humanitarian Law Project v. United States DOJ*, 393 F.3d 902 (9th Cir. 2004) (invalidating provisions of the USA PATRIOT Act barring the provision of aid to designated terrorist organizations as unconstitutionally vague).

39. See, for e.g., Walter F. Murphy, "Who Shall Interpret? The Quest for the Ultimate Constitutional Interpreter," *Review of Politics* 48 (1986): 411–412.

40. *McCulloch v. Maryland*, 17 U.S. 316 (1819); see *United States President: A Compilation of the Messages and Papers of the Presidents*, ed., James D. Richardson (New York: Bureau of National Literature, 1896), 2:576, 2:581–583. President Jackson insisted that "the authority of the Supreme Court must not . . . be permitted to control the Congress or the Executive when acting in their legislative capacities, but to have only such influence as the force of their reasoning may deserve." Ibid.

41. Moore, "Reconceiving Interpretive Autonomy," 345.

42. As Professor Moore has demonstrated, this view of state interpretive autonomy does not depend on the Virginia and Kentucky Resolutions's more controversial adoption of a "compact" theory of the Constitution, but rather on the more widely shared notion that the Constitution created a government of limited powers. See Moore, "Reconceiving Interpretive Autonomy," 348–351.

43. See Bradford R. Clark, "Separation of Powers as a Safeguard of Federalism," *Texas Law Review* 79 (2001): 1332.

44. See, for e.g., Lynn A. Baker, "Conditional Federal Spending After Lopez," *Columbia Law Review* 95 (1995): 1911–1990.

45. Viet Dinh, Remarks at the LBJ School of Government, Austin, TX (November 2003). See also Richard B. Schmitt, "Anti-Terror Policy Under Criticism from Ex-Insiders," *Houston Chronicle*, November 30, 2003, 6.

46. See, for e.g., Edward L. Rubin & Malcolm Feeley, "Federalism: Some Notes on a National Neurosis" (hereinafter as "Federalism: Some Notes"), *University of California Law Review* 41 (1994): 928–929.

47. Justice Stevens's dissent in *Printz* itself, discussed below, is the most prominent example. Most commentators seem to have assumed instead that the Court would simply create an exception to *Printz* if national security were at stake. See, for e.g., Seth Waxman, "Federalism, Law Enforcement, and the Supremacy Clause: The Strange Case of Ruby Ridge," *Kansas Law Review* 51 (2002): 152 ("After September 11th, . . . it is difficult to imagine the Court treating lightly the federal government's need to respond to problems of national dimension."). The important point, however, is that few observers stress the political dynamics that would buttress national authority in the terrorism context.

48. See, for e.g., *Garcia v. San Antonio Metropolitan Transit Authority*, 469 U.S. 528, 550–54 (1985); Jesse H. Choper, *Judicial Review and the National Political Process: A Functional Reconsideration of the Supreme Court* (Chicago, IL: University of Chicago Press, 1980), 161–259. This position has generally drawn inspiration from the more moderate view advanced in Herbert Wechsler, "The Political Safeguards of Federalism: The Role of the States in the Composition and Selection of the National Government," *Columbia Law Review* 54 (1954): 543–560.

49. *Printz v. United States*, 940 (J. Stevens, dissenting) (emphasis added).

50. Ibid., 957.

51. Ibid., 956. Justice Stevens also joined Justice Blackmun's majority opinion in *Garcia*, which is the locus classicus of the modern "political safeguards" argument. See *Garcia v. San Antonio Metropolitan Transit Authority*, 530.

52. See Ernest A. Young, "Two Cheers for Process Federalism" (hereinafter as "Two Cheers") *Villanova Law Review* 46 (2001): 1380–1384. For an example of Justice Stevens's defense of state autonomy, see *Geier v. American Honda Motor Co.*, 529 U.S. 861, 887 (2000) (J. Stevens, dissenting).

53. I develop that view in Ernest A. Young, "The Rehnquist Court's Two Federalisms," *Texas Law Review* 83 (2004): 1–166.

54. See, for e.g., Larry Kramer, "Putting the Politics Back into the Political Safeguards of Federalism" (hereinafter as "Putting the Politics Back") *Columbia Law Review* 100 (2000): 220–227; Saikrishna B. Prakash & John C. Yoo, "The Puzzling Persistence of Process-Based Federalism Theories" (hereinafter as "The Puzzling Persistence") *Texas Law Review* 79 (2001): 1459–1524; Lynn A. Baker & Ernest A. Young, "Federalism and the Double Standard of Judicial Review" (hereinafter as "Federalism and the Double Standard"), *Duke Law Journal* 51 (2001): 75–164. For the Court's arguable rejection, see *U.S. Term Limits, Inc. v. Thornton*, 514 U.S. 779, 821 (1995) (rejecting the notion that members of Congress serve on behalf of state political institutions rather than the citizens directly). It's hardly surprising, however, that the nationalist justices in the *Term Limits* majority would reject *Garcia*'s theory of representation in a case where that theory favored state autonomy.

55. See, for e.g., Robert F. Nagel, *The Implosion of American Federalism* (New York: Oxford University Press, 2001), 9–10 (explaining why national politicians have incentives to take over local responsibilities from state and local politicians); ibid., 29 (observing that when Congress does devolve power to states, it is likely to do so to shift responsibility for costly failures).

56. See Kramer, "Putting the Politics Back," 278–287. Professor Kramer's view is criticized in Prakash & Yoo, "The Puzzling Persistence," and Baker & Young, "Federalism

and the Double Standard." The truth is likely that political parties and shared administration protect states some of the time, but probably not as often as Kramer supposes.

57. See, for e.g., "Note, No Child Left Behind and the Political Safeguards of Federalism," *Harvard Law Review* 119 (2006): 885–906 (describing how Republican members of Congress sacrificed concerns about federal intrusion into state and local prerogatives on education policy because of the need to support the newly elected Republican president).

The linkage between national and state political parties may also cause partisan warfare at the center to undermine local governance. The recent battles in the Texas legislature over congressional redistricting illustrate how political parties at the national level may distort internal state politics. See, for e.g., Laylan Copelin & Michele Kay, "D.C. Keeps Eye on Special Session," *Austin American-Statesman (Texas)*, June 19, 2003 (describing pressure on Texas state officials from House Majority Leader Tom DeLay and presidential advisor Karl Rove to convene a contentious special legislative session to redraw federal House districts, in order to help Republican party fortunes in Congress); Dave Harmon, "Representatives Seek Senate's Help for Threatened Bills," *Austin American-Statesman (Texas)*, May 14, 2003 (describing how the attempt to push redistricting legislation through the state legislature, at the behest of federal officials, endangered important state legislation). See generally Steve Bickerstaff, *Lines in the Sand: Congressional Redistricting in Texas and the Downfall of Tom DeLay* (Austin, TX: University of Texas Press, 2007).

58. These pressures should at least be enough to overcome libertarian resistance to antiterror measures in most jurisdictions. The more doubtful question arises from the massive financial and other resource costs that the war on terror imposes on states and localities. See Jack Weiss, "Orange Crunch," *New York Times*, January 14, 2004 (final edition). As antiterror begins to trade off with core law enforcement priorities, pressures to opt out of federal measures may increase.

59. *Creek v. Village of Westhaven*, 80 F.3d. 186, 193 (7th Cir. 1996).

60. See, for e.g., *National Foreign Trade Council v. Natsios*, 181 F.3d 38, 61 (1st Cir. 1999) (expressing doubt whether a state possesses first amendment rights against federal regulation), aff'd on other grounds, *Crosby v. National Foreign Trade Council*, 530 U.S. 363 (2000).

61. See, for e.g., Matthew C. Porterfield, "State and Local Foreign Policy Initiatives and Free Speech: The First Amendment as an Instrument of Federalism" (hereinafter as "State and Local Foreign Policy Initiatives"), *Stanford Journal of International Law* 35 (1999): 33–47; Meir Dan-Cohen, "Freedoms of Collective Speech: A Theory of Protected Communications by Organizations, Communities, and the State," *California Law Review* 79 (1991): 1258–1266.

62. *Pacific Gas & Electric. Co. v. Public Utilities Commission*, 475 U.S. 1, 8 (1986) (quoting *First Nat'l Bank of Boston v. Bellotti*, 435 U.S. 765, 783 (1978)).

63. Akhil Reed Amar, "Some New World Lessons for the Old World," *University of Chicago Law Review* 58 (1991): 504.

64. See, for e.g., *Brentwood Academy v. Tennessee Secondary School Athletic Association*, 531 U.S. 288 (2001) (holding that a statewide interscholastic athletic association of both public and private schools was sufficiently "entwined" with government activities to be subject to the First Amendment); *Marsh v. Alabama*, 326 U.S. 501 (1946) (holding that private authorities in a "company town" are bound by the First Amendment).

65. See, for e.g., *Connick v. Meyers*, 461 U.S. 138, 154 (1983); *Pickering v. Board of Education*, 391 U.S. 563, 573 (1968).

66. James Forman, "Note, Driving Dixie Down: Removing the Confederate Flag from Southern State Capitols," *Yale Law Journal* 101 (1991): 518–519.

67. See, for e.g., *U.S. Term Limits v. Thornton*, 514 U.S. 779, 838–842 (1995) (J. Kennedy, concurring).

68. See, for e.g., *Santa Clara County v. Southern Pacific Railroad Co.*, 118 U.S. 394 (1886).

69. See Porterfield, "State and Local Foreign Policy Initiatives," 33.

70. See *Barnes v. Glen Theatre, Inc.*, 501 U.S 560, 565–566 (1991) (plurality opinion).

71. See, for e.g., *R.A.V. v. City of St. Paul*, 505 U.S. 377, 385–386 (1992); *United States v. O'Brien*, 391 U.S. 367, 376–377 (1968).

72. *Creek v. Village of Westhaven*, 80 F.3d. 186, 193 (7th Cir. 1996).

73. For a description of the Serrano controversy, see Jacqueline Trescott, "NEA Balks at Funding Serrano: Critics See Rejection As Politically Motivated," *Washington Post*, August 6, 1994 (final edition). For a similar controversy that occurred not far from the site of the Brooklyn Law School symposium, see Kit R. Roane, "Arguments Heard in Museum's Legal Battle with Mayor," *New York Times*, October 9, 1999 (final edition).

74. Compare *Brandenburg v. Ohio*, 395 U.S. 444, 447 (1969) (permitting restriction of private incitement only "where such advocacy is directed to inciting or producing imminent lawless action and is likely to incite or produce such action").

75. *Wooley v. Maynard*, 430 U.S. 705, 714 (1977).

76. See *Arkansas Educational Television Commission v. Forbes*, 523 U.S. 666, 674–675 (1998) (holding that a state public television station had a protected first amendment interest in deciding which candidates to include, and which to exclude, in a televised political debate).

77. For a similar argument, see Cox, "Expressivism in Federalism."

78. Rubin & Feeley, "Federalism: Some Notes," 909.

79. Kate Zemike, "'No Child Left Behind' Brings a Reversal: Democrats Fault a Federal Education Plan," *New York Times*, January 12, 2004 (final edition) (quoting Andrew J. Rotherham, director of education policy for the Progressive Policy Institute).

80. Kreimer, "Federalism and Freedom," 67.

81. See Baker & Young, "Federalism and the Double Standard," 147–149.

82. See *Parents Involved in Community Schools v. Seattle Independent School District No. 1, Nos. 05–908 and 05–915*, 2007 U.S. LEXIS 8670 (June 28, 2007) (holding that race-based student assignment plans designed to promote racial balance failed strict scrutiny under the Equal Protection Clause).

83. See, for e.g., *Raich v. Ashcroft*, 352 F.3d 1222 (9th Cir. 2003) (holding that plaintiffs challenging federal prohibitions on medical marijuana use were entitled to a preliminary injunction on Commerce Clause grounds), *reversed, Gonzales v. Raich*, 545 U.S. 1 (2005); see also *Conant v. Walters*, 309 F.3d 629, 645–647 (9th Cir. 2002) (J. Kozinski, concurring) (making an anti-commandeering argument against aspects of the federal law restricting medical marijuana use); Stephanie Hendricks, "Death with Dignity;" Nelson & Pushaw, "Rethinking the Commerce Clause" (discussing same-sex marriage). In light of the Court's recent decision upholding the federal ban on medical marijuana, statutory arguments restricting the reach of federal preemption are likely to be more fruitful than Commerce Clause claims. See, for e.g., *Gonzales v. Oregon*, 546 U.S. 243 (2006) (holding that a federal regulation seeking to preempt Oregon's right-to-die law exceeded the agency's statutory authority); Ernest A. Young, "Just Blowing Smoke? Politics, Doctrine, and the Federalist Revival after *Gonzales v. Raich*," *Supreme Court Review 2005*: 1–50.

84. Paul Finkelman, "The Roots of *Printz*: Proslavery Constitutionalism, National Law Enforcement, Federalism, and Local Cooperation" (hereinafter as "The Roots of *Printz*").

85. Ibid.

86. *Meyer v. Nebraska*, 262 U.S. 390 (1923) (involving a state law prohibiting the teaching of foreign languages to young children).

87. See Finkelman, "The Roots of *Printz*" (citing Meyer and William G. Ross, *Forging New Freedoms: Nativism, Education, and the Constitution, 1917–1927* (Lincoln, NE: University of Nebraska Press, 1994)).

88. See Stuntz, "Terrorism, Federalism, and Police Misconduct," 674. This much is clear: the FBI is less accountable than local police forces.... FBI agents also have more freedom to target the wrong people than do local cops—in part because the local cops have primary responsibility for day-to-day law enforcement. If we are to add to the FBI's power, we would do well to worry about those two problems.

89. See Chemerinsky, "Empowering States When It Matters."

90. See Ernest A. Young, "State Sovereign Immunity and the Future of Federalism," *Supreme Court Review 1999*: 39–40 (arguing that preemption cases are much more important for state autonomy than cases involving state sovereign immunity, despite the Court's focus on the latter); Young, "Two Cheers," 1375–1376 (arguing that preemption cases are the most important class of federalism cases from the perspective of state autonomy); see also S. Candice Hoke, "Preemption Pathologies and Civic Republican Values," *Boston University Law Review* 71 (1991): 694 (noting the "jurispathic" effect of federal preemption in killing off state policy choices). For the notion of "jurispathic" effects, see generally, Robert M. Cover, "The Supreme Court, 1982 Term: Foreword—Nomos and Narrative," *Harvard Law Review* 97 (1983): 40.

91. For some representative decisions, see, for example, *Lorillard Tobacco Co. v. Reilly,* 533 U.S. 525 (2001), and *Geier v. American Honda Motor Co.*, 529 U.S. 861 (2000). Several scholars in addition to Professor Chemerinsky have noted this pattern. See Daniel J. Meltzer, "The Supreme Court's Judicial Passivity," *Supreme Court Review 2002*: 362–378; Calvin Massey, "Federalism and the Rehnquist Court," *Hastings Law Journal* 53 (2002): 502–512; Richard H. Fallon, Jr., "The 'Conservative' Paths of the Rehnquist Court's Federalism Decisions," *University of Chicago Law Review* 69 (2002): 429–430; Young, "Two Cheers," 1349. I develop and analyze this pattern at much greater length in Young, "The Rehnquist Court's Two Federalisms."

92. See Young, "Two Cheers," 1384.

93. See generally, Richard A. Epstein and Michael S. Greve, eds., *Federal Preemption: States' Powers, National Interests* (Washington, DC: AEI Press, 2007).

94. See, for e.g., *Federal Maritime Commission v. South Carolina State Ports Authority,* 535 U.S. 743, 788 (2002) (J. Breyer, dissenting) ("Today's decision reaffirms the need for continued dissent—unless the consequences of the Court's approach prove anodyne, as I hope, rather than randomly destructive, as I fear."); *Kimel v. Florida Board of Regents*, 528 U.S 62, 98–99 (2000) (J. Stevens, dissenting) (asserting that "the kind of judicial activism manifested in [the Court's 11th Amendment cases] represents such a radical departure from the proper role of this Court that it should be opposed whenever the opportunity arises"); see also Charles Fried, "Five to Four: Reflections on the School Voucher Case," *Harvard Law Review* 116 (2002): 178 (observing that "such explicit commitments to keep dissenting until the dissent becomes the doctrine of the Court are rare"). It may be that the dissenters' unwillingness to accord stare decisis effect to the Court's federalism decisions is confined

to the Eleventh Amendment cases, which are harder to see in libertarian terms. We simply don't have enough commandeering or commerce clause cases to tell for sure. But certainly we have no evidence of the *Printz* and *Lopez* dissenters' willingness to accept the legitimacy of those decisions in future cases.

95.  Lucas A. Powe, Jr., *The Warren Court and American Politics* (Cambridge: Belknap Press, 2000). I would certainly not argue that we have reached national consensus on race issues in general, but I think it is safe to say that the basic equality norms embodied in the 1964 Civil Rights Act or the Equal Protection Clause's prohibition on overt, malign, racial discrimination enjoy far broader popular support than, say, a right to gay marriage. See, for e.g., "US Opposed to Gay Marriage," *Birmingham Post*, April 12, 2004 (first edition) (reporting that respondents to a poll opposed gay marriage by a margin of 55 to 41 percent).

96.  Eugene Volokh has argued—persuasively, in my view—that the portion of the Defense of Marriage Act that relieves states of their full faith and credit obligations to recognize gay marriages permitted in other states may actually promote social change on this issue. E-mail posting of Eugene Volokh, CONLAWPROF listserv (November 18, 2003) (on file with author; cited with permission). The reason is that if, say, Vermont's recognition of gay marriage can bind all other states to recognize such unions entered into in Vermont, then any state opposed to the practice has a stake in snuffing out Vermont's policy. Better, Professor Volokh argues, to defuse this pressure for a national solution and let each state determine how to handle the issue on its own. The critical point, however, is that this aspect of the Defense of Marriage Act may facilitate incremental reform precisely by decentralizing resolution of the issue. See also "States Represent Best Forums for Gay-Marriage Debate," USAToday.com, April 1, 2004, http://www.usatoday.com/news/opinion/editorials/2004-04-01-our-view_x.htm.

97.  See Baker & Young, "Federalism and the Double Standard," 151.

98.  See "Eatanswill Revisited: America's Election," *The Economist*, January 31, 2004 (U.S. edition).

99.  See Edward A. Purcell, Jr., *Brandeis and the Progressive Constitution: Erie, The Judicial Power, and the Politics of the Federal Courts in Twentieth-Century America* (New Haven, CT: Yale University Press, 2000), 1–2, 12–16.

100.  See Finkelman, "The Roots of *Printz*"; Baker & Young, "Federalism and the Double Standard," 121–124.

101.  One can argue that, to the extent federalism fosters incremental change and caters to risk aversion about political defeat at the national level, it is inherently related to a Burkean form of conservatism. See Ernest A. Young, "The Conservative Case for Federalism," *George Washington University Law Review* 74 (2006): 874–887. But that is quite different from the sort of conservative/liberal dichotomy that we generally refer to when we speak of contemporary politics. See generally Young, "Judicial Activism," 1181–1203.

102.  See, for e.g., E. J. Dionne, Jr., "When States' Rights Get in the Way," editorial, *Washington Post*, June 25, 2002 (final edition): "The doctrine of states' rights, so often invoked as a principle, is almost always a pretext to deny the federal government authority to do things that conservatives dislike.... How do I know this? Because when states have the temerity to try doing progressive things . . . , conservatives are quick to use federal power to stop them from exercising their right to act."

103.  James Madison, *The Federalist No. 51*. Madison's discussion seems most immediately directed at separation of powers within the national government, but there is little

doubt that it applies to federalism as well. Both federalism and separation of powers are part of the "double security" for the "rights of the people," which figures prominently in the essay. See ibid., at 351.

104. Ibid., 349.
105. Ibid. (emphasis added).
106. Ibid.
107. Ibid.
108. Ibid.

# Collapsing Spheres: Joint Terrorism Task Forces, Federalism, and the War on Terror

Susan N. Herman

The war on terror has already created new frontiers in federalism by attempting to enlist state and local law enforcement officials as the "hands and feet" of federal strategists.[1] An early example was a fall 2001 FBI program of interviewing, with the aid of local law enforcement officials, thousands of Arab and Muslim men around the country.[2] A more recent example is the expanded use of Joint Terrorism Task Forces. These hybrid federal/local law enforcement programs operate on the frontiers of federalism by creating a variety of ambiguous relationships between federal and state or local officials and muddling the lines of authority and accountability that have characterized our dual sovereignty model of federalism. Both of these programs met with general acceptance throughout most of the country, but not in Portland, Oregon, one of the country's best-known "laboratories" for experiments in federalism.[3]

Portland decided to withdraw its officers from a Joint Terrorism Task Force after discovering that the secrecy surrounding federal antiterrorism investigations makes it a real challenge to maintain local control of local law enforcement officials engaged in joint federal/local enterprises. Withdrawal turned out to be the only way Portland could maintain autonomy within its own sphere of operations, accountability of its own executive branch officials, and legislative control of policy decisions that otherwise might disappear into the city's executive branch. The debates that took place over these issues in Portland provide a provocative model for the rest of the country, where the issues Portland took so seriously barely seem to have been noticed.

The war on terror has precipitously shifted a tremendous amount of power to the executive branch of the federal government and minimized the role of Congress and the courts,[4] at the risk of undermining the United States Constitution's horizontal system of checks and balances. Joint federal and state/local enterprises risk weakening the Constitution's vertical checks and balances by collapsing previously autonomous spheres of authority. Portland's experience with the Joint Terrorism Task Force, like other federal/state skirmishes over the allocation of decision-making authority, also shows that the federal government's antiterrorism campaign can disrupt a locality's internal system of governance by forcing a shift of the center of policymaking gravity away from legislative bodies and toward the executive branches, where accountability and transparency are minimized.

In addition to discussing Portland's experience with the Joint Terrorism Task Force program, I will also explore another example of a city legislative body attempting to maintain control of its employees in the context of federal antiterrorism efforts: an ordinance in Arcata, California threatened city officials with a fine of $57 if they officially assisted or voluntarily cooperated with federal agents wielding PATRIOT Act powers, which Arcata disliked.[5] By way of contrast, in New York City, city executive officials were allowed to make essentially unilateral decisions about the manner of their cooperation with federal antiterrorism efforts. In one instance, the New York Police Department went into federal court to ask to be relieved of limitations on its surveillance powers imposed by an earlier consent decree. In another, three different New York City mayors coped with the issue of city/federal relations with respect to the local enforcement of immigration law. In neither case did the New York City Council play any significant policymaking role.

Finally, I will describe several instances in which all branches of state or local government have been preempted by federal law or policy from making their own decisions about their manner of cooperating in the federally led war on terror. As is more fully discussed by Ronald Chen ("Whose Jail Is It Anyway?"), during the fall of 2001 a New Jersey court applied a state freedom of information law to require disclosure of the identities of federal detainees being held in the state's jails under contract with the federal government. While that case was pending appeal, the state law was preempted by an interim rule issued by a federal agency, prohibiting such disclosure. If such preemption is valid, could the Oregon law whose integrity was at the center of the Portland City Council's debates be simply swept out of the way by the United States Attorney General? May executive officials at the local, state, or federal level preempt state or local legislative decisions?


## THE DUAL-SOVEREIGNTY PARADIGM AND THE TENTH AMENDMENT

Although federal and state/local law enforcement officers have sometimes worked together in the area of crime control,[6] our paradigmatic model for such relationships has been a dual sovereignty model. Under this model, each "sovereign"[7] has a sphere of operations[8] in which it makes its own policy decisions; each controls the executive branch officials it hires to implement its policies; each decides how and to whom its officers will be accountable for their actions, including the extent of civilian review of its law enforcement activities. Although state and local officials must follow the dictates of the federal Constitution, any state may decide to exceed the floor of federal constitutional protection by providing more rights for suspects and defendants within its own sphere. Through its own state constitutional decisions, statutes, regulations, and common law, each state (and to some extent local governments) can define what will be considered to constitute intolerable abuse of law enforcement and can decide what measures to take to counter what it defines as abusive. Law enforcement agents must follow the law of each higher entity in the hierarchy—city police, for example, must follow applicable city, state, and federal restrictions—and may ignore the restrictions of those lower in the hierarchy. Thus, because the law is cumulative, the officers are not placed in the position of Pavlov's dogs, asked to follow inconsistent sets of commands. A state may not impose any rules or restrictions that conflict with its federal obligations; a locality may not impose any rules that conflict with its federal or state obligations. Officers need only combine the applicable sets of rules and, by following the most demanding, they will be in compliance with all.

The Supreme Court's double jeopardy jurisprudence has created a strong incentive for keeping federal and state criminal enforcement efforts discrete. Under the Court's "dual sovereignty exception" to double jeopardy rules, a person may be prosecuted by two different jurisdictions for the same offense, but only if the officers of those jurisdictions have not cooperated too much during the initial investigation and prosecution.[9] As I have explained in a law review article, this double jeopardy doctrine can actually impede the implementation of federal interests.[10] Federal officials are discouraged, for example, from offering their assistance in a state civil rights prosecution. The law encourages them to sit by and watch a state prosecution flounder so that they can preserve the possibility of initiating their own successive prosecution.[11]

Going a step further in enforcing the separation of federal and state crime control efforts, the Supreme Court in *Printz v. United States*[12] interpreted the Tenth Amendment and principles of federalism to prohibit the federal government from "commandeering" state or local law enforcement officials to assist in implementing federal criminal law. The federal government was prohibited from enlisting local law enforcement officials to help conduct background checks on people within their jurisdictions who applied for gun permits.[13] As in the dual sovereignty area, one of the Court's chief concerns in *Printz* was its desire to preserve separate spheres in which the dual sovereigns will operate.[14] According to Justice Scalia, author of the majority opinion, the lines of federalism are fixed[15] and no matter what the circumstances, the federal government must hire its own enforcement officials to implement federal programs. It may only enlist state enforcement officials if the state is given a choice whether or not to cooperate and voluntarily decides to do so (often because the state receives federal funding in exchange for its cooperation).[16] The federal program, no matter how important, can be permitted to fizzle unless Congress musters the funding to employ sufficient federal personnel to implement the program or to bribe state and local officials to participate.[17] Justice Scalia's opinion in *Printz* suggests that in addition to the Tenth Amendment, various provisions of Articles I to III of the Constitution embed the principle that there must be dual spheres of sovereignty.[18]

During the fall of 2001, there was a moment where it appeared that this anti-commandeering model might spawn an exception for federal antiterrorism efforts. The FBI wished to question thousands of Arab and Muslim men around the country not because they were suspected of terrorism or any crime, but to find out whether they had any useful information. Lacking the manpower to conduct so many interviews, the FBI asked local police chiefs and sheriffs to assist with the interviewing process.[19] The request for local assistance was reminiscent of the request to local law enforcement officers condemned in *Printz*: the local officers were asked to share their experience with and knowledge of local residents as well as to provide sheer manpower to assist with the federal investigation.

Most local law enforcement officials were eager to cooperate, but not all. Portland, Oregon Chief of Police, Mark Kroeker, noted that Oregon had a state law[20] which prohibited police from collecting or maintaining information about the political, religious, or social views, associations, or activities of any individual or group unless the information relates to a criminal investigation and there are reasonable grounds to suspect that the subject is or may be involved with criminal conduct.[21] The Portland City Attorney expressed the opinion that some of the questions the FBI wished to pose, if asked of people as to whom there was no "criminal nexus," would violate the state law.[22] While federal agents are empowered, under the Supremacy Clause,[23] to ignore state law while implementing a federal program, state and local officers are not. Whether the Portland police might be violating their own employer's law by participating in the interviews was not the only issue that surfaced. The Chief of Police of Detroit, a community with a substantial number of Arab and Muslim residents, expressed his own concern that playing the role of a federal terrorism investigator and questioning Arab and Muslim men in his community on behalf of the FBI could compromise his relations with members of his community and impede his ability to do the job Detroit was paying him to do.[24]

In the fall of 2001, any objection or refusal to cooperate in any respect with the federal government's antiterrorism program was politically loaded. Chief Kroeker, in a subsequent appearance on a nationally televised program on CNN,[25] protested repeatedly that he and the Portland police were "participating 100 percent" with "every effort of the federal government in Portland," including the Joint Terrorism Task Force. "Our heart is there," he said, "but it's the law."[26] The Portland interpretation of how Oregon law applied to these interviews proved controversial. Both the Oregon Attorney General and the Multnomah County District Attorney opined that state law did not prevent Portland police from asking the questions on the FBI's list because the interviews were voluntary.[27] The interviews proceeded, after some negotiations about who would ask what. The FBI might have had to negotiate harder in some areas of the country—like Portland—to work out who, as between federal and local agents, would ask what questions under what conditions, but the tension between federal and state law was resolved politically, under the watchful eye of the media and the public. Therefore, there was no need for any court to decide whether or not, as in *Printz*, the local law enforcement officials had a constitutional basis for declining to render their assistance or whether or not the FBI might constitutionally have compelled cooperation under an exception to *Printz*.

Time has passed and it is no longer politically impossible for a state or local official to question aspects of the federal government's antiterrorism program or even to threaten to withhold cooperation. Eight states and over 400 cities and counties have now passed resolutions, based on a Bill of Rights Defense Committee [BORDC] model, condemning provisions of the USA PATRIOT Act[28] and other aspects of the federal government's antiterrorism activities,[29] Portland passed such a resolution on October 29, 2003; Multnomah County passed a similar resolution on December 9, 2004.[30] These resolutions are based on three premises: (1) under the Supremacy Clause, a state or local entity cannot impede a federal investigation that conforms to federal law,[31] no matter how much the local residents dislike the federal powers being used; (2) in our system of federalism, localities can and should weigh in on the making of federal policy;[32] and (3) state and local governments are entitled to make decisions governing the conduct of their own employees. Some of these resolutions recognize and assert that state and local law enforcement officials need not themselves follow federal procedures with which they disagree, even if those procedures are found to be acceptable under the federal Constitution, and they may instruct local officers not to use the disapproved tactics in their own investigations.[33] Some of the resolutions also raise questions about how far the Supremacy Clause requires state and local entities to go in actively cooperating with federal enforcement efforts with which they disagree.[34]

The same day the Portland City Council passed its own version of this resolution, the Council also agreed to renew Portland's participation in a Joint Terrorism Task Force for that year.[35] It was only after several years of debate and a change of the relevant elected officials that Portland decided in 2005 not to renew its participation.

### Joint Terrorism Task Forces and Federalism

According to the FBI's website, Joint Terrorism Task Forces ("JTTFs") are "teams of state and local law enforcement officers, FBI Agents, and other federal agents and personnel who work shoulder-to-shoulder to investigate and prevent terrorism."[36] Although JTTFs were first used in 1980, their number has doubled since September 11, 2001.[37] There are now sixty-six JTTFs, including one in each FBI field office and others in smaller offices.[38] More than 2,300 personnel work on these task forces nationwide.[39] The task forces are supposed to be a two-way street, enlisting the numerically superior manpower of the states and localities[40] to complement federal efforts, on the one hand, and sharing information gathered by the federal government with state and local enforcement officials on the other. Some have questioned whether the states and localities are indeed giving more than they receive,[41] but this is one of the many questions that cannot be publicly debated in any meaningful manner because of the level of secrecy surrounding the operations of the JTTFs.

The terms governing each of these cooperative ventures are set forth in a Memorandum of Understanding ("MOU") between the locality and the FBI, the terms of which are often kept secret from the public.[42] The draft MOU the Portland City Council considered was made public.[43] Under its terms, it appears that Portland police officers assigned to the Portland JTTF ("PJTTF") continued to be paid by the city, although their overtime was paid by the federal government.[44] Local officers were sworn in and deputized as Special Federal Officers and received appropriate federal security clearances; they were required to sign nondisclosure agreements agreeing not to disclose any classified or sensitive information to non-JTTF members without the express permission of the FBI; and they were considered to be federal employees "for the limited purpose of defending claims arising out of JTTF activity."[45]

These sections created a somewhat ambiguous, hybrid status for the Portland police participants. On the one hand, they continued to be Portland employees by dint of their salaries and supervision; but on the other hand, they were subject to control by the FBI in a number of respects, including the need to get the FBI's permission before disclosing information about investigations and their own roles in those investigations. The section constituting the Portland police officers as federal employees for purposes of defending claims could be read as an attempt to provide those officers with immunity against any lawsuit for violating a state law that provided more rights to targets of investigation than federal law—like the Oregon State law limiting surveillance of political and religious groups described above.[46] Other sections of the memorandum, however, provided that state law was not to be supplanted or undermined. Responsibility for the conduct of the Portland officers remained with their Portland police supervisors; their participation was subject to review by the Portland police lieutenant "to insure compliance with applicable Oregon statutes and laws," and the memorandum explicitly stated that "in situations where the statutory or common law of Oregon is more restrictive of law enforcement than comparable federal law, the investigative methods employed by the state and local law enforcement agencies shall conform to the requirements of such Oregon statutes or common law."[47]

Thus Portland contractually agreed that its officers would remain subject to state and local law and not fully become federal agents permitted to operate under less constrained federal procedures. For example, Department of Justice guidelines permit placing an undercover agent in a political or religious meeting even in the absence of any suspicion that anyone present would meet the criminal nexus requirement Oregon law imposes.[48] Oregon officers were prohibited from acting in the absence of a criminal nexus, and required to limit their involvement in immigration raids.[49] The document is fairly clear in its instruction to the Portland police officers to follow the greater demands of state law. Former Mayor Vera Katz had declared herself satisfied that the Portland police were complying with state law.[50] Her successor, Mayor Tom Potter, proved more difficult to satisfy.

Opponents of PJTTF participation regarded the MOU's attempts to assure respect for the more demanding Oregon state law as insufficient. First, they were wary of simply trusting assurances that state law would be respected when they would not be able to review whether or not those assurances were well founded.[51] (One commissioner said, "I'm not going to take it on faith that the federal government is using our officers in compliance with Oregon law.")[52] The chief issue became how to provide for civilian oversight of the police given the veil of secrecy surrounding the operations of the JTTF. Opponents alleged that abuses of the antiterrorism authority had already occurred elsewhere[53] and that there was no way for the City Council or the public to know whether or not there had been or would be abuses, as defined by Oregon law, in Portland.[54] Several different concerns were raised about the MOU's blurring of the lines of accountability. Under the MOU, information could be shared with Oregon's United States Senators and Representatives and with the Mayor if the Mayor could obtain an adequate security clearance, but not with other civilians, including the members of the City Council.[55] During the final round of negotiations, the FBI declined to offer either the Mayor or the council members the same top level security clearance as the officers assigned to the PJTTF.[56] (Mayor Potter, who was a former Portland chief of police, acted as police commissioner with oversight of the police department[57] according to Portland tradition.) And because of the nondisclosure agreements, the local police officers might not have been able to inform the City Council, the public, or the press if any state, local, or federal agents were intruding on religious or political groups or violating the state's law in any other manner.

The nondisclosure agreement thus created a distinct possibility that any violation of the state law by Portland employees would go undiscovered. Although the MOU instructed the Portland officers to comply with state law, it is not clear, given the nondisclosure agreement, that one of the Portland police officers would have been permitted either to report a police colleague for joining in a federal effort in disregard of Oregon law, or even to confess his or her own violation of state law, as this might entail divulging the details of a clandestine federal operation. Since investigations conducted by the JTTF, especially surveillance of a suspect group, are carried out in secret, the targets of surveillance would not be likely to know if Portland police officers were violating state law, or even that they were involved in an investigation, and so it might be that no one would be able to complain of a violation if one did occur.[58] There was also concern that the activities of the JTTF might not actually be confined to antiterrorism activities in practice, but might invisibly spill over to ordinary criminal law enforcement.[59]

The MOU's command to follow state law respecting the gathering of information was clear but, other than sheer trust, there were no mechanisms for enforcing those commands that were not under the control of the FBI. In addition, because the files created by the JTTF were considered to be FBI files, they were not subject to the requirement of state laws that such files be reviewed and purged, which would have made it impossible to enforce the Oregon statute's provision against the maintenance of such files.[60]

Another type of accountability argument focuses on the lines of funding rather than supervision. The JTTFs offer a way for the federal government to use local law enforcement officers as its "hands and feet" without footing the bill for their services. As in *Printz*, the argument can be made that if the federal government wants manpower, it must pay instead of conscripting even willing state or local employees.[61] If the federal government is not paying these officers, under this line of argument, the federal government should not be controlling them even to the extent provided in the draft MOU. The forms of federal control under the MOU, particularly control over the dissemination of information relevant to whether state law has been violated, are in some respects tantamount to federal preemption of state law, but accomplished by contract rather than by congressional action. The people of Portland, through their elected representatives, should have some means of reviewing the extent of the resources they are providing the federal government. As Jason Mazzone argues in "The Security Constitution," there is also an independent constitutional basis, in the Protection Clause of Article IV, for arguing that it is the responsibility of the federal government to protect the people of Portland against terrorist attacks that are directed not specifically against Portland, but against the United States. If this is true, the salaries of all of the JTTF participants should be paid by federal rather than state or local tax dollars.

Not all of the arguments outlined above were raised during the course of the Portland debates, but the Mayor and City Council's concerns about accountability were decisive. Negotiations ultimately proved fruitless when the FBI refused to offer top security clearances to the Mayor or City Council members. The City Council therefore voted to withdraw the Portland officers from the PJTTF.[62]

The agent in charge of the Portland FBI office remarked (perhaps wistfully) that he knew of no other local government that had pulled out of a JTTF.[63]


### The PJTTF and the Law of Federalism

The Portland City Council provided a dramatic model of dual sovereignty federalism in action by taking its responsibilities very seriously. Portland's withdrawal from the JTTF was a logical culmination of the arguments the Supreme Court has accepted in the dual sovereignty arena and in *Printz*. The City Council's debates demonstrated how difficult it is for local policymakers to fulfill their supervisory and policymaking roles when they cannot have access to relevant information. This difficulty could have become an excuse for the Council to cede all decisions to federal decision makers, but the council members were unwilling to do so. As one Portland Commissioner said "the onus rests on those of us who were elected to govern the city to make sure that here in Portland things are going well."[64] The policymakers in other jurisdictions may or may not have inserted provisions in their secret MOUs to ensure that local law would be respected and civilian oversight and accountability preserved. It seems that only in Portland did an official body publicly debate the value of the words on paper.

The federal government cannot, because of *Printz*, compel local participation in a JTTF, so whether or not to participate is a political decision. Localities are offered the expertise and intelligence gathering capabilities of federal antiterrorism agents in exchange for remitting some of their employees to a certain degree of federal control. But the policymakers who must decide whether the tradeoff is worthwhile cannot know how much intelligence or expertise is actually being offered, to what extent federal agents actually control operations in practice, or whether local officials have actually disregarded or colluded in disregard of state or local restrictions on investigations. The members of the PJTTF and their supervisor at the Portland Police Bureau would have been the only city employees to know what was happening. The Mayor and council members, with a lower security clearance, would have been able to share some but perhaps not all of that information. If the Portland police had become disillusioned or dissatisfied with the workings of the PJTTF, they could have advised the City Council not to renew its agreement and the City Council would then have had to decide whether to accept their recommendation, probably without having access to the information on which that recommendation was based. Under those circumstances, it is likely that the City Council would defer to the officers' superior knowledge of what had been happening. Thus the real decisions about whether the tradeoff of accountability for information is worthwhile would actually be made by executive branch officials who are less accountable to the public than the legislature and who would be acting in the absence of informed public debate.[65]

The JTTF structure, mostly because of the secrecy of its operations, thus impeded the City Council's ability to supervise the activities of its employees and also, as a practical matter, allowed those employees to have a weighty influence on the decision about whether to participate. These joint ventures do not commandeer, but they do interfere with the state or city's usual methods of creating accountability and allocating decision-making authority. The Tenth Amendment, as defined in *Printz*, prohibits coercion; it does not so far prohibit interference with a state's decision about how to organize its policymaking authority—the state's separation of powers.[66] Many of the same issues of accountability and autonomy described in *Printz* and the dual sovereignty doctrine are implicated, however, even if Portland's participation is voluntary.

How sharp is the line between cooperation and cooptation? I do not expect or recommend that the Supreme Court will develop a new facet to its Tenth Amendment jurisprudence to render this a judicial rather than a political question. And so it will be the states and localities themselves, through their policymaking bodies, the legislatures, which will have to try to draw these lines. The Portland City Council tried to negotiate the terms of the MOU to provide a greater role for itself in order to fulfill its obligation to its constituents, but this proved impossible.[67]

Perhaps the reason the MOUs in other jurisdictions have been kept secret is that one or both of the parties was reluctant to publicize the terms of their deal. The federal government might well be loath to tell Portland if it has agreed to a sweetheart deal in some other city; the city officials might well be loath to let their constituents know that they have signed away their authority and are simply trusting their own police and the FBI to avoid abuses, including violations of state or local law. It is certainly an inconvenience for the FBI to have to negotiate the terms of each JTTF separately, but this balkanization is the essence of "Our Federalism."

## LEGISLATIVE ACCOUNTABILITY

### Arcata and Accountability

Another jurisdiction that was notably assertive in trying to maintain legislative control over local executive branch officials in the face of potential federal investigations was Arcata, California. Like many other communities, Arcata objected to various provisions of the PATRIOT Act, but recognized that it did not have the power to prohibit federal agents from using those powers in Arcata. Unlike other communities, which passed only resolutions condemning various tactics federal agents were empowered to use, Arcata passed an actual ordinance, not just a resolution, prohibiting its law enforcement officials from officially assisting or voluntarily cooperating with surveillance activities by federal agents who employed the disapproved procedures.[68] To give its ordinance teeth, the Arcata City Council provided for a fine of $57 for violating the ordinance. This provision, which applied only to the top nine managers of the city, instructed them that they must refer any PATRIOT Act investigation request to the City Council itself.[69]

To the extent that the Arcata ordinance might be read as instructing or allowing city officials to interfere with federal enforcement efforts, it would be considered unconstitutional in light of the Supremacy Clause. Regardless of a locality's negative opinion of the tactics of federal officers, the locality cannot bind federal officers to its own standards or enforce its own standards in a manner that impedes the federal government's investigation.[70] But the word "cooperation" is vague, and in light of *Printz*, loaded. Would it improperly impede federal officers for Arcata employees to decline to provide them with information about local residents from their own files or computer database? To decline to allow them to use the office copy machine? To decline to provide them with office space? It will be years before the Supreme Court spells out the limits of what a locality may be required to do, or not do, when operating in the no man's land between the protection of the *Printz* anti-commandeering principle and the prohibition of the Supremacy Clause. Meanwhile, the Arcata City Council does seem to have some space in which to decide that it will not go beyond required noninterference by providing assistance of the sort that could not be commandeered.

What is clear is that the Arcata City Council, like the Portland City Council, wanted to preserve for itself the responsibility to make sure that things in Arcata were "going well" in their own estimation instead of leaving the critical policy decisions to their executive branch employees. Even if the City Council rather than local executive officials were to consider federal agents' requests for assistance with PATRIOT Act authorized investigations, it might well be that the debate over how far such assistance should go would be no more visible to the public than it would have been in a police department office. The federal investigations will still be shrouded in secrecy, which might envelop local decision-making in any venue. But the decision, even if not made publicly, would be made in a forum with greater accountability and perhaps diversity of viewpoint. And it would be made by the body the people of Arcata trusted with the authority to make policy. If its ordinance does not violate the Supremacy Clause by going too far in the direction of actually interfering with federal investigators, is there anything unconstitutional about the City Council compelling its employees to abide by its policy decisions by fining them for violations?[71]

### New York City and Accountability

Not all local legislative bodies have been as assertive as the Portland and Arcata City Councils. In New York City, for example, the City Council has allowed the executive branch to decide several significant issues that have arisen about the relationship of federal and city policies. First, the New York Police Department went to court to seek relief from a pre-September 11 consent decree that, like the Oregon law described above, had prohibited sending undercover agents to infiltrate religious or political organizations.[72] The litigation over this matter was complex and went through multiple stages,[73] but the City Council made no serious attempt to wrest the policy decisions in question from the city's executive branch.[74]

Similarly, the City's "Don't Ask Don't Tell" approach to immigration status was forged and then superseded by mayors. Beginning in 1989 with an Executive Order issued by Mayor Ed Koch, New York City had a sanctuary policy, which provided that city employees could not ask the immigration status of people they encountered in the course of doing their jobs and, with limited exceptions, could not share with federal officials any information about immigration status that they happened to acquire in their official capacity.[75] In 1996, Congress enacted a statute providing that no person or agency may prohibit, or in any way restrict, a federal, state, or local government entity from sending information regarding an individual's immigration status to the federal immigration authorities, maintaining such information, or exchanging such information with any other federal, state, or local government entity.[76] Mayor Rudolph Giuliani challenged the constitutionality of this statute as applied to New York City, arguing (*inter alia*) that the Tenth Amendment entitled New York City to make policy decisions respecting control of its own employees.[77] When the court ruled that the federal law preempted the city's policy under the circumstances presented by the case, successor Mayor Michael Bloomberg embarked on the difficult and politically charged task of forging a new policy. The city's sanctuary policy had been motivated by concern that undocumented aliens might fear to approach or cooperate with city agencies if they had reason to fear that the City would turn them over to federal authorities for deportation, and this would hamper the City in performing such functions as providing protection to crime victims or obtaining the cooperation of witnesses. In his Executive Order, the Mayor created a modified "Don't Ask Do Tell" policy, attempting to accommodate the requirements of the federal statute and the local policy objectives.[78] Throughout the deliberations and public discussions about the content of this controversial policy, the New York City Council considered weighing in, but did not actually do so. The New York City Council did adopt a resolution opposing various PATRIOT Act provisions, similar to the resolution adopted by Portland, on February 4, 2004.[79]

Other localities, of course, have different stories to tell. The City of Los Angeles, for example, developed a policy opposing providing immigration information to federal authorities.[80] Under this policy, a Los Angeles police officer who notifies federal immigration authorities about an illegal alien picked up for minor violations faces disciplinary sanctions.[81] Los Angeles adopted a Bill of Rights Defense Campaign resolution on January 21, 2004, around the same time as New York City.[82] But Los Angeles was not willing to disclose the terms of its Memorandum of Understanding for its Joint Terrorism Task Force.[83]

At the federal level, critics of the Bush administration antiterrorism policies have complained that Congress is not providing sufficient oversight over the executive branch's investigations and other operations.[84] The same concern about unconstrained executive authority should echo in state and local assemblies as well.

## PREEMPTION AND ACCOUNTABILITY

The New York City sanctuary policy, no matter what branch of the City government adopted it, was displaced by a federal statute in which Congress valued federal interests—in enforcing immigration law—above what the City had determined to be its own local interest—in minimizing incentives for undocumented aliens to remain underground even if they became crime victims or necessary witnesses.[85] The Second Circuit ruling that the federal statute preempted the city policy, however, was quite narrow and left room for a Tenth Amendment based argument that Congress may not interfere with the city's ability to set policy for and control its own employees.[86]

The power of the federal government to preempt state or local law is restrained by the Tenth Amendment, but the contours of the Tenth Amendment with respect to issues like these are far from fully defined. The Supreme Court has decided only two cases explicating its current view of the Tenth Amendment's anti-commandeering principle. Before *Printz*, the Court had ruled in *New York v. United States*[87] that the Tenth Amendment prohibits federal commandeering of a state legislature. In her opinion for the Court, Justice O'Connor expressed a concern about accountability and transparency that was later reiterated in *Printz*: If the federal government orders a state legislature to take a certain action, how will voters know whom to blame if they dislike that action?[88]

The same concern could be raised about the revised New York City sanctuary policy. If city residents are angry when a city employee discloses someone's immigration status to federal officials, pursuant to federal request, the lines of accountability are blurred regardless of whether the inquiry was mandatory.[89] City taxpayers pay the salary of the employee but can control neither the employee's actions nor the use of information acquired in an official capacity. Even if city employees are not being "commandeered," because they are not actually compelled by the federal government to do anything, the city is being prohibited from creating policy that its employees must follow and from sanctioning them if they fail to follow that policy. This means that the city council, the legislative branch, cannot make final policy decisions and that executive branch officials, perhaps even low level employees, will have the power to decide when to disclose information to the federal government. Policy and practice could vary among the city's agencies. Power shifts to the executive branch again, where decisions in individual cases may be made in a manner invisible to the public and where the state or locality's own decision about how to allocate policymaking authority is subverted.

Another interesting example of a judicial finding of federal preemption of a state policy decision respecting the conduct of the war on terror within that state is the one discussed by Ronald Chen in "Whose Jail Is It Anyway?" Among those detained by federal authorities in the aftermath of September 11, 2001, were some 762 "special interest" aliens, primarily men from Arab or South Asian countries who were detained by the INS for some number of months prior to their eventual deportation. Many of these detainees were housed in New Jersey jails, including the Hudson and Passaic County jails, pursuant to a voluntary agreement the federal government had previously entered with New Jersey state authorities to house federal detainees in New Jersey's excess jail space.

Even after being sued under the federal Freedom of Information Act, the Department of Justice refused to release the names of these special interest detainees.[90] A lawsuit brought in New Jersey state court, *ACLU of New Jersey, Inc. v. County of Hudson*,[91] sought to compel the sheriffs and wardens of the Hudson and Passaic jails to comply with a long-standing provision of New Jersey state law mandating public disclosure of the identities of the inmates of New Jersey jails.[92] The trial court ordered the county to comply with the state law, after a limited stay of ten days granted at the request of the United States (which had been allowed to intervene in the lawsuit).[93] The United States promptly filed an appeal of this decision; on the same day, April 17, 2002, INS Commissioner James Ziglar signed an emergency interim regulation superseding state law by prohibiting state jail officials from disclosing the identities of the detainees held on behalf of the INS, whether by contract or otherwise. The plaintiffs argued that this ad hoc regulation exceeded the authority delegated to the Attorney General by Congress, violated the Administrative Procedure Act in that there had been no notice and comment period, and violated the Tenth Amendment.[94] The New Jersey appellate court held that New Jersey law had been validly preempted and reversed the trial court's order of disclosure.[95]

As in the PJTTF controversy, a local interest in the use of local resources— here in the use of jail space maintained by New Jersey taxpayers—was pitted against the federal interest in conducting the war on terror in whatever manner the federal government deemed appropriate—in this case a claim of need for secrecy of the identities of detainees. As in Portland, those who had to make decisions about the use of the local resources had no meaningful way to evaluate the federal claim of need. Because the federal claim was held to prevail, New Jersey was left with the same choice as Portland: to deny the use of its local resources to the federal government or to abide by the federal government's impenetrable decisions about how those resources would be used. Only by refusing to contract with the federal government for use of New Jersey jail space could New Jersey implement its own disclosure policies and preserve its own autonomy to make policy decisions. As in Portland, a negotiated contract that would allow the state's interest to be served would not be a likely result. The federal government would be as unlikely to cede to New Jersey the decision of when it is appropriate for inmates to be held in secret or incommunicado, as it was to grant high-level security clearances to Portland officials. The federal/local joint enterprise is based on asymmetrical power and so the only true power of the locality is to decline to participate at all.

Erwin Chemerinsky ("Empowering States When It Matters") questions whether a federal administrative official, rather than Congress, should be considered to have the authority to preempt state law, especially in such a peremptory fashion. The use of the preemption doctrine in the New Jersey case accomplished exactly what residents of Portland feared—federal policy supplanted competing local concerns, even when the state's own policy choices, providing a greater level of protection than federal constitutional law would require, were embodied in a state statute. Portland residents feared even the subtle possibilities for encroachment presented by a JTTF agreement that on its face purported to honor state law. There was nothing subtle about the federal government's blunt action with respect to the New Jersey sunshine law. The law was perceived as conflicting with the manner in which the federal government wished to conduct the war on terror, and so it was swept aside.

If Commissioner Ziglar could preempt New Jersey law in this manner, without congressional action or even a notice and comment period, could the United States Attorney General simply preempt the Oregon law that the Portland City Council has been struggling to honor by providing that participants in a PJTTF should follow the more lenient federal rather than the more demanding state restrictions on their conduct? Would politics prevent the Attorney General from taking such an action, making it unnecessary for the courts to define the limits of the Tenth

Amendment? If Portland remains the only jurisdiction to have insisted on its autonomy, it is less likely that other jurisdictions would rise up to defend Portland's right to implement its own state and local policies. If such a federal action were politically feasible, would the Tenth Amendment be interpreted as limiting the federal preemption power in the Oregon hypothetical or with respect to New York City's sanctuary policy, perhaps on the basis Chemerinsky suggests?

How sharp is the line between commandeering and generous application of the preemption doctrine? How much space is there for a local policy that is more protective of rights than the federal Constitution requires and a local policy where that local policy might be deemed to conflict with federal law or interests?


## CONCLUSION

Because the examples given above all concern the conduct of the "war on terror," some will argue that our usual models of federalism must give way to an extraordinary and exceptional need for federal power. If the war powers can justify incommunicado detention of citizens who have not been charged with or convicted of a crime or allowing the government to withhold information about how it is using its surveillance powers,[96] might a majority of the Supreme Court find the Tenth Amendment prohibition against commandeering inconclusive in this exceptional setting? If federal war powers were found to provide a basis for the FBI to commandeer Portland, Arcata, or New York City law enforcement officials, then questions about how to draw boundaries under *Printz* could become moot. I believe that it would be a poor idea for the Court to create exceptions to our usual structures of federalism for this amorphous "war" of indefinite duration.[97] The examples of federal/state/local interactions discussed in this article show the practical utility of federalism as a political rather than a judicial doctrine. It is noteworthy that the FBI did not need to seek any exception to the Tenth Amendment to get the Portland Chief of Police to help to interrogate Arab and Muslim men not suspected of any crime, and that the Detroit Chief of Police did not need the shield of a judicial declaration of tenth amendment rights in order to decline to do so. The politics of the day pressured many local law enforcement officials to cooperate. If most communities agree with a federal program, isolated instances of rebellion will not impede the federal program. It is feasible for the FBI to send a few extra agents to Portland or Detroit if local agents in a few locations cannot or will not participate in their interrogation program. It is only if many communities disagree with an FBI program that federal resources will be challenged. At that point, the FBI will be pressured to change its tactics because it may not have the resources to conduct a program that is widely unpopular. Thus, as Ann Althouse argues ("The Vigor of Anti-Commandeering Doctrine in Times of Terror"), federalism can act as a popular check on controversial federal tactics, which neither the courts nor Congress have prohibited. The Bill of Rights Defense Committee resolutions are one interesting source of information about what concerns people around the country have had about federal surveillance techniques. The negotiations over JTTFs, at least in Portland, have been another.

Daniel Richman has argued that the political process of federal/state negotiations over the terms of JTTF participation will promote both accountability and effectiveness in the war on terror because local officials, having an important service to sell, will have the bargaining power to insist on accountability and to protect their own vision of the appropriate balance between security and liberty.[98] Under this optimistic theory, one might argue that the same dialectic could work to achieve a proper balance between state, local, and federal concerns about the local enforcement of immigration law and other issues of apparent conflict. New Jersey, having jail space the federal government desires, has the bargaining power to decide whether to continue to contract with the federal government if the state's policy about disclosure of the identities of residents is not to be honored. And perhaps the political dialectic could generally act as a "self-correcting constitutional compass"[99] that would inspire the federal government to take greater account of grassroots concerns about providing adequate privacy for people's religious and political activities, library records, and Internet surfing.

This view may be overly optimistic. One of the very few other academic commentators to have focused on the role of local policing in the war on terror, William Stuntz, predicts that the courts will not find anything unconstitutional about the federal legislative powers that communities like Portland, Arcata, and New York City have condemned and that rather than operating as a brake on a federal juggernaut, states will feel encouraged to board the bandwagon and confer the same broad powers on their own law enforcement personnel.

Perhaps pessimistically, I think that Stuntz is more likely to be right in predicting a constitutional race to the bottom than Richman is in predicting a happy synthesis resulting from the federalism dialectic being conducted in the Portland City Council. For one thing, Portland is no more typical of the rest of the country than Arcata. Only if there were widespread opposition to federal policies would the federal government have to change its policies in any significant way, even if it is inconvenient to negotiate individual deals. Furthermore, the fact that so many MOUs are not public and so contracts between the federal government and individual local governments cannot be compared means that there is little possibility of collective action having an impact. Private deals may exist that differ from jurisdiction to jurisdiction, but if they are secret, other communities will not be inspired to insist on a similar deal and the public will not be aware that so many issues are being swept under the rug.

The fact that cities are not "sovereigns" of the same constitutional status as states complicates the application of federalism doctrine to most of the examples described above. In *Printz*, county sheriffs, described as state employees, spurred a discussion of federal interference with the state's sphere of operations. In many of the examples described above, individual cities were objecting to tactics their states might not have found objectionable. After the Portland City Attorney expressed the opinion that the FBI's proposed questioning of Arab and Muslim men would violate Oregon State law, lawyers for the county and the state declared that it would not.[100] How much autonomy a city has will vary depending on the state's local government law. One commentator has argued that our notions of federalism are actually an impediment to effective federal and local joint ventures because a state government with discrete legal rights is interposed between the national government and the cities, the principal partners of federal law enforcement officials in antiterrorism efforts.[101] In the PJTTF example, the city was negotiating directly with the FBI, but the county and the state always loomed in the background, and sometimes stepped out to pressure Portland's decisions. After Portland withdrew from the JTTF, in fact, Multnomah County assigned its own officers to the task force.[102]

It is not surprising that the shock waves of the war on terror are shaking relationships among political entities within the states. The horizontal checks and balances among the three branches of the federal government have been profoundly shaken.[103] As described above, the vertical checks of federalism—the relationships among federal, state, and local powers—are also challenged, although mostly in ways that are not generally apparent. The discussion of the Portland debates about the problems created by even a heavily negotiated MOU suggests that in most other cities where JTTFs operate, some quantum of local power and money may well have been transferred to federal control, out of the view of the public.

In times of national crisis, power tends to flow to the federal executive branch from all directions, as if by centripetal force. What may be a more surprising outcome is that the same forces that are leading to expanded presidential authority—the desire to enable secret, coordinated, and prompt action—are leading to trickle-down dislocation of power within municipalities. The discussion of the PJTTF demonstrates how policymaking authority over antiterrorism investigations—including questions about how much power and money to cede to the federal government and how vigorously to implement special state or local protections of privacy and liberty—tends to lodge in the executive branch of local governments instead of the local policymaking bodies. But not in Portland.

## Notes

1. See Chief Joseph Samuels, "Strengthening the Relationship with Our Federal Partners," President's Message at the Meeting of the International Association of Chiefs of Police, April 17, 2003 (quoting Attorney General John Ashcroft), http://www.theiacp.org/documents/index.cfm?fuseaction=document&document_type_id=1&document_id=438.

2. See Fox Butterfield, "Police Force Rebuffs F.B.I. on Querying Mideast Men," A Nation Challenged: The Interviews, *New York Times*, November 21, 2001 (late edition) (hereinafter as "Police Force Rebuffs F.B.I.").

3. See *New State Ice Co. v. Liebmann*, 285 U.S. 262, 311 (1932) (J. Brandeis, dissenting) ("It is one of the happy incidents of the federal system that a single courageous

state may, if its citizens choose, serve as a laboratory; and try novel social and economic experiments without risk to the rest of the country.").

4. See, for e.g., Neal K. Katyal & Laurence H. Tribe, "Waging War, Deciding Guilt: Trying the Military Tribunals," *Yale Law Journal* 111: (2002): 1259–1310 (discussing separation of powers and checks and balances issues created by the President's military tribunal order).

5. See *An Ordinance of the City Council of the City of Arcata Amending the Arcata Municipal Code to Defend the Bill of Rights and Civil Liberties: Ordinance No. 1339*, City of Arcata, CA, April 2, 2003, http://www.bordc.org/detail.php?id=119 (hereinafter as "Arcata Ordinance No. 1339").

6. See Daniel C. Richman, "The Changing Boundaries between Federal and Local Enforcement," *Boundary Changes in Criminal Justice Organizations* 2 (2000): 81–111, http://www.ncjrs.gov/criminal_justice2000/vol_2/02d2.pdf.

7. Under the dual sovereignty model, states are sovereigns; the role of state subdivisions, counties, and municipalities, is more ambiguous.

8. See Ann Althouse, "How to Build a Separate Sphere: Federal Courts and State Power," *Harvard Law Review* 100 (1987): 1485–1538 (exploring the different motivations of judges in drawing the boundary lines between the separate state and federal spheres).

9. *Bartkus v. Illinois*, 359 U.S. 121, 123–124 (1959) (describing an exception to dual sovereignty successive prosecutions where the dual nature of the proceedings is a "sham" because authorities from the second jurisdiction have been heavily involved in the investigation or prosecution of the first).

10. See Susan N. Herman, "Reconstructing the Bill of Rights: A Reply to Amar and Marcus's Triple Play on Double Jeopardy," *Columbia Law Review* 95 (1995): 1094–1106 (hereinafter as "Reconstructing the Bill of Rights") (arguing that the Supreme Court's decision to adopt a competitive dual sovereignty model as opposed to a cooperative federalism model was not dictated by the Constitution).

11. This, of course, happened in the case of the prosecution of the Los Angeles police officers charged in federal court with violating the civil rights of Rodney King after having been acquitted in state court, as well as in other notorious cases like that of Lemrick Nelson, who was acquitted in state court of murdering Yankel Rosenbaum in Crown Heights, Brooklyn, and then charged in federal court. The order of prosecution can also be reversed. Paul Hill, who was convicted of a federal offense under the Freedom of Access to Clinic Entrances statute, *U.S. Code 18* (1994), sec. 248, for killing a doctor who worked at an abortion clinic, was reprosecuted in state court for murder because the state wished to impose a heavier penalty than had been available under federal law. See "Reconstructing the Bill of Rights," 1090 nn. 1–3.

12. *Printz v. United States*, 521 U.S. 898 (1997).

13. Ibid., 902–904. The local law enforcement officers were being asked to provide assistance on an interim basis until a federal system became operative.

14. Ibid., 921–922. Justice Scalia quoted *The Federalist No. 51*, positing that the separation of the two spheres provides a "double security" for protecting liberty and checking tyranny. Ibid.

15. See ibid., 932–933 (describing the Court's conclusion that the states cannot be compelled to administer a federal program as "categorical" and declaring that balancing federal against state interests is inappropriate where the federal law in question compromises the structural framework of dual sovereignty).

16. Ibid., 928. If the states do not have a choice, maintained Scalia, they could become the "puppets of a ventriloquist Congress."

17. Ibid., 929–930 (suggesting that the Constitution contemplates that the state governments will represent and remain accountable to their own citizens).

18. Ibid., 924.

19. See Butterfield, "Police Force Rebuffs F.B.I."

20. *Oregon Revised Statutes Annotated*, sec. 181.575 (West 2003).

21. The law evidently was enacted as part of a compromise to allow employers to get criminal background information on prospective workers. It has not been interpreted by any appellate court, although Portland has been sued a few times for retaining information about political activists, including in the intriguingly named case of (Douglas) *Squirrel v.* (then Chief of Police Charles) *Moose*, in which the plaintiff alleged that the police had gathered information on Squirrel and other activists who participated in political demonstrations. See Rop Zone, "Portland Chief Denies City Not Cooperating: He Says Police Aiding U.S. Terror Probe," *The Seattle Times*, December 3, 2001 (fourth edition) (hereinafter as "Portland Chief Denies City Not Cooperating").

22. See Sam Howe Verhovek, "Federal Effort Does Not Violate Law, Oregon Attorney General Says," *New York Times*, November 28, 2001 (final edition) (hereinafter as "Federal Effort Does Not Violate Law").

23. U.S. Constitution Art. VI.

24. Fox Butterfield, "Police Are Split on Questioning of Mideast Men," A Nation Challenged: The Interviews, *New York Times*, November 22, 2001 (final edition).

25. "FBI May Be Easing Restrictions about Spying on Domestic Organizations," *Mornings with Paula Zahn*, CNN television broadcast, December 3, 2001.

26. Chief Kroeker's solution was that to be on the safe side, federal agents (rather than state or local agents) should question the twenty-three men involved. See Zone, "Portland Chief Denies City Not Cooperating."

27. Zone, "Portland Chief Denies City Not Cooperating;" Verhovek, "Federal Effort Does Not Violate Law."

28. *USA PATRIOT Act*, Public Law No. 107–156, *U.S. Statutes at Large* 115 (2001): 272.

29. See *Bill of Rights Defense Committee*, http://www.bordc.org (listing the eight states as Alaska, California, Colorado, Hawaii, Idaho, Maine, Montana, and Vermont).

30. *Portland, Oregon: USA PATRIOT Act Resolution*, October 29, 2003, http://www.bordc.org/detail.php?id=86 (affirming that the war on terrorism requires cooperation of cities and states) and also (1) affirming Portland's "strong support for the First Amendment right of public demonstrations, vigils, protests, marches, and similar forms of protected expression of ideas and views without fear of prosecution under federal terrorism laws"; (2) expressing Portland's "strong opposition to the indefinite detention of people who have not been charged with a crime; and measures that target individuals for legal scrutiny or enforcement activity based solely on their religion or country of origin"; and (3) requesting Oregon's members of Congress to work to limit the PATRIOT Act and to enact other legislation attentive to civil liberties concerns); *Multnomah County, Oregon: USA PATRIOT Act Resolution*, December 9, 2004, http://www.bordc.org/detail.php?id=67.

31. The constitutionality of most of the controversial provisions of the PATRIOT Act has not yet been established for a number of reasons, including the secrecy surrounding their use. See Susan N. Herman, "The USA PATRIOT Act and the Submajoritarian Fourth Amendment," *Harvard Civil Rights-Civil Liberties Law Review* 41 (2006): 67–132.

32. See Vikram David Amar, "Is It Appropriate, Under the Constitution, for State and Local Governments to Weigh in on the War on Terror and a Possible War with Iraq?" *Find Law's Writ*, March 7, 2003, http://writ.corporate.findlaw.com/amar/20030307.html (comparing the BORDC resolutions to the traditional role state and local governments have played in fighting disfavored federal legislation ever since the Virginia and Kentucky resolutions condemned the federal Alien and Sedition Acts in 1798).

33. See, for e.g., "Arcata Ordinance No. 1339," http://www.bordc.org/detail.php?id= 119.

34. See, for e.g., *Senate Concurrent Resolution No. 18*, Hawaii, http://www.capitol. hawaii.gov/session2003/bills/SCR18_.htm (opposing use of state funds to monitor political and religious gatherings exercising their First Amendment rights "to the extent legally possible").

35. See Henry Stern, "Portland May Pull Out of FBI Task Force," *The Oregonian*, December 21, 2004 (sunrise edition) (hereinafter as "Portland May Pull Out of FBI Task Force") ("Debate on the task force, as in past years, deeply divided the community.").

36. *Joint Terrorism Task Force*, http://columbia.fbi.gov/jttf.htm.

37. Ibid.

38. Ibid.

39. Ibid.

40. State and local police officers outnumber FBI agents sixty to one. Ibid.

41. See Alasdair Roberts, "Big Brother Keeps Secrets Under Wraps," *The Post-Standard (Syracuse, NY)*, December 19, 2004 (final edition) (hereinafter as "Big Brother").

42. See ibid. (Discussing requests for disclosure of MOUs that were denied by Los Angeles and New York Police Departments). The ACLU filed a Freedom of Information Act request seeking information about the terms of those agreements. See American Civil Liberties Union to Federal Bureau of Investigation, December 2, 2004, http://www.aclu.org/FilesPDFs/foia_jttf.pdf; Noelle Crombi, "ACLU Wants FBI to Lift Its 'Cloak' on Surveillance," *The Oregonian*, December 3, 2004 (sunrise edition) (hereinafter as "ACLU Wants FBI to Lift Its 'Cloak'").

43. See Draft of Oregon's *Memorandum of Understanding*, http://www.aracnet. com/~copwatch/JTTFmou2005.html.

44. Ibid., section VIII.

45. Ibid., sections VIII, IX.

46. *Oregon Revised Statutes Annotated*, sec. 181.575 (West 2004).

47. Draft of Oregon's *Memorandum of Understanding*, sec. III B, IV C, December 16, 2004, http://www.aracnet.com/~copwatch/JTTFmou2005.html. See also ibid., at sec. III. C. ("Failure to abide by local, state, or federal law by a Portland Police Bureau officer can result in the suppression of evidence in criminal trials, in civil liability against the City of Portland or individual officers, and in the criminal prosecution of officers.").

48. See *The Attorney General's Guidelines on Federal Bureau of Investigation Undercover Operations*, May 30, 2002, http://www.usdoj.gov/olp/fbiundercover.pdf.

49. See Zone, "Portland Chief Denies City Not Cooperating" (discussing a 1987 Oregon law that prevents police from enforcing federal immigration law).

50. Stern, "Portland May Pull Out of FBI Task Force."

51. Ibid.

52. Ibid. (Quoting Randy Leonard).

53. See, for e.g., *Testimony of Andrea Meyer*, ACLU of Oregon, Portland City Council, October 2003, http://www.aclu-or.org/site/DocServer/JTTF_meyer_testimony_10_03.pdf?

docID=967 (testifying that "an anti-terrorism officer of the Sheriff's department in Fresno, California, infiltrated Peace Fresno," a local political group that "was and is not suspected of criminal activity").

54. The ACLU FOIA suit was designed to uncover whether agents investigating terrorism were spying on religious or political activities in Oregon, see Crombi, "ACLU Wants FBI to Lift Its 'Cloak.'" Brandon Mayfield, a Portland lawyer who was arrested for participating in the bombing in Madrid (a charge later dropped when federal authorities realized that his fingerprint did not actually match one found at the scene), was said in court documents to have traveled to and from a mosque, an activity that constituted one of several reasons proffered as justifying issuance of an arrest warrant. Ibid.

55. Draft of Oregon's *Memorandum of Understanding*, sec. IV B, December 16, 2004, http://www.aracnet.com/~copwatch/JTTFmou2005.html.

56. See Sarah Kershaw, "In Portland, Ore., A Bid to Pull Out of Terror Task Force," *New York Times*, April 23, 2005 (final edition) (hereinafter as "A Bid to Pull Out of Terror Task Force").

57. Ibid.

58. The Fresno episode surfaced by accident when the local undercover agent involved died in a motorcycle accident and his actual name was published in the newspaper together with his photograph. Some of the peace activists who had been at meetings the agent had attended recognized his picture, registered the difference in the name he had given them, learned of his actual employment, and figured out that he had been assigned to spy on their meeting. This sort of sequence of events is not likely to happen very often. "Accord Peace Group Infiltrated By Government Agent," *Democracy Now!* October 9, 2003, http://www.democracynow.org/article.pl?sid=03/10/09/1556226%20.

59. For an example of mission creep occurring in Las Vegas, see Jeffrey Rosen, "Prevent Defense," *The New Republic*, September 6, 2004.

60. *Testimony of David Fidanque*; Executive Director, ACLU of Oregon, March 30, 2005, http://www.aclu-or.org/site/DocServer/jttf_fidanque_3_05.pdf?docID=963. The files presumably would also be immune from state disclosure laws and subject only to federal FOIA requests, which may be more burdensome and time-consuming to litigate, and subject to national security exceptions.

61. See, for e.g., *Printz v. United States*.

62. See Kershaw, "A Bid to Pull Out of Terror Task Force."

63. Stern, "Portland May Pull Out of FBI Task Force."

64. Ibid.

65. See Daniel C. Richman, "Federal Criminal Law, Congressional Delegation, and Enforcement Discretion," *UCLA Law Review* 46 (1999): 757–814 (discussing the low level of accountability of federal law enforcement agents).

66. *Printz v. United States*, 923.

67. See Kershaw, "A Bid to Pull Out of Terror Task Force."

68. See, for e.g., "Arcata Ordinance No. 1339," http://www.bordc.org/detail.php?id=119. See also Kevin Fagan, "Arcata The Defiant; Town Ordinance Penalizes Officials Who Cooperate with PATRIOT Act, but Law May Not Stand Up in Court," *San Francisco Chronicle*, April 13, 2003 (final edition).

69. "Arcata Ordinance No. 1339," http://www.bordc.org/detail.php?id=119.

70. See, for e.g., *Olmstead v. United States*, 277 U.S. 438 (1928) (permitting federal officers to use wiretap evidence obtained in violation of a Washington state statute).

71. The Second Circuit, in *City of New York v. United States*, 179 F.3d 29, 35 (2d Cir. 1999), held that states do not have an "untrammeled" right to prohibit voluntary cooperation.

72. *Handschu v. Special Services Division*, 273 F. Supp. 2d 327, 329–335 (S.D.N.Y. 2003).

73. See Jerrold L. Steigman, Note, "Reversing Reform: The *Handschu* Settlement in Post-September 11, New York City," *Brooklyn Journal of Law & Policy* 11 (2003): 765–770.

74. Several resolutions calling for oversight hearings were introduced, see, for e.g., Resolution No. 548, N.Y. City Council (2002), http://webdocs.nyccouncil.info/textfiles/Res%200548-2002.htm?CFID-474918&CFTOKEN=, but do not seem to have been enacted or to have led to any actions on the part of the City Council.

75. *Executive Order No. 124*, New York City, August 7, 1989 (providing that no New York City officer or employee shall transmit information respecting any alien to federal immigration authorities unless the disclosure was either required by law, authorized by the alien, or respecting an alien suspected by the agency of criminal activity).

76. *Illegal Immigration Reform and Immigrant Responsibility Act of 1996*, sec. 642, Public Law No. 104–208, *U.S. Statutes at Large* 110 (1996): 3009–3546, 3009–3707.

77. *City of New York v. United States*, 31–34.

78. *Executive Order No. 41*, New York City, September 17, 2003. The order authorizes a New York City officer or employee to inquire about immigration status only if (1) that status is necessary for determination of eligibility for some program, service, or benefit or (2) the officer is required by law to make such inquiry. Law enforcement officers may not inquire about immigration status unless investigating criminal activity other than mere status as an undocumented alien; police officers may not inquire about the immigration status of crime victims, witnesses, or others seeking assistance, and may authorize disclosure of immigration status if "such disclosure is necessary in furtherance of an investigation of potential terrorist activity." The Mayor's original attempt at a revised policy, in May 2003, was narrower in a number of respects and generated a public outcry, demonstrating that executive officials are indeed subject to political accountability. Alisa Solomon, "Don't Ask Don't Tell: Outcry Over New City Policy on Reporting the Undocumented Stuns the Mayor," *Village Voice*, July 9, 2003, http://www.villagevoice.com/news/0328,solomon, 45387,1.html.

79. *Resolution 60-2004*, New York City Council, Bill of Rights Defense Committee, http://www.bordc.org/detail.php?id=69.

80. *Special Order No. 40*, November 27, 1979, from LAPD Police Chief Daryl F. Gates (mandated by the Los Angeles City Council).

81. Ibid. The order also prohibits officers from "initiating police action where the objective is to discover the alien status of a person." Ibid.

82. *USA PATRIOT ACT / Repeal: No. 03-0002-S162*, Los Angeles, CA, January 21, 2004, Bill of Rights Defense Committee, http://www.bordc.org/detail.php?id=58.

83. Roberts, "Big Brother."

84. See, e.g., Rafael Lorente, "Attacks Left Americans Fearing for their Security and their Liberties," *Sun-Sentinel (Fort Lauderdale, FL)*, September 7, 2003 (Broward metro edition) (quoting a former Army Intelligence officer as stating that "[w]e are in a situation now where our fear of the terrorist threat has driven us to create the intelligence apparatus of a police state," and that "modern computer technology, in the hands of an overzealous Department of Justice with little congressional oversight, could be a dangerous

new weapon"); "First Things First," Editorial, *Washington Post*, November 8, 2004 (final edition) (citing a report from the American Enterprise Institute purporting to show that "neither Congress nor the Bush administration ever conducted any real risk assessment or applied any real oversight" to the Department of Homeland Security").

85. *City of New York v. United States*, 32–33.

86. See ibid., 35–37. The court found that neither the City nor the state had in fact made a general policy decision about the need to protect confidential information like immigration status. The Executive Order creating the sanctuary policy was very specific and provided only that one particular type of information—immigration status—could not be disclosed to one particular type of recipient—federal immigration officials. If New York City or State were to adopt a general confidentiality policy, the court suggested, a preemption argument might then fail because federal interests, as *Printz* found, cannot be exalted at the price of subjugating state or local employees and compelling them to serve federal interests above the interests of their own employer. Ibid., 34–37.

87. *New York v. United States*, 505 U.S. 144, 161–66 (1992).

88. Ibid., 168–169.

89. I have always had doubts about the accuracy of the public relations assumptions underlying Justice O'Connor's accountability argument. Local officials, unless muzzled by federal insistence on secrecy, would be quick to proclaim that they were acting under federal government compulsion and should not be blamed for unpopular actions if they ever wanted to be reelected.

90. See *Center for National Security Studies v. United States Department of Justice*, 331 F.3d 918, 920 (D.C. Cir. 2003) (upholding federal government's refusal to make this information available under the Freedom of Information Act).

91. *ACLU of New Jersey, Inc. v. County of Hudson*, 799 A.2d 629, 635 (N.J. Super. Ct. App. Div. 2002).

92. *New Jersey Statutes Annotated*, sec. 30:8–16 (West 1997).

93. *ACLU of New Jersey, Inc. v. County of Hudson*, 636.

94. Ibid., 639.

95. Ibid., 655.

96. See, e.g., *Hamdi v. Rumsfeld*, 542 U.S. 507, 516 (2004) (administration argument that plenary war powers derived from Article II support detention of "enemy combatants" even in the absence of congressional authorization).

97. See Richard T. Ford, "Police Don't Fight Wars," *Boston Review* (December 2004/January 2005), http://bostonreview.net/BR29.6/ford.html (suggesting that the war powers analogy is inapt because local police do not fight wars).

98. See Daniel Richman, "The Right Fight: Enlisted by the Feds, Can Police Find Sleeper Cells and Protect Civil Rights, Too?" *Boston Review* 29 (December 2004/January 2005), http://bostonreview.net/BR29.6/richman.html.

99. See Burt Neuborne, "Toward Procedural Parity in Constitutional Litigation," *William & Mary Law Review* 22 (1981): 731.

100. In fact, after Portland withdrew from the JTTF, Multnomah County offered its own officers to the task force. See Anna Griffin, "Multnomah Sheriff, FBI Discuss Task Force Posts," *The Oregonian (Portland, OR)*, June 29, 2005 (sunrise edition) (hereinafter as "Multnomah Sheriff, FBI Discuss Task Force Posts."

101. Edward Rubin, "Federalism Won't Work," *Boston Review* 29 (December 2004/January 2005), http://bostonreview.net/BR29.6/rubin.html.

102. Griffin, "Multnomah Sheriff, FBI Discuss Task Force Posts."

103. See Susan N. Herman, "The USA PATRIOT Act and the USA Department of Justice: Losing Our Balances?" *The Jurist*, December 4, 2001, http://jurist.law.pitt.edu/forum /forumnew40.htm.

# State Incarceration of Federal Prisoners After September 11: Whose Jail Is It Anyway?

Ronald K. Chen

## INTRODUCTION

Among the many ways in which fidelity to our legal institutions and constitutional principles has been sorely tested in the aftermath of the September 11 terrorist attacks, adherence to the principles of federalism counts as a prominent example. Involvement by state law enforcement agencies in controversial federal antiterrorism techniques, including secret incarceration, raises the issue of the appropriate balance between traditional state police power and federal supremacy.

As the Supreme Court has noted, "It is difficult to imagine an activity in which a State has a stronger interest, or one that is more intricately bound up with state laws, regulations, and procedures, than the administration of its prisons."[1] But since the capacity of state jails and prisons has always far surpassed that of federal institutions, the practice of voluntarily housing federal prisoners in state jails has a long history. As Justice Scalia noted in *Printz v. United States* (1997):[2]

On September 23, 1789—the day before its proposal of the Bill of Rights—the First Congress enacted a law aimed at obtaining state assistance of the most rudimentary and necessary sort for the enforcement of the new Government's laws: the holding of federal prisoners in state jails at federal expense. Significantly, the law issued not a command to the States' executive, but a recommendation to their legislatures. Congress "recommended to the legislatures of the several States to pass laws, making it expressly the duty of the keepers of their gaols, to receive and safe keep therein all prisoners committed under the authority of the United States," and offered to pay 50 cents per month for each prisoner. Moreover, when Georgia refused to comply with the request, Congress's only reaction was a law authorizing the marshal in any

State that failed to comply with the Recommendation of September 23, 1789, to rent a temporary jail until provision for a permanent one could be made.[3]

From the outset of our constitutional experience, therefore, reception of federal prisoners in state jails was understood to be the result of voluntary assistance provided to the federal government by a coequal sovereign. "The Framers' experience under the Articles of Confederation had persuaded them that using the States as the instruments of federal governance was both ineffectual and provocative of federal-state conflict."[4] In the place of direct federal control over the mechanisms of state government, therefore, federal prisoners were housed in state jails purely at the discretion of state legislatures or state jailers, as a matter of free contract and agreement.

After September 11, 2001, federal law enforcement authorities made aggressive use of immigration laws to detain aliens suspected of having possible ties to terrorism, detaining more than 1,200 persons within two months.[5] Some were questioned and subsequently released. Many others, however, were held indefinitely, ostensibly for overstaying or being out of status under the terms of their visa, although they normally would not have been incarcerated for such relatively minor violations.[6] The Department of Justice adopted a "no bond" policy to hold those who were "of interest" in the terrorism investigation,[7] and as a direct result the Immigration and Naturalization Service ("INS")[8] detained 762 aliens who were primarily men from Arab or South Asian countries.[9] "Of these 762 aliens, 24 were in ins custody on immigration violations prior to the September 11 attacks. The remaining 738 aliens were arrested between September 11, 2001, and August 6, 2002, as a direct result of the FBI's investigation" into the September 11 attacks.[10] Yet the government never charged any of these so-called "special interest" detainees with a terrorism-related offense,[11] and in the end simply deported almost all to their countries of origin.

The unprecedented circumstances associated with the incarceration of the September 11 detainees created, at least temporarily, the very practical problem of where to house them when their number exceeded the capacity of federally operated facilities. Even under normal circumstances federal law enforcement agencies, including the INS, regularly place federal prisoners or detainees in state facilities pursuant to contracts entered into with state officials.[12] Of the 762 special interest detainees, a majority were apparently held in state jails in New Jersey,[13] since most of the detainees were arrested in the New York metropolitan area,[14] and since various counties of New Jersey, with their excess jail capacity, had previously entered into intergovernmental service agreements with the INS for this purpose.

Although at first willing to give an aggregate count of the INS detainees, the Justice Department soon ordered that the detainees' individual names be withheld. A complete list of those arrested and held by the INS has never been made public. Attorney General Ashcroft gave two reasons for keeping these detentions secret: (1) the release of the identities of the detainees would assist Al Qaeda operatives and (2) such release would violate the privacy interests of the detainees.[15] The policy of withholding the names of the INS detainees, however, met with heavy criticism from editorial pages[16] and civil liberties groups. Throughout our history, antipathy toward such secret arrests has resonated among those who otherwise occupied opposite ends of the political spectrum. Thus, in a *Federalist Paper*, Alexander Hamilton commented:

> To bereave a man of life . . . or by violence to confiscate his estate, without accusation or trial, would be so gross and notorious an act of despotism, as must at once convey the alarm of tyranny throughout the whole nation; but confinement of the person, by secretly hurrying him to jail, where his sufferings are unknown or forgotten, is a less public, a less striking, and therefore a more dangerous engine of arbitrary government.[17]

The American Civil Liberties Union ("ACLU") sued in federal court, seeking disclosure under the federal Freedom of Information Act as well as under the common law and First Amendment right of access to government information.[18] It also sued to overturn a related policy of categorically closing immigration hearings to the public.[19]

Apart from the general merits of the federal policy refusing to make public the names of the September 11 detainees, however, the competence of the federal government, in a manner consistent with both statutory and constitutional principles, to extend its decision of secret detention to govern the operation of state jails in which it chooses to house federal detainees pursuant to voluntary agreements with state governmental authorities, raises fundamental issues of allocation of powers among coordinate sovereignties. The enthusiasm of those who, while promoting limits on federal power in other contexts, would quickly sweep aside the traditional prerogatives of the states in the area of antiterrorism, gives support to the accusation of fair weather federalism.

### The Case: ACLU of New Jersey, Inc. v. County of Hudson

In *ACLU of New Jersey, Inc. v. County of Hudson* (2002),[20] the plaintiffs sought to compel the sheriffs and wardens of the county jails of Hudson and Passaic Counties to abide by provisions of New Jersey state law mandating public disclosure of the identities of those committed to their care. Since the nineteenth century, the New Jersey Legislature has mandated that basic pedigree information relating to inmates housed in New Jersey county jails be made public. The so-called New Jersey "Jailkeeper's Statute," enacted in 1898, provides:

> The keeper of every jail or other penal or reformatory institution supported by public moneys of any county or municipality, shall keep a book provided by the board of freeholders in the county where the institution shall be, in which he shall set forth

the date of entry, date of discharge, the description, age, birthplace and such other information as he may be able to obtain as to the inmates committed to his care, which book shall be exposed in a conspicuous place in the institution and shall be open to public inspection.[21]

Similarly, since 1877, a New Jersey statute has required that county sheriffs and jailkeepers record the names of all federal prisoners committed to county jails,[22] which records must then be made public pursuant to New Jersey's Right to Know Law.[23] Because the Jailkeeper's Statute, by its terms, creates an unqualified and absolute right of public access to the roster of inmates housed in county jails, it provided a seemingly indefeasible mechanism to force the state jailers to disclose the identities of "the inmates committed to his care."

In December 2001, the ACLU of New Jersey made a formal request to inspect the records of inmates held in the Hudson County Correctional Center and the Passaic County Jail, where the largest number of INS detainees were being held. The local sheriffs refused these requests, claiming that such information was under the exclusive control of the INS. The ACLU then filed suit on January 22, 2002, in the Superior Court of New Jersey, Hudson County, naming as defendants only the county sheriffs and wardens who operate the jails according to state law. No federal officer or agency was impleaded (that is, included as a party in the case).

The cause of action was distinctively local in character. In New Jersey practice, an "action in lieu of prerogative writs"[24] is the procedural device by which the state's courts review the actions of state or local governmental agencies and officers to ensure that such agencies are acting within their jurisdiction and according to law. Akin to a common law petition for writ of mandamus (an order to an official to perform a ministerial, i.e., legally required, act or duty), the complaint demanded the performance of a ministerial act or duty, namely nondiscretionary obedience by the county jail officials to the mandate of a state statute requiring disclosure of the names and other identifying information of all the inmates of the jails then in their care, including those housed on behalf of the INS in accordance with intergovernmental service agreements.[25] Although the United States was not named as a party to the action, it sought and was granted status as a defendant-intervenor (one who voluntarily enters a lawsuit because of a personal stake in it) and in effect became the principal counsel for the defendants.

On March 26, 2002, Superior Court Assignment Judge Arthur N. D'Italia heard argument on the cross-motions for summary judgment and rendered a bench opinion the same afternoon, granting the plaintiffs partial summary judgment.[26] The trial judge found that, in referring to "inmates committed to [the jailer's] care," the New Jersey Legislature intended to include all persons housed in the county jail, including federal prisoners or detainees. He thereby rejected the United States's contention that the statute applied only to inmates incarcerated in county jails pursuant to state criminal processes.[27] Initially, Judge D'Italia granted the United States's motion for a stay pending appeal, meaning that the government would not be required to comply with the order while their appeal was pending.

On April 12, 2002, however, during a hearing to settle the form of order, Judge D'Italia announced that he had reconsidered the stay, pending appeal. In light of the need for timely action, he granted a limited stay of ten days, after which he ordered the state jailors to comply with the state law.

On April 17, 2002, the United States and the various county defendants filed notices of appeal and cross-appeal to the Appellate Division of the New Jersey Superior Court. That same day, in Washington DC, however, INS Commissioner James W. Ziglar signed an emergency interim regulation, without following the notice and comment period normally required under the federal Administrative Procedures Act.[28] The regulation provided:

> No person, including any state or local government entity or any privately operated detention facility, that houses, maintains, provides services to, or otherwise holds any detainee on behalf of the Service (whether by contract or otherwise), and no other person who by virtue of any official or contractual relationship with such person obtains information relating to any detainee, shall disclose or otherwise permit to be made public the name of, or other information relating to, such detainee. Such information shall be under the control of the Service and shall be subject to public disclosure only pursuant to the provisions of applicable federal laws, regulations and executive orders. Insofar as any documents or other records contain such information, such documents shall not be public records. This section applies to all persons and information identified or described in it, regardless of when such persons obtained such information, and applies to all requests for public disclosure of such information, including requests that are the subject of proceedings pending as of April 17, 2002.[29]

The rule therefore prohibited all persons, including state jail officials, from disclosing basic identifying information regarding inmates committed to their care, and made clear that it "superseded State or local law relating to the release of such information."[30] Moreover, the regulation applied to "requests that are the subject of proceedings pending as of April 17, 2002," an obvious reference to the pending appeal in the *County of Hudson* case.

Faxed copies of Commissioner Ziglar's regulation were provided immediately to the Appellate Division, with a request by the United States that it stay Judge D'Italia's order pending an expedited appeal. Mindful of the possibility that INS detainees might be deported or transferred outside of New Jersey during the pendency of the appeal, on April 19, 2003, the Appellate Division held a teleconference with the counsel, in which it attempted to fashion a mutually agreeable temporary standstill agreement while the appeal was heard. When no such agreement could be reached, the appellate court issued a stay of the lower court order on the condition that the status quo be maintained—that no INS detainee be removed from his or her present confinement without consent. The purpose of the requirement, the court later explained, "was simply to forestall the eventuality that the individual rights and interests at the heart of the complaint for relief would become moot in ways that would unreasonably disadvantage the detainees in respect of the fundamental rights asserted on their behalfs."[31] The response of the INS in the following days to the conditions imposed by the Appellate Division was somewhat draconian. It forbade any detainee housed in the Hudson or Passaic County jails from leaving those facilities, even if the detainee was willing to accept voluntary departure from the United States to his home country, and even if the detainee had been granted release on bond by an immigration judge. At least one detainee who had agreed to voluntary departure and who was literally in the departure lounge of JFK International Airport waiting to return home, was reincarcerated in the county jail where she had been originally kept, ostensibly in order to abide literally by the stay order.[32] A second teleconference with the Appellate Division quickly ensued, in which the court provided further clarification of its April 19 order: "It is not the court's intention to limit unduly the government's discharge of its essential functions; nor will the court tolerate any steps pendente lite (during the course of the litigation) that worsen the procedural lot of the detainees before the ultimate issues are resolved."[33] The court maintained its original order, but made clear that detainees could be removed from the jails under certain conditions in which they themselves consented to the removal, including voluntary departure or release on bond.[34]

Oral argument before the Appellate Division was held on May 10, 2002. On June 12, 2002, the court issued an opinion in which it upheld the efficacy of the interim regulation promulgated on April 17, finding that the century-old New Jersey state statute mandating public access to jail rosters had been retroactively preempted by Commissioner Ziglar's sweep of the pen, and it therefore reversed the trial court's order based solely on application of the new federal rule.[35] The New Jersey Supreme Court ordered expedited consideration of the petition for certification and denied review on July 9, 2002. The ACLU elected not to seek certiorari in the United States Supreme Court.

Of all the statements made by the federal government in the course of the litigation, perhaps the most noteworthy, and also the most facially troubling, was the statement accompanying the promulgation of the interim regulation:

This rule will not have substantial direct effects on the States, on the relationship between the National Government and the States, or on the distribution of power and responsibilities among the various levels of government. This rule merely pertains to the public disclosure of information concerning Service detainees housed, maintained or otherwise served in state or local government or privately operated detention facilities under any contract or other agreement with the Service. In effect, the rule will relieve state or local government entities of responsibility for the public release of information relating to any immigration detainee being housed or otherwise maintained or provided service on behalf of the Service. Instead, the rule reserves that responsibility to the Service with regard to all Service detainees. Therefore, in accordance with section 6 of Executive Order 13132, it is determined that this rule does not have sufficient Federalism implications to warrant the preparation of a federalism summary impact statement.[36]

This statement was required under Executive Order 13,132,[37] which provides in part:

> To the extent practicable and permitted by law, no agency shall promulgate any regulation that has federalism implications and that preempts State law, unless the agency, prior to the formal promulgation of the regulation,
> (1) consulted with State and local officials early in the process of developing the proposed regulation;
> (2) in a separately identified portion of the preamble to the regulation as it is to be issued in the Federal Register, provides to the Director of the Office of Management and Budget a federalism summary impact statement, which consists of a description of the extent of the agency's prior consultation with State and local officials, a summary of the nature of their concerns and the agency's position supporting the need to issue the regulation, and a statement of the extent to which the concerns of State and local officials have been met; and
> (3) makes available to the Director of the Office of Management and Budget any written communications submitted to the agency by State and local officials.[38]

The contention that a federal regulation expressly preempting a state statute that governs the way that state officers operate state jails will not have serious federalism implications is facially remarkable. Indeed, the observation that "the rule will relieve state or local government entities of responsibility for the public release of information" is functionally equivalent to the observation that the federal rule relieved state and local government entities of the responsibility to abide by the dictates of state law. The result in *County of Hudson* has potentially profound implications for traditional assumptions about the allocation of power between the federal and state sovereignties in one of the most basic governmental functions— operating places of incarceration.

## THE HISTORICAL FEDERAL/STATE RELATIONSHIP IN HOUSING FEDERAL PRISONERS IN STATE JAILS

In the exercise of that discretion, most states have provided by statute for housing of federal prisoners in their jails, and have either directed or permitted state jailers to receive federal prisoners.[39] New Jersey, for instance, included a typical provision in the *Sheriff's Act of 1877*.

> Each sheriff and keeper of a jail in any county of this state shall receive all prisoners committed to his custody by authority of the United States and safely keep them until discharged in due course of the laws of the United States. Any sheriff or keeper who neglects or refuses to perform the services and duties required of him by this section, or who offends in the premises shall be subject to like penalties, forfeitures and actions as if such prisoners had been committed under authority of this state.[40]

Thus, unlike other states that permitted but did not require its sheriffs and jailers to receive federal prisoners,[41] New Jersey commands its inferior officers to receive those prisoners, and holds them responsible as if the prisoners were detained by the state. In New Jersey, the state officer was always understood to be acting pursuant to his state legislature's command, rather than as a servant of the federal sovereignty. In *Board of Chosen Freeholders of Hudson County v. Kaiser* (1908),[42] for instance, a county sheriff claimed that he should be able to keep excess monies paid to him by the federal government for housing federal prisoners, contending that he was an agent of the United States Marshal and not a state official. The state court disagreed:

> The county jail is not furnished to the sheriff to conduct a private business in, and ... if his only authority to receive federal prisoners within its walls was a private bargain made with the United States marshal, his conduct would be a clear violation of official duty. But such is not the case. Section 33 of the act concerning sheriffs ... makes it the duty of the sheriff of every county to receive all persons committed to his custody by the authority of the United States. He takes them into his custody as sheriff; he remains responsible for them as sheriff, and all moneys paid to him on their account are paid to him as, and received by him as, sheriff. That being so, moneys paid to him by the federal government in excess of what was needed for the food and care of federal prisoners was paid to him as compensation for services rendered and duties performed with relation to them as sheriff.... [43]

The New Jersey court therefore rejected the contention that, in housing federal prisoners, the sheriff enjoyed a dual existence as part federal officer and part state officer. The state jailer serves a unitary master, and is answerable solely to the state sovereignty.

Federal courts have consistently adopted the same model of state jail officials as acting purely in their capacities under state law. In 1815, the Supreme Court observed in *Randolph v. Donaldson* that:

> The keeper of a state jail is neither in fact nor in law the deputy of the [United States] marshal. He is not appointed by nor removable at the will of the marshal. When a prisoner is regularly committed to a state jail by the marshal, he is no longer in the custody of the marshal, nor controllable by him. The marshal has no authority to command or direct the keeper in respect to the nature of the imprisonment.[44]

Similarly, in *Saunders v. United States* (1896), the federal court observed:

> But the state jailer is not an officer of the United States, and the commissioner has no power to call upon him to perform any service. The United States uses the jails of the state for the confinement of prisoners under sentence or awaiting trial. The Revised Statutes of the United States (section 5539) subject prisoners so confined to the same discipline and treatment as convicts sentenced under the laws of the state, and place them under the control of the officer having charge of the jail under the laws of the state.[45]

This characterization of state jail officials as acting exclusively as creatures of state sovereignty even when housing federal prisoners has been embraced by the United States Supreme Court in modern cases, as a matter of federal statutory interpretation. In *Logue v. United States* (1973), a federal prisoner confined in a county jail pending trial committed suicide, and his parents sued both the state jailer and the United States marshal for damages under the *Federal Tort Claims Act* ("FTCA") contending that both officers' negligence was the proximate cause of their son's death.[46] In finding that the state sheriff was an independent contractor of the United States and therefore not within the control of a federal officer, the Court concluded that the state officer could not be liable under the FTCA. The Court construed the general federal statute that authorizes federal law enforcement agencies to enter into contracts with state authorities to house federal detainees.[47] In authorizing such contracts, "Congress . . . clearly contemplated that the day-to-day operations of the contractor's facilities were to be in the hands of the contractor, with the federal Government's role limited to the payment of sufficiently high rates to induce the contractor to do a good job."[48] Thus, the Court has found that such an intergovernmental service agreement "gives the United States no authority to physically supervise the conduct of the jail's employees."[49] Each county defendant in this case is an "independent contractor who contracts with another to do something for him but who is not controlled by the other nor subject to the other's right to control with respect to his physical conduct in the performance of the undertaking."[50] Particularly with respect to the policies and practices regarding the treatment of federal prisoners, the Court has made it clear that the state rules govern, an axiom that presumably embraces state laws, such as the Jailkeeper's Statute, which mandate the manner of public disclosure of jail records.[51]

To save expense and travel, the federal government has found it convenient with the consent of the respective States to use state prisons in which to confine many of its prisoners, and the United States Attorney General is the agent of the government to make the necessary contracts to carry this out. In order to render the duty thus assumed by the state governments as free from complication as possible, the actual authority over, and the discipline of, the federal prisoners while in the state prison are given to the state prison authorities. If the treatment or discipline is not satisfactory, the Attorney General can transfer them to another prison, but while they are there, they must be as amenable to the rules of the prison as are the state prisoners.[52]

At the most specific level, the intergovernmental service agreements between the United States and Hudson and Passaic Counties for the housing of INS detainees in effect at the time County of Hudson was litigated were fully consistent with the characterization of the Hudson and Passaic County Jails as purely state entities, not under the control of a federal agency. The Hudson County agreement provided, for instance:

> The contractor will provide housing, safekeeping, subsistence and other services for INS detainee(s) within its facility . . . consistent with the types and levels of services

and programs routinely afforded its own population, and fully consistent with all applicable laws, standards, policies, procedures and court orders applicable to its facility ... unless, or as specifically modified by this Agreement.

Admission and discharge of INS detainee(s) shall be fully consistent with the Contractors policies and procedures, and shall ensure positive identification and recording of both detainee(s) and officer(s).[53]

Similarly, the Passaic County agreement provided: "The County agrees to accept and provide for the secure custody, care and safekeeping of USINS detainees in accordance with state and local laws, standards, policies, procedures, or court orders applicable to the operations of the facility."[54]

It is evident from the contractual agreement that the United States not only consented to (but indeed also mandated) that Hudson and Passaic County Jails keep the records pertaining to inmates committed to their care pursuant to the federal agreements in accordance with state law.

Thus, pursuant to (a) the state statutes that first authorized local jailers to cooperate with federal authorities and receive federal detainees in local facilities; (b) the federal statutes that authorized the Attorney General to solicit such voluntary cooperation from state officers; and (c) the actual agreements entered into by Hudson and Passaic Counties for the housing of INS detainees, two consistent characterizations of the relationship between federal and state officers emerge:

(1) The state jailers were exclusively officers of the state sovereignty, and not subject to the control or command of the federal authorities in the manner in which federal detainees were handled while in state custody.
(2) It was the expectation of the federal authorities when entering into contracts with the state jailers that state and local laws, policies and practices would be applied in the treatment of federal prisoners held by state jails, and that, for all essential purposes, such federal prisoners would be treated identically to state prisoners.

Given the venerable heritage of these two propositions, it would seem to have been well established, both under relevant state and federal statutes (and under the assumptions undergirding federal-state relations since the infancy of the nation) that federal agencies neither sought, nor were empowered, to instruct state jailers on the manner of operation of their institutions. That historical understanding was severely tested by the interim regulation, promulgated on April 17, 2002, in order to address the consequences of one case.

## STATUTORY AUTHORIZATION FOR PREEMPTION OF THE NEW JERSEY JAILKEEPER'S STATUTE BY ADMINISTRATIVE REGULATION

The weighty considerations of federalism usually invite considerable rhetorical flourish in cases where congressional intent to permit preemption is not express. As the Supreme Court held in *Gregory v. Ashcroft* (1991):

> If Congress intends to alter the "usual constitutional balance between the States and the Federal Government," it must make its intention to do so "unmistakably clear in the language of the statute." Congress should make its intention "clear and manifest" if it intends to pre-empt the historic powers of the States. . . . "In traditionally sensitive areas, such as legislation affecting the federal balance, the requirement of clear statement assures that the legislature has in fact faced, and intended to bring into issue, the critical matters involved in the judicial decision."[55]

This plain statement rule is nothing more than an acknowledgment that the States retain substantial sovereign powers under our constitutional scheme, powers with which Congress does not readily interfere.[56] Thus, many cases speak of a heavy presumption against preemption of state law, particularly in areas traditionally committed to state police power.[57]

In determining whether a federal administrative regulation preempts preexisting state law, however, the cases yield a surfeit of axioms and often conflicting guidance; consequently, they are difficult to rationalize into a coherent framework. It is certainly true that "federal regulations have no less pre-emptive effect than federal statutes."[58] But the Court also cautions with equal assurance that a federal agency "literally has no power to act, let alone pre-empt the validly enacted legislation of a sovereign State, unless and until Congress confers power upon it."[59] In determining whether Congress intended to confer that power, however, there is a strange analytical disconnect. When the issue is whether Congress itself intends to displace state law, then the federal statute effecting preemption must usually speak with a loud voice,[60] as the "plain statement" rule operates to create a "presumption against preemption." But when an individual federal administrator, acting pursuant to a general delegation of regulatory authority by Congress, decides to preempt a state law, then the presumption against preemption is vitiated.

Where Congress has directed an administrator to exercise his discretion, his judgments are subject to judicial review only to determine whether he has exceeded his statutory authority or acted arbitrarily. When the administrator promulgates regulations intended to preempt state law, the court's inquiry is similarly limited: "If his choice represents a reasonable accommodation of conflicting policies that were committed to the agency's care by the statute, we should not disturb it unless it appears from the statute or its legislative history that the accommodation is not one that Congress would have sanctioned."[61]

Thus, "a pre-emptive regulation's force does not depend on express congressional authorization to displace state law."[62] So long as an administrative agency is acting within the general scope of rule-making authority granted by Congress, it appears that such delegation implicitly includes within it the power to preempt state law, even absent any clear indication that Congress intended to bestow such power.

The Supreme Court has noted the empirical existence of this odd distinction between legislative and administrative preemption in *New York v. FERC* (2002), but did little to justify or explain it. The Court stated:

> Pre-emption of state law by federal law can raise two quite different legal questions. The Court has most often stated a "presumption against pre-emption" when a controversy concerned not the scope of the Federal Government's authority to displace state action, but rather whether a given state authority conflicts with, and thus has been displaced by, the existence of Federal Government authority.
>
> . . . .
>
> The other context in which "pre-emption" arises concerns the rule "that a federal agency may pre-empt state law only when and if it is acting within the scope of its congressionally delegated authority[,] . . . for an agency literally has no power to act, let alone pre-empt the validly enacted legislation of a sovereign State, unless and until Congress confers power upon it." . . . Such a case does not involve a "presumption against pre-emption," . . . but rather requires us to be certain that Congress has conferred authority on the agency. As we have explained, the best way to answer such a question—i.e., whether federal power may be exercised in an area of pre-existing state regulation—"is to examine the nature and scope of the authority granted by Congress to the agency." In other words, we must interpret the statute to determine whether Congress has given FERC the power to act as it has, and we do so without any presumption one way or the other.[63]

When Congress—which of course is elected from the several states and is presumably sensitive to the proper balance between federal and state sovereignties—desires to displace state law itself, it is held to the requirement that it articulate its intent with convincing clarity. It therefore seems counterintuitive not to impose a similar requirement of clearly articulated legislative intent when Congress delegates rule-making powers to an unelected administrator in the executive branch, who is neither inherently responsible nor responsive to the electoral process. As one federal judge noted in rejecting one attempt by the Justice Department to overrule state law by administrative fiat, "To allow an attorney general—an appointed executive whose tenure depends entirely on whatever administration occupies the White House—to determine the legitimacy of a particular medical practice without a specific congressional grant of such authority would be unprecedented and extraordinary."[64]

In the context of modern statutory schemes in which a general delegation of rule-making power to an administrative agency is often quite broad, the absence of such a requirement that Congress plainly state its intent to permit preemption of state law grants potentially sweeping powers to individual administrators whose political legitimacy in overruling the decisions of elected state legislators is questionable at best. Indeed, as a matter of self-imposed restraint the executive branch itself has made at least some attempt to restore the balance of power between the states and the federal government by applying the traditional presumption against preemption to limit the scope of an administrative agency's power even when Congress has bestowed it with a general delegation of rule-making authority. In 1999, President Clinton issued Executive Order 13,132, encaptioned simply

"Federalism," by which he ostensibly attempted to curb the potentially immense power of administrative agencies to unilaterally displace state legislatures. Among the provisions of Executive Order 13,132 is the following rule of construction:

> Section 4. Special Requirements for Preemption.
> (a) Agencies shall construe, in regulations and otherwise, a Federal statute to preempt State law only where the statute contains an express preemption provision or there is some other clear evidence that the Congress intended preemption of State law, or where the exercise of State authority conflicts with the exercise of Federal authority under the Federal statute.
> (b) Where a Federal statute does not preempt State law (as addressed in subsection (a) of this section), agencies shall construe any authorization in the statute for the issuance of regulations as authorizing preemption of State law by rulemaking only when the exercise of State authority directly conflicts with the exercise of Federal authority under the Federal statute or there is clear evidence to conclude that the Congress intended the agency to have the authority to preempt State law.[65]

Thus, Executive Order 13,132 in effect attempts to restore the "presumption against preemption" even when Congress has made a general delegation of rulemaking authority to an administrative agency, since it requires "clear evidence to conclude that the Congress intended the agency to have the authority to pre-empt State law,"[66] unless the statute itself preempts state law. By its terms however, Executive Order 13,132 creates no legally enforceable rights, since Section 11 provides: "This order is intended only to improve the internal management of the executive branch, and is not intended to create any right or benefit, substantive or procedural, enforceable at law by a party against the United States, its agencies, its officers, or any person."[67] The substantive provisions of the presidential edict are therefore completely hortatory. Even the procedural requirements that an agency consult with state officials and prepare a federalism impact statement before promulgating a regulation preempting state law[68] can be dispensed with unilaterally by the administrator promulgating the regulation, without the possibility of review, by the convenient device of finding that the rule "will not have substantial direct effects on the States, on the relationship between the National Government and the States, or on the distribution of power and responsibilities among the various levels of government."[69]

Applying the rule that a federal administrative agency may preempt state law so long as it is acting within the general scope of authority delegated by Congress, the Appellate Division in County of Hudson found that New Jersey's century-old policy against secret detentions had been overridden by the sweep of Commissioner Ziglar's pen. The court first noted the uncontroversial proposition that Congress has exclusive authority over matters involving naturalization and immigration,[70] and then observed that the Immigration and Nationality Act ("INA") provides that the Attorney General "shall establish such regulations; prescribe such forms of bond, reports, entries, and other papers; issue such instructions; and perform such other acts as he deems necessary for carrying out his authority under the provisions of this Act."[71] Combining these two provisions, the Appellate Division found that the Attorney General, through his delegate, the Commissioner of the INS, was authorized to promulgate the interim regulation preempting state law mandating public disclosure of the names of inmates in New Jersey county jails.

The Appellate Division did express reservations, however, about the initial contention that the conditions of confinement of INS detainees in state jails fell within the scope of the INA:

> Although there can be no question that, under the INA and its implementing regulations, the Commissioner has the authority to promulgate regulations relating to immigration and naturalization, it may be open to question whether [section 236.6 of the *Code of Federal Regulations 8*] actually "relates" to immigration and naturalization, for the rule itself does not purport to regulate the conduct or status of aliens, nor does it address the legal processes afforded INS detainees. Rather, the regulation deals solely with public access to records concerning detainees. Thus, the real focus of the regulation, as evidenced by the rationale presented in its preamble, may be seen to be on the facilitation of law enforcement efforts in the wake of September 11.[72]

Nevertheless, the court ultimately concluded that "we would breach faith with overarching principles of our federalism if we were to see this case as an occasion for viewing the grant of authority to the Commissioner as anything but very broad."[73] It therefore held, albeit in somewhat reserved language, that the regulation fell within the ambit of federal immigration laws:

> We accept as not patently unrealistic the government's assertion that the regulation bears upon the privacy interests of those detainees who may not want to have their names made public and that it tends to affect the safety of the detainees and their families as well as others involved in the detention scheme. The further assertion that the regulation affects ongoing investigations into violations of the immigration laws is also not so far-fetched as to invite disbelief.[74]

The correctness of this conclusion, however, is not self-evident. The authority of the Attorney General and the Commissioner under the INA to issue regulations pertaining to immigration cannot extend any further than the scope of the Act itself. Despite the general breadth of the rule-making authority granted relative to the overall scope of the Act, the boundaries of what Congress actually intended to govern pursuant to the INA are limited. It overstates the law considerably to assert that any regulation dealing with aliens must therefore be a regulation of immigration and thus subject to the plenary power of Congress to legislate and the Attorney General and Commissioner to regulate. As Justice Brennan stated for the Court in *DeCanas v. Bica* (1976), "the Court has never held that every state enactment which in any way deals with aliens is a regulation of immigration and thus per se pre-empted by this constitutional power, whether latent or exercised."[75] The Court then gave guidance to construing the meaning and scope of the immigration power exercised by Congress under the INA: "The fact that aliens are the subject of a state statute does not render it a regulation of immigration, which is essentially a determination of who should or should not be admitted into the country, and the conditions under which a legal entrant may remain."[76]

The plaintiffs in *County of Hudson* therefore asserted that the Attorney General had not been given the power to regulate in an area beyond the scope of the INA itself. Whether the inmates held for the INS are subject to deportation, voluntary departure, release on bond, are entitled to asylum, or are subject to some other substantive immigration policy, is concededly a matter subject to exclusive federal control. The New Jersey statutes that require that a county jail's inmate records be open to public inspection, however, do not address "who should or should not be admitted into the country, and the conditions under which a legal entrant may remain." Substantive immigration issues are not implicated by the requirement that the names of all inmates in New Jersey jails (including but not limited to inmates held pursuant to contract with the INS) be subject to public disclosure.

Once the Appellate Division concluded that the public disclosure of the identities of INS detainees in county jails fell within the ambit of federal immigration laws, however, it quickly concluded that the general grant of authority delegated to the Attorney General to "establish such regulations; . . . issue such instructions; and perform such other acts as he deems necessary for carrying out his authority under the provisions of this Act"[77] empowered him to adopt the interim regulation.[78]

But while the INA certainly bestows broad rule-making authority, that authority has its limits, and authorizes the Attorney General only to promulgate regulations necessary "for carrying out his authority under the provisions of this chapter." The only relevant reference contained in the INA to federal interaction with state government is the empowerment of the Attorney General to arrange for "the housing, care, and security of persons detained by the Service pursuant to Federal law under an agreement with a State or political subdivision of a State."[79] This authorization to enter into a voluntary agreement or contract with a state (or its political subdivisions) hardly qualifies as a clear statement authorizing the Attorney General to preempt state law governing the substantive conditions under which state jails are operated. To the contrary, such language circumscribes the Attorney General's power by authorizing him to enter only into those contractual relationships to which the State chooses to agree. The relationship intended by Congress between the federal government and state entities expressed in the INA is therefore one of arm's-length contracting partners, not one of a superior preempting authority over an inferior.

Interpreting the INA as imposing such a limitation on the grant of rule-making authority is consistent with—and perhaps constitutionally mandated by—the longstanding historical understanding that federal prisoners are kept in state jails purely at the sufferance of state sovereignty. Indeed, not only is the limitation on the Attorney General's rule-making power with regard to state-operated jails inherent in the text of the INA itself, but that is how the Attorney General himself interpreted his power—at least before the exigencies of the September 11 detainees arose—when he entered into contracts with the Hudson and Passaic County jail facilities expressly providing that the manner of detention of the inmates shall be governed by state law and local policies and procedures. The interim regulation of April 17 was, therefore, not only not "necessary for carrying out his authority under the provisions of this Act,"[80] but in fact was in direct contradiction to that authority under section 1103(a)(9)(A) of the *U.S. Code 8*, as both the Attorney General himself exercised it when he entered into intergovernmental service agreements with the state jails,[81] and as Congress intended it under the general statutory scheme permitting such agreements. Even under the less deferential standards currently applied in determining the efficacy of federal administrative regulations that endeavor to preempt state law, therefore, the Attorney General's attempt to regulate the manner in which New Jersey state authorities record and disclose the identities of inmates held in their care represents a marked departure not only from the text of the relevant statutes, but perhaps more importantly, also from the consistent historical practice, which the federal government had itself promoted, of exclusive local control of federal prisoners in state jails.

## CONSTITUTIONAL LIMITATIONS ON FEDERAL REGULATION OF THE OPERATION OF STATE JAILS: ANTI-COMMANDEERING

Perhaps the most novel claim raised by the plaintiffs in *ACLU of New Jersey v. County of Hudson* was the constitutional argument that "commandeering" state officials to engage in secret detentions of federal inmates in a manner contrary to state law is an unconstitutional derogation of state autonomy and sovereignty that violates the Tenth Amendment of the United States Constitution. The actual defendants in the case, the Counties of Hudson and Passaic and the wardens and keepers of the respective county jails, are entities and offices created under the authority of the State of New Jersey. Their power arises solely from the sovereignty of the State, and they owe their obligations to the State. Even when they act as jailors of federal prisoners, they do so in their capacity as state officers, not federal employees. For the federal government to enact a regulation that forbids state officials from complying with the dictates of state law raises at least the suggestion of federal assumption of the powers of the state sovereign over its own state officials.

Several recent United States Supreme Court cases have rediscovered previously unexplored constitutional limits on the ability of the federal government to control the apparatus of state government. In *New York v. United States* (1992),[82] the Court held unconstitutional a provision of federal law regulating the disposal of radioactive wastes. The law required a state to "take title" to any wastes within its borders that were not otherwise properly disposed of. Justice O'Connor, writing for the Court, found that putting states to the choice of "either accepting own-ership of waste or regulating according to the instructions of Congress" would impermissibly "commandeer" state government to implement federal law.[83] The scheme embodied in the original Constitution, according to O'Connor, was that the federal sovereignty could regulate individuals but not the States.[84] "While Congress has substantial powers to govern the Nation directly, including in ar-eas of intimate concern to the States, the Constitution has never been understood to confer upon Congress the ability to require the States to govern according to Congress' instructions."[85]

New York's somewhat metaphorical reference to "commandeering" state gov-ernments into the service of federal regulatory purposes left some uncertainty con-cerning the type of federal mechanisms it intended to forbid, and in *Printz v. United States* (1997), the Court attempted to provide greater clarity. *Printz* struck down a provision in the Brady Act requiring state law enforcement officers to conduct background checks on prospective handgun purchasers. The Court held that "[t]he Federal Government may neither issue directives requiring the States to address particular problems, nor command the States' officers, or those of their political subdivisions, to administer or enforce a federal regulatory program. It matters not whether policymaking is involved, and no case-by-case weighing of the burdens or benefits is necessary; such commands are fundamentally incompatible with our constitutional system of dual sovereignty."[86]

Thus, in the words of one commentator, *Printz* "expressly rejected function-alism as a consideration in the state sovereignty context, replacing it with a struc-tural formalism."[87] The Court expressly rejected the United State's argument that "[t]he Brady Act serves very important purposes, is most efficiently administered by [local law enforcement officers] . . . and places a minimal and only temporary burden upon state officers."[88] *Printz* therefore declared "categorically" that the "Federal Government may not compel the States to enact or administer a federal regulatory program,"[89] regardless of the salutary purposes it might serve or the harm to federal interests that might result as a consequence.

Definitional problems still arose after *Printz*, however, as to the meaning of "commandeering" and the limits of federal compulsion of state activities. In *Reno v. Condon* (2000),[90] the Court resolved the conflict among lower courts on the application of *New York* and *Printz* to the *Driver's Privacy Protection Act of 1994*,[91] ("DPPA") which banned disclosure of state driver's license per-sonal information without the driver's consent.[92] The Act's provisions did not apply solely to States; it also regulated the resale and redisclosure of drivers' personal information by private persons who had obtained that information from a state agency.[93] The Court unanimously held that the federal statute did not run afoul of the federalism and dual sovereignty principles embodied in its previ-ous cases. Although it agreed that compliance with the federal law would "re-quire time and effort on the part of state employees," it rejected the State's argument that the Act violated the principles laid down in either *New York* or *Printz*.[94]

> We think, instead, that this case is governed by our decision in *South Carolina v. Baker*, 485 U.S. 505 (1988). In *Baker*, we upheld a statute that prohibited States from issuing unregistered bonds because the law "regulated state activities," rather than "seeking to control or influence the manner in which States regulate private parties."
>
> . . . .
>
> Like the statute at issue in *Baker*, DPPA does not require the States in their sovereign capacity to regulate their own citizens. The DPPA regulates the States as the owners of databases. It does not require the South Carolina Legislature to enact any laws or regulations, and it does not require state officials to assist in the enforcement of federal statutes regulating private individuals.[95]

The Court further noted that the *Driver's Privacy Protection Act* regulated not merely the states, but "the universe of entities that participate as suppliers to the market for motor vehicle information," and thus was a law of general application that did not regulate the states qua states.[96]

With only three modern cases to serve as points of reference for a somewhat opaque constitutional doctrine, it might be overreaching to assert the existence of a clear outcome with respect to the April 17 interim regulation. The Appellate Division relied exclusively on *Condon* to reject the plaintiff's contention that the April 17 interim regulation promulgated by Commissioner Ziglar amounted to federal "commandeering" of state officers to enforce federal law under *New York*, and amounted to the Federal Government compelling the States to "administer a federal regulatory program" under *Printz*.[97] But apart from the April 17 regulation's superficial similarity with the statute at issue in *Condon*—both of which forbade disclosure of personal information—there are several factors that separate the two. *Condon* distinguished *Printz* and *New York* by noting that the statute at issue "does not require state officials to assist in the enforcement of federal statutes regulating private individuals."[98] Nor did the federal government in that case seek "to control or influence the manner in which States regulate private parties."[99] But that is precisely what Commissioner Ziglar's directive did in this case, since it affirmatively enmeshed state officials in a federal regulatory program—there being no clearer example of "regulation" than incarceration—in a manner that affirmatively violated state law. Requiring that holders of private individual information, including state agencies, not disclose that information is one thing; but both as an aspect of historical understanding and doctrinal application, requiring that state jailers physically incarcerate inmates in secret in contravention of state law is quite another. Thus, a federal mandate that county jails take custody of federal inmates in the secretive manner required by federal policies and procedures appropriates the apparatus of state government to implement a federal policy.

In *Condon*, the restraints placed upon state officials (as well as private vendors in possession of the drivers license data) were purely passive; they were not required to engage in any affirmative activity in furtherance of a federal program, but merely to refrain from distributing such information. Here, however, the inexorable effect of the April 17 regulation and the post hoc reneging on the terms of the intergovernmental service agreements with Hudson and Passaic Counties, is that state officials must now engage in the affirmative activity of maintaining INS inmates in secret detention according to the commands of their new federal superiors. And thus, unlike the statute in *Condon*, the federal regulation "requires state officials to assist in the enforcement of federal statutes regulating private individuals."[100]

As a practical matter, local state officials are attracted to dealing directly with the federal government through lucrative intergovernmental service agreements[101] and have little incentive to be passionate about state policy against secret detentions. But the willingness of jail officials in Hudson and Passaic Counties to cede their authority to the federal government should be constitutionally irrelevant. "Where Congress exceeds its authority relative to the States, therefore, the departure from the constitutional plan cannot be ratified by the 'consent' of state officials."[102] The state autonomy and sovereignty that is at issue in this case is not for any individual state official to give away. Moreover, state officials cannot unilaterally abrogate a controlling state statute. Inmates detained pursuant to the INS directive were held at the Hudson and Passaic County jails only because county officials entered into voluntary contracts with the INS. The express terms of the service agreements between the counties and the INS provide that local laws govern the manner of identification and recording of detainees.[103]

The structural "detour" mechanism validated by the April 17 regulation has profound implications for federal-state programs in the future, since it allows federal officials to (1) contract with individual local state officials; (2) excise by appropriate preempting regulation any inconvenient limitations imposed by state law on the conduct of its own officers; and (3) thereby effectively bypass the state as the empowering sovereignty. The United States can thus provide immunity from a state official's obligation to abide by state law, simply by promulgating a regulation that forbids him to follow that state law. In light of ongoing attempts to shift, or at least share, law enforcement responsibilities previously exercised by federal officers with state officials in connection with the war on terrorism,[104] validation of this mechanism of federal-local cooperation, thereby bypassing state limitations, could have significant federalism implications.

But counties and their officials are bound whenever possible to exercise their prerogatives and official discretion consistent with state law and policy, and thus could not initially enter into a voluntary contract that requires them to violate such state law. To do so would amount to a breach of a fiduciary duty owed by state officials to their sovereign and employer. The only solution to this conundrum would be for county officials, in order to reconcile their obligations to the State of New Jersey with the proscriptions of the Ziglar directive, to terminate immediately the intergovernmental service agreements with the INS and refuse to enter into any further contracts that require them to violate state law prohibiting secret detentions. But a federal agency should not, through unilateral and retroactive imposition of a "secret detention" rule upon state officials, be able to force those state officials to become complicit in a federal detention program whose terms violate a state statute's policy.

## CONCLUSION

The directive of Commissioner Ziglar of April 17, 2002, is an attempt to turn a voluntary obligation assumed by a state official pursuant to an intergovernmental contract into an involuntary duty to violate state law. For the federal government to be able to impose conditions on the county jails to compel them to engage in secret detention—conduct that the New Jersey Legislature has declared to be against public policy—signals a significant reworking of the structures by which federal and state agencies engage in cooperative efforts. It is unclear that Congress, in granting rule-making power to the Attorney General, intended to authorize such restructure. Moreover, the practical implications of permitting direct agreements between federal and local law enforcement officials to bypass state control over those local officials may encourage a novel method of intergovernmental cooperation that could dilute the historical and constitutional understandings underlying our Federalism.

## Notes

1. *Preiser v. Rodriguez*, 411 U.S. 475, 491–492 (1973).

2. *Printz v. United States*, 521 U.S. 898 (1997).

3. Ibid., 909–910 (internal citations omitted).

4. Ibid., 919.

5. Office of the Inspector General, United States Department of Justice, "The September 11 Detainees: A Review of the Treatment of Aliens Held on Immigration Charges in Connection with the Investigation of the September 11 Attacks" (April 2003): 1 [hereinafter as "OIG Report"], http://www.usdoj.gov/oig/special/0306/full.pdf.

6. See Amnesty International, *Amnesty International's Concerns Regarding Post-September 11 Detentions in the USA*, March 14, 2002 [hereinafter as "Amnesty International Report"], http://web.amnesty.org/library/Index/ENGAMR510442002?open&of=ENG-USA.

7. OIG Report, 72.

8. On March 1, 2003, the Immigration and Naturalization Service became part of the Department of Homeland Security and its functions were divided into various bureaus of that department, including U.S. Immigration and Customs Enforcement (ICE). *Homeland Security Act of 2002*, Public Law No. 107-296, *U.S. Statutes at Large* 116 (2002): 2135.

9. Ibid., 20

10. OIG Report, 2.

11. The only person charged for or convicted of complicity in the terrorist attacks of September 11, 2001, Zacarias Moussaoui, was arrested in Minnesota on August 17, 2001, and was not a special interest detainee. Some of the detainees were charged with

crimes unrelated to September 11 or other terrorist activity. See, for e.g., Laura Parker, Kevin Johnson, and Richard Willing, "Terror Network Remains Crouched in Shadows," *USA Today*, September 28, 2001 (final edition).

12. See generally *U.S. Code 18* (2000) sec. 4002 (Attorney General may contract with State for imprisonment, subsistence, care, and proper employment of persons held under authority of federal law.); *U.S. Code 8* (2004), sec. 1103(a)(11) (Attorney General is authorized to make payments for housing, care, and security of persons detained by Service pursuant to Federal law under agreement with a State or political subdivision of a State.).

13. The Hudson County Correctional Center in Kearny, New Jersey, and the Passaic County Jail in Paterson, New Jersey, housed most of the September 11 detainees, with some others housed in the Middlesex County Jail in North Brunswick, New Jersey. Special interest detainees whom the FBI considered to be especially dangerous were usually housed in the Metropolitan Detention Center in Brooklyn, NY. See Anne-Marie Cusac, "Ill-Treatment on Our Shores; Detainees Arrested After Terrorist Attacks Lodge Allegations of Abuse While in Custody," *The Progressive*, March 1, 2002, 24.

14. Of the total 762 detainees, 491 were arrested in New York, and 70 in New Jersey (74%). OIG Report, 21. The place of arrest of the remainder has not been disclosed. Ibid.

15. General Ashcroft noted: "I am not interested in providing, when we are at war, a list to Osama bin Laden, the al Qaeda network, of the people that we have detained that would make in any way easier their effort to kill American citizens—innocent Americans. That will remain the policy of this department, which will scrupulously adhere to the law." (Department of Justice Briefing with Attorney General John Ashcroft, *Federal News Service*, November 27, 2001 [hereinafter as "Ashcroft Briefing"]).

16. See, for e.g., Editorial, "Justice Deformed; War and the Constitution," *New York Times*, December 2, 2001 (final edition); Editorial, "Secret Detainees; Ashcroft Should Be More Forthcoming," *Dallas Morning News*, November 30, 2001 (second edition); Editorial, "An Un-American Secrecy," *Los Angeles Times*, November 17, 2001 (home edition); Editorial, "Secret Detentions Needlessly Undercut Public Justice," *USA Today*, November 2, 2001 (final edition).

17. *The Federalist No. 84* (Alexander Hamilton) (emphasis in original) (quoting Blackstone, Commentaries on the Laws of England). "The requirement that arrest books be open to the public is to prevent any 'secret arrests,' a concept odious to a democratic society. . . ." *Morrow v. District of Columbia*, 417 F.2d 728, 741–742 (D.C. Cir. 1969).

18. *Center for National Security Studies v. United States Department of Justice*, 215 F. Supp. 2d 94 (D.D.C. 2002), aff'd in part and rev'd in part, 331 F.3d 918 (D.C. Cir. 2003), cert. denied, 540 U.S. 1104 (2004).

19. *Detroit Free Press v. Ashcroft*, 195 F. Supp. 2d 937 (E.D. Mich. 2002), aff'd, 303 F.3d 681 (6th Cir. 2002) (holding that the First Amendment grants right of public access to immigration proceedings); *North Jersey Media Group, Inc. v. Ashcroft*, 205 F. Supp. 2d 288 (D.N.J.), rev'd, 308 F.3d 198 (3d Cir. 2002) (holding no First Amendment right of public access to immigration proceedings), cert. denied, 538 U.S. 1056 (2003).

20. *ACLU of New Jersey, Inc. v. County of Hudson*, No. HUD-L-463-02 (N.J. Super. Ct. filed January 22, 2002).

21. *New Jersey Statutes Annotated*, sec. 30:8-16 (West 2002).

22. The statute provides:

Each such sheriff and keeper shall, on or before the first days of April and October, make out the names of all prisoners who, since the last settlement, shall have been committed to his custody, under the authority of the United States, and the time they shall have been respectively confined, with an account of the amount thereof, at fifty cents per month for the use and keeping of such jail, for every person so committed, together with an account of their subsistence, at the rate established by law for state prisoners, and transmit the same to the United States marshal for the proper district, for payment.

New Jersey Statutes Annotated, sec. 30:8-2 (West 2002).

23. *New Jersey Statutes Annotated*, sec. 47:1A-2 (West 2002). The Right-to-Know Law in effect at the time required that "all records which are required by law to be made, maintained or kept on file" by a government body be made public. Since section 30-8-2 of the New Jersey Statutes Annotated expressly requires that the names of federal prisoners housed in New Jersey jails be recorded, the Right-to-Know Law thereby mandated public disclosure of those records.

The Right-to-Know Law has since been superseded by an even more expansive *Open Public Records Act*, 209th Legis., 2d Annual Session, *New Jersey 2001 Session Law Service*, Ch. 404 (2002), which requires disclosure of any documents regularly kept by a state agency, regardless of whether it was required to do so by law. Both the Right-to-Know Law and the Open Public Records Act contained exemptions for certain documents, including documents related to ongoing law enforcement investigations.

24. See *New Jersey Statutes Annotated*, New Jersey Rules of the Court, Part IV, Ch. VII, Rule 4: 69 (2002).

25. See Intergovernmental Service Agreement between County of Hudson and the U.S. Department of Justice, Immigration and Naturalization Service (Agreement No. ACB-5-I-0001); Intergovernmental Service Agreement between Passaic County Jail and U.S. Department of Justice, Immigration and Naturalization Service (January 28, 1985).

26. The trial judge originally granted summary judgment on the complaint's first cause of action under section 30:8–16 of the *New Jersey Statutes Annotated* and second cause of action under section 10A: 31-6.5 of the *New Jersey Administrative Code*, but granted summary judgment in favor of defendants on the third cause of action under the *New Jersey Right-to-Know Law*, *New Jersey Statutes Annotated,* sec. 47: 1A-1 to 4; and dismissed the fourth cause of action under the common-law right of access to government records. On April 12, 2002, however, Judge D'Italia informed counsel that he was issuing a revised written opinion that would supersede the oral opinion rendered on March 26, and noted that he was entering summary judgment in favor of plaintiffs on the first three causes of action, including the third cause of action based upon the Right-to-Know Law. *ACLU of New Jersey v. County of Hudson*.

27. In his bench opinion, Judge D'Italia held:

> The argument . . . that the statute applies only to inmates charged with state crimes and being held as pre-trial detainees pursuant to state charges or those sentenced to prison pursuant to state law is rejected. The statute contains no such qualifying language. It refers to all inmates committed to the care of the keeper of the jail without regard to the authority by which the inmate is committed, whether it be federal, state or local.

*ACLU of New Jersey v. County of Hudson*.

28. *U.S. Code 5* (2000), sec. 553.

29. Interim Rule, Release of Information Regarding Immigration and Naturalization Service Detainees in Non-Federal Facilities, *Federal Register 67* (2002), 19,508, as

confirmed at *Federal Register 68* (2003), 4364 (codified at *Code of Federal Regulations 8* (2003), sec. 236.6) [hereinafter as "Interim Rule"].

30. *Federal Register 67* (2002), 19,510.

31. Ibid.

32. See Jim Edwards, "Stay on Release of Detainee Names Leads to Chaos for Sept. 11 Cases; ACLU, INS at Odds Over Meaning of Appellate Order," *New Jersey Law Journal* (April 29, 2002): 337.

33. *ACLU of N.J. v. County of Hudson*, No. A-4100-00T5, 2002 N.J. Super. LEXIS 201 (N.J. Super. Ct. App. Div. April 29, 2002).

34. The stay order was refined to permit the following:

(1)  The removal of any detainee who has agreed to voluntary departure.

(2)  The removal of any detainee with a final removal order who exhibits his consent to such removal by signing a form setting forth that consent.

(3)  The removal of any detainee who is authorized to leave the jail on bond.

(4)  The temporary removal of any detainee, such as for transportation to immigration or other court hearings, medical matters, or the like.

(5)  The removal of any detainee who is actually represented by counsel.  Ibid.

35. *ACLU of NJ v. County of Hudson*, 799 A.2d 629 (N.J. Super. Ct. App. Div. 2002), cert. denied, 803 A.2d 1162 (N.J. 2002).

36. Interim Rule at 19,511.

37. *Executive Order No. 13,132* (August 4, 1999), *Federal Register 64* (August 1999): 43,255. President Clinton issued the executive order "to ensure that the principles of federalism established by the Framers guide the executive departments and agencies in the formulation and implementation of policies. . . . " Ibid.

38. Ibid., 43,258

39. For e.g., Code of Alabama, sec. 14-6-4 (West 2003); Arizona Revised Statutes Annotated, sec. 31-122 (West 2004); West's Arkansas Code Annotated, sec. 12-41-503 (West 2003); West's Annotated California Penal Code, sec. 2902 (West 2004); *West's Colorado Revised Statutes Annotated*, sec. 17-26-123 (West 2003); Kansas Statutes Annotated, sec. 19-1930 (West 2003); *Baldwin's Kentucky Revised Statutes Annotated*, sec. 441.035 (West 2004); *West's Louisiana Statutes Annotated: Louisiana Revised Statutes*, sec. 15:707 (West 2004); *Maine Revised Statutes Annotated*, Title 30-A, sec. 1554 (West 2004); *Michigan Compiled Laws Annotated*, sec. 801.101 (West 2004); *West's Annotated Mississippi Code*, sec. 19-25-81 (West 2004); *Vernon's Annotated Missouri Statutes*, sec. 221.270 (West 2004); *Nebraska Revised Statutes of 1943*, sec. 83-420 (West 2003); *West's Nevada Revised Statutes Annotated*, sec. 211.060 (West 2004); *McKinney's Consolidated Laws of New York Annotated*, sec. 612 (West 2004); *West's North Carolina General Statutes Annotated*, sec. 162-34 (West 2004); *Oklahoma Statutes Annotated*, Title 57, sec. 16 (West 2004); *West's Oregon Revised Statutes Annotated*, sec. 169.540 (West 2003); *Code of Laws of South Carolina 1976 Annotated*, sec. 23-19-20 (West 2003); *West's Tennessee Code Annotated*, sec. 41-4-105 (West 2004); *Vernon's Texas Statutes and Codes Annotated*, sec. 351.043 (West 2004); *West's Annotated Code of Virginia*, sec. 53.1-79 (West 2004); *Michie's West Virginia Code Annotated*, sec. 7-8-8 (Michie 2003); W*est's Wyoming Statutes Annotated*, sec. 18-6-305 (West 2003).

40. *New Jersey Statutes Annotated*, sec. 30:8-2 (West 2002). This provision is first found in the Sheriff's Act of 1877, *New Jersey Revised Statutes Annotated*, sec. 33, at 1105 (West 1877).

41. Georgia's original reluctance, noted in *Printz*, to house federal prisoners apparently survives to some extent to this day. The current Georgia statute provides: "The keeper of a county jail may decline to receive a person from the custody of anyone acting under the authority of the United States government. He may receive the person if the consent of the authority having control of county matters is first obtained." *West's Code of Georgia Annotated*, sec. 42-4-9 (2002).

42. *Board of Chosen Freeholders of Hudson County v. Kaiser*, 69 A. 25 (N.J. Sup. Ct.), aff'd, 71 A. 1133 (N.J. 1908).

43. Ibid., 28.

44. *Randolph v. Donaldson*, 13 U.S. 76, 86 (1815).

45. *Saunders v. United States*, 73 F. 782, 783 (C.C.D. Me. 1896).

46. *Logue v. United States*, 412 U.S. 521 (1973); Federal Tort Claims Act, U.S. Code 28 (1997), sec. 1346(b),

47. The statute currently provides: "For the purpose of providing suitable quarters for the safekeeping, care, and subsistence of all persons held under authority of any enactment of Congress, the Attorney General may contract, for a period not exceeding three years, with the proper authorities of any State, Territory, or political subdivision thereof, for the imprisonment, subsistence, care, and proper employment of such persons." *U.S. Code 18* (2000), sec. 4002. At the time that *Logue* was decided, the statute named the Director of the Bureau of Prisons as the federal officer authorized to enter into contracts with state authorities for housing federal prisoners. (*U.S. Code 18* (1976), sec. 4002.) In 1978, the statute was amended to substitute the Attorney General for the Director, thus broadening its scope to include all federal detainees held by the Department of Justice, including those held by the INS. (Public Law No. 95-624, sec. 8, *U.S. Statutes at Large* 92 (1978): 3459.)

48. *Logue v. United States*, 529.

49. Ibid., 530.

50. Ibid., 527 n.5 (quoting *Restatement (Second) of Agency* sec. 2(3) (1958)).

51. New Jersey is not unique in providing by statute for the public disclosure of the identities of inmates held in state institutions, and the existence of such provisions could hardly have been a surprise to federal authorities. Over fifty years ago, New York adopted a law requiring the maintenance of public records on prisoners, which now provides that:

Each keeper [of a local correctional facility] shall keep a daily record, to be provided at the expense of the county, of the commitments and discharges of all prisoners delivered to his charge, which shall contain the date of entrance, name, offense, term of sentence, fine, age, sex, place of birth, color, social relations, education, secular and religious, for what and by whom committed, how and when discharged, trade or occupation, whether so employed when arrested, number of previous convictions. The daily record shall be a public record, and shall be kept permanently in the office of the keeper.

*McKinney's Consolidated Laws of New York Annotated*, Correction Law, sec. 500-f (2004).

Similarly, a Louisiana statute, initially enacted in 1928, requires every jail to keep a book setting forth the name and other information "as to each prisoner received" and provides that "the book and booking information summaries shall always be open for public inspection." *West's Louisiana Statutes Annotated*, Louisiana Code of Criminal Procedure, Art. 228(B) (West 2004). A New Mexico statute, successor to a similar law enacted in

1961, provides that "each county sheriff, jail administrator or independent contractor shall keep a written record showing the exact time of confinement and release of each prisoner incarcerated in the jail under his jurisdiction." *West's New Mexico Statutes Annotated*, sec. 4-44-19 (West 2004). A Nebraska statute, originally part of a law enacted in 1866, requires the sheriff of each jail to keep "a suitable book to be called the jail register, in which he or she shall enter (1) the name of each prisoner, with the date and cause of his or her commitment. . . . " *Nebraska Revised Statutes of 1943*, sec. 47-106 (West 2003). See also *Massachusetts General Laws Annotated*, ch. 127, sec. 5, (originally enacted in 1784); *Code of Alabama*, sec. 36-22-8 (West 2004); *District of Columbia Official Code 2001 Edition*, sec. 5-113.01 (West 2004) (requiring record keeping); *District of Columbia Official Code 2001 Edition*, sec. 5-113.06 (West 2004) (stating that the records "shall be open to the public inspection"). Congress, in enacting the predecessor statute to section 5-113.01 of the *District of Columbia Official Code 2001 Edition*, noted the underlying justification for making arrest records public:

> It is felt that the keeping of such records and their availability to the public should be matters of law and not of administrative discretion, both for the protection of the public against secret arrests and to guard against the abuse in any way of the arrest power.

U.S. House Report No. 2332, 83rd Cong., 2d sess. (1954). See also *White v. United States*, 164 U.S. 100, 104 (1896) (recognizing that then-sections 4537, 4538, 4539, and 4555 of the Criminal Code of Alabama required a local jailor to keep such a register).

52. *Ponzi v. Fessenden*, 258 U.S. 254, 264 (1922).

53. Intergovernmental Service Agreement between County of Hudson and U.S. Department of Justice, Immigration and Naturalization Service (Agreement No. ACB-5-I-0001) Arts. II(1), III(1), and IV(1).

54. Intergovernmental Service Agreement between Passaic County Jail and U.S. Department of Justice, Immigration, and Naturalization Service Art. III (January 28, 1985).

55. *Gregory v. Ashcroft*, 501 U.S. 452, 460–461 (1991) (quoting *Will v. Michigan Department of State Police*, 491 U.S. 58, 65 (1989)) (internal citations omitted).

56. Ibid., 461.

57. See, for e.g., *Hillsborough County v Automated Medical Laboratories, Inc.*, 471 U.S. 707, 715 (1985).

58. *Fidelity Federal Savings & Loan Association v. De La Cuesta*, 458 U.S. 141, 153 (1982); *Capital Cities Cable, Inc. v. Crisp*, 467 U.S. 691, 699 (1984) (quoting *Fidelity Federal Savings & Loan Association v. De La Cuesta*).

59. *Louisiana Public Service Commission v. Federal Communications Commission*, 476 U.S. 355, 374 (1986).

60. In the absence of an explicit preemption provision, a federal statute will be deemed to have superseded state law only where Congress has legislated so thoroughly across a field "as to make reasonable the inference that Congress left no room for the States to supplement it . . . ," or if an irreconcilable conflict exists between a state law and a federal statute that address the same general subject area. See generally *Louisiana Public Service Commission v. Federal Communications Commission, Pacific Gas & Electric Co. v. State Energy Resources Conservation and Development Commission*, 461 U.S. 190 (1983); *Jones v. Rath Packing Co.*, 430 U.S. 519 (1977); *Rice v. Santa Fe Elevator Corp.*, 331 U.S. 218 (1947). The Court has applied the same interpretive principles to determine the preemptive

intent of administrative regulations. See *Geier v. American Honda Motor Co.*, 529 U.S. 861 (2000).

61. *Fidelity Federal Savings & Loan Association v. De La Cuesta*, 153–154 (citations omitted).

62. Ibid., 154 (emphasis added).

63. *New York v. Federal Energy Regulatory Commission*, 535 U.S. 1, 17–18 (2002).

64. *Oregon v. Ashcroft*, 192 F. Supp. 2d 1077, 1092 (D. Ore. 2002) (finding Congress did not intend to authorize Attorney General to preempt Oregon's Death with Dignity Act through administrative regulation), review granted, 368 F.3d 1118 (9th Cir. 2004), aff'd, 546 U.S. 243 (2006). See generally Comment, "Questioning the Foundation of Attorney General Ashcroft's Attempt to Invalidate Oregon's Death with Dignity Act," *Oregon Law Review* 81 (2002): 505.

65. Executive Order No. 13,132, sec. 4 (August 4, 1999), *Federal Register* 64 (August 1999): 43,255, 43,257. For a discussion of Executive Order 13,132 and its predecessors, see Note & Comment, "Presidential Power Grab or Pure State Might? A Modern Debate Over Executive Interpretations on Federalism," *Brigham Young University Law Review 2000*: 293–325.

66. *Federal Register* 64 (1999): 43,257.

67. Executive Order No. 13,132, sec. 11, *Federal Register* 64 (1999): 43,259.

68. Ibid., sec. 6(c), 43,258.

69. Interim Rule. 19,511.

70. *ACLU of New Jersey v. County of Hudson*, 799 A.2d 629, 647 (N.J. Super. Ct. App. Div. 2002), cert. denied, 803 A.2d 1162 (N.J. 2002).

71. *ACLU of New Jersey v. County of Hudson*, 648 (quoting *U.S. Code 8* (2004), sec. 1103(a)(3)). The statute further provided that the Attorney General was empowered to delegate his rule-making authority to the Commissioner of the INS. (Ibid.) The INA has since been amended to vest general rule-making power in the Secretary for Homeland Security. *Homeland Security Act of 2002*, Public Law No. 107-296, sec. 1102, *U.S. Statutes at Large* 116 (2002): 2135, 2273 (November 25, 2002).

72. *ACLU of New Jersey v. County of Hudson*, 648.

73. Ibid., 648–649.

74. Ibid., 649.

75. *DeCanas v. Bica*, 424 U.S. 351, 355 (1976) (holding that a state law regulating employment of illegal aliens not preempted by INA).

76. Ibid.

77. *U.S. Code 8* (2004), sec. 1103(a)(3).

78. The United States also asserted the Attorney General has authority under section 1103(a)(2) of the *U.S. Code 8* (2004) to "control, direct[], and supervise ... all of the files and records of the Service," empowering him to adopt the interim regulation. The Appellate Division, however, declined to base its ruling on that provision, thus perhaps accepting the argument that section 1103(a)(2) does not apply to the records maintained by Hudson and Passaic Counties, because those records are not "records of the Service."

79. *U.S. Code 8* (2004), sec. 1103(a)(9)(A).

80. *U.S. Code 8* (2004), sec. 1103(a)(3).

81. The practical explanation as to why the INS often insisted in its agreements that its detainees be treated under the same state and local laws and procedures as state prisoners was to enhance its argument that state officials, not the INS, were responsible

for any substandard living conditions. See, for e.g., "United States, Locked Away: Immigration Detainees in Jails in the United States," *Human Rights Watch*, Vol. 10, No. 1(G) (September 1998): 1–44, http://www.hrw.org/reports98/us-immig; "Lost in the Labyrinth: Detention of Asylum-Seekers," *Amnesty International USA* (September 1999), http://www.amnestyusa.org/document.php?lang=e&id=86646DC7B706F38B8025690000693284.

82. *New York v. United States*, 505 U.S. 144 (1992).

83. Ibid., 161, 175.

84. Ibid., 166.

85. Ibid., 162 (citing *Coyle v. Smith*, 221 U.S. 559, 565 (1911)).

86. *Printz v. United States*, 935.

87. Andrew S. Gold, "Formalism and State Sovereignty in *Printz v. United States*: Cooperation by Consent," *Harvard J. of Law and Public Policy* 22 (1998): 247–277.

See also Vicki C. Jackson, "Federalism and the Uses and Limits of Law: *Printz* and Principle?" *Harvard Law Review* 111 (1998): 2180–2259 (criticizing *Printz* for its "categorical" approach and arguing for more flexible multifactored standard).

88. *Printz v. United States*, 931–932.

89. Ibid., 933.

90. *Reno v. Condon*, 528 U.S. 141 (2000).

91. *U.S. Code 18* (1994), secs. 2721–2725.

92. Some states had historically sold drivers' information for use by insurers, manufacturers, direct marketers, and others engaged in interstate commerce to contact drivers with customized solicitations. *Reno v. Condon*, 141.

93. Ibid., 146.

94. Ibid., 150.

95. Ibid., 150–151.

96. Ibid., 151.

97. The Appellate Division rejected plaintiff's Tenth Amendment argument on the basis of similarities with *Condon*.

In *Reno v. Condon*, the United States Supreme Court upheld a federal statute that established a regulatory scheme to restrict the authority of the states to disclose personal information contained in the records of state motor vehicle departments. The Court observed that the Tenth Amendment precludes the federal government from issuing directives requiring states to address particular problems or commanding state officers to administer or enforce federal regulatory programs.... Similarly, [section 236.6 of *Code of Federal Regulations* 8 (2003)] does not require New Jersey to enact any legislation, nor does it require State officials to administer a federal regulatory scheme, or even to accept federal prisoners or detainees. [Section 30:8–2 of the *New Jersey Statutes Annotated* (1997)] represents a choice made by the State of New Jersey, not one imposed by the federal government. Viewed in this light [section 236.6 of *Code of Federal Regulations 8*] simply controls the type of information the State can release to the public in respect of a subject matter committed to the plenary authority of the federal government. ACLU of *New Jersey v. County of Hudson*, 654–655 (citations omitted).

98. *Reno v. Condon*, 151.

99. Ibid., 150.

100. Ibid., 151.

101. The intergovernmental service agreements with Hudson and Passaic Counties provided for $77 per day per inmate to be paid by the United States. Housing 200 detainees

for 100 days would therefore yield over $1,500,000 paid directly into the local county sheriff's budget. (Intergovernmental Service Agreement between County of Hudson and the U.S. Department of Justice, Immigration and Naturalization Service (Agreement No. ACB-5-I-0001); Intergovernmental Service Agreement between Passaic County Jail and U.S. Department of Justice, Immigration and Naturalization Service (January 28, 1985)).

102. *New York v. United States*, 505 U.S. 144, 182 (1992).

103. Intergovernmental Service Agreement between County of Hudson and U.S. Department of Justice, Immigration, and Naturalization Service (Agreement No. ACB-5-I-0001) Art. IV(1).

104. See, for e.g., *Clear Law Enforcement for Criminal Alien Removal Act of 2003*, House of Representatives 2671, 108th Cong., 1st sess. (2003), http://www.govtrack.us/congress/billtext.xpd?bill=h108-2671 ("CLEAR Act"). The controversial CLEAR Act would authorize "law enforcement personnel of a State or a political subdivision of a State . . . to investigate, apprehend, detain, or remove aliens in the United States . . . in the enforcement of the immigration laws of the United States." Ibid., sec. 101. The bill further provides, however, that a State that fails to have in effect a statute that expressly authorizes law enforcement officers of the State, or of a political subdivision within the State, to enforce Federal immigration laws in the course of carrying out the officer's law enforcement duties shall not receive any of the funds that would otherwise be allocated to the State under section 241(i) of the *Immigration and Nationality Act* (*U.S. Code 8* (2006), 1231(i)). *CLEAR Act*, sec. 102(a). Moreover, state and local law enforcement must provide information about apprehended illegal aliens to the Department of Justice and the Department of Homeland Security within ten days "in such form and in such manner as the Attorney General may by regulation or guideline require." Ibid., sec. 105(a). Failure to provide such information likewise would result in deprivation of federal funding.

# Empowering States When It Matters: A Different Approach to Preemption

## Erwin Chemerinsky

### INTRODUCTION

When historians look back at the Rehnquist Court, undoubtedly they will say that its most significant impact on the law has been with regard to federalism. In the last decade, the Court has limited the scope of Congress's power to legislate under the Commerce Clause and Section Five of the Fourteenth Amendment;[1] revived the Tenth Amendment as a constraint on federal power;[2] and greatly expanded the scope of state sovereign immunity.[3]

One would expect that a Court concerned with federalism and states' rights also would be narrowing the scope of federal preemption of state laws. Narrowing the circumstances of federal preemption leaves more room for state and local governments to act. The Court has done quite the opposite, though. Over the last several years, the Supreme Court repeatedly has found preemption of important state laws, and done so when federal law was silent about preemption or even when it explicitly preserved state laws.

For example, in *Geier v. American Honda Motor Co.*,[4] the Court found preemption of a state products liability common law cause of action notwithstanding a statutory provision that expressly provided that "[c]ompliance with" a federal safety standard did "not exempt any person from any liability under the common law."[5] In *Lorillard Tobacco Co. v. Reilly*,[6] the Court found that federal law preempted state regulation of outdoor billboards and signs in stores advertising cigarettes. In *Crosby v. National Foreign Trade Council*,[7] the Court invalidated a Massachusetts law that restricted the ability of the state and its agency to purchase goods and services from companies that did business with Burma. Most recently, in *American Insurance Association v. Garamendi*, the Supreme Court found preemption of a California law requiring that insurance companies doing business in that state disclose Holocaust-era insurance policies.[8] The Court invalidated the California statute despite the absence of any federal law expressing an intent to preempt state law, basing its holding on the murky idea that the President has "dormant foreign affairs power" even though such a power is not specified in the Constitution.

At the very least, these and other cases like them are inconsistent with the Supreme Court's oft-stated presumption against preemption. One illustrative example of the statement appears in *Medtronic, Inc. v. Lohr*:

> [B]ecause the States are independent sovereigns in our federal system, we have long presumed that Congress does not cavalierly pre-empt state-law causes of action. In all pre-emption cases, and particularly in those in which Congress has "legislated . . . in a field which the States have traditionally occupied," we "start with the assumption that the historic police powers of the States were not to be superseded by the Federal Act unless that was the clear and manifest purpose of Congress."[9]

Contrary to this statement and its homage to the presumption against preemption, this Article will argue that the recent Supreme Court preemption cases clearly put the presumption in favor of preemption.[10]

More profoundly, the Court's recent decisions finding preemption expose the political content of its federalism rulings. The Court has eagerly found preemption of state laws regulating business, such as tobacco companies, the auto industry, and insurance companies. On the other hand, most of the Supreme Court's federalism decisions invalidating federal laws have struck down civil rights laws—such as the Violence against Women Act, the Religious Freedom Restoration Act, the Age Discrimination in Employment Act, and the Americans with Disabilities Act. Comparing the Court's preemption rulings with its decisions limiting Congress's powers to legislate under the Commerce Clause and Section Five (the enforcement provision) of the Fourteenth Amendment reveals that what animates the Rehnquist Court is not a concern for states' rights and federalism. Rather, the Court is hiding its value choices to limit civil rights laws and to protect business from regulation in decisions that seem to be about very specific doctrines of constitutional law, such as the scope of the commerce power and the circumstances of preemption.

This chapter is divided into four sections altogether. The next section describes the broad view of preemption reflected in the Supreme Court's recent decisions. The third section explains why these decisions are undesirable, and the fourth section offers a different approach to federalism, followed by a brief conclusion. My broad thesis is that federalism should be reconceptualized as being about empowering government at all levels, rather than limiting power. The genius of having multiple levels of government is there are several different actors to advance rights and liberties. From this perspective, congressional authority under the Commerce Clause and Section Five of the Fourteenth Amendment should be broadly interpreted, as it was from 1937 until the 1990s. Correspondingly, preemption of state and local laws should be narrowed. My specific thesis in the arena of preemption is that courts should find preemption only if a law expressly preempts state and local action or if there is a direct conflict between federal and state law. From this perspective, the Supreme Court's recent preemption cases are wrong in invalidating desirable state and local laws creating liability for injured consumers, protecting children from tobacco advertisements, and requiring insurance companies to disclose their Holocaust-era policies.

Obviously, a full exposition and defense of my federalism-as-empowerment thesis is beyond the scope of this chapter. But I do want to argue that such a radically different approach to federalism would mean a dramatic change for the better in the area of preemption analysis. States' rights are not an end in themselves. They are a means to the crucial objectives of advancing freedom and enriching the lives of those in the United States. Unfortunately, the Supreme Court's decisions limiting federal power in the area of civil rights and invalidating desirable state laws based on preemption have had exactly the opposite effects.

## THE DENIAL OF STATES' CHOICES: THE COURT'S BROAD VIEW OF PREEMPTION

Article Six of the Constitution contains the Supremacy Clause, which provides that the Constitution, and laws and treaties made pursuant to it, are the supreme law of the land. When a state law conflicts with federal law, the federal law controls and the state law bows under the principle of federal supremacy.[11] As the Supreme Court declared: "[U]nder the Supremacy Clause, from which our pre-emption doctrine is derived, any state law, however clearly within a State's acknowledged power, which interferes with or is contrary to federal law, must yield."[12] In *Gade v. National Solid Waste Management Association*, the Court summarized the tests for preemption:

> Pre-emption may be either expressed or implied, and is compelled whether Congress' command is explicitly stated in the statute's language or implicitly contained in its structure and purpose. Absent explicit pre-emptive language, we have recognized at least two types of implied pre-emption: field pre-emption, where the scheme of federal regulation is so pervasive as to make reasonable the inference that Congress left no room for the States to supplement it, and conflict pre-emption, where compliance with both federal and state regulations is a physical impossibility, or where state law stands as an obstacle to the accomplishment and execution of the full purposes and objectives of Congress.[13]

The Supreme Court has recognized that these categories are often difficult to apply. The Court once remarked that there is not "an infallible constitutional test or an exclusive constitutional yardstick. In the final analysis, there can be no one crystal clear distinctly marked formula."[14] In the vast majority of cases in which a court must decide whether state law is rendered invalid by related federal law, the federal law itself is ambiguous as to whether it precludes state and local law. Therefore, a choice must be made as to whether federal law should be presumed to preempt state law.

The Supreme Court correctly has said that concerns about federalism and state authority justify a presumption against preemption. The Court has observed: "Congress . . . should manifest its intention [to preempt state and local laws] clearly . . . The exercise of federal supremacy is not lightly to be presumed."[15] Recently, the Court emphasized that states "are independent sovereigns in our federal system" and therefore there is a presumption against finding preemption.[16]

The Supreme Court's recent preemption decisions are striking because they are so at odds with the Court's insistence on deference to the states in Commerce Clause and state sovereign immunity cases. To illustrate, I want to briefly describe several recent cases and how they put the presumption in favor of preemption. In this section, my focus is descriptive, focusing on how the Court has placed the presumption in favor of preemption; the normative criticism of this approach and these rulings is in the following section.

### Geier v. American Honda Motor Co., Inc.

Alexis Geier bought a 1987 model Honda Accord. She was seriously injured when the car crashed into a tree. She sued, claiming that the absence of airbags was a design defect that was responsible for her injuries. The Department of Transportation had issued rules pursuant to the *National Traffic and Motor Vehicle Safety Act* for 1987 automobiles. The regulations required that cars have passive restraint systems and gave manufacturers choices as to how to comply; one choice was to install airbags, another choice was to install the lap and shoulder belts that were in Geier's car. The defendant argued that Geier's suit was preempted by federal law because it built the car in compliance with the federal safety requirements.

The problem with this regulatory framework is that the *National Traffic and Motor Vehicle Safety Act*, which was the basis for the Department of Transportation regulations, contained a "savings clause" providing that nothing within the law was meant to preempt any other cause of action that might exist. The law expressly said that "[c]ompliance with" a federal safety standard does "not exempt any person from any liability under the common law."[17] Geier argued that this provision prevented a finding of federal preemption.

The Supreme Court rejected Geier's argument and found federal preemption notwithstanding the savings clause. Justice Breyer, writing for the majority, said that this was not a situation of express preemption, but instead conflict preemption.[18] The Court found that allowing state liability for cars made in compliance with the federal safety standard would conflict with the federal law. Justice

Breyer said that the savings clause did not foreclose preemption because there was no indication that Congress wanted to permit lawsuits when cars were made in compliance with the Department of Transportation's safety regulations.[19]

The only way to make sense of the case is to see it as putting a presumption in favor of preemption.[20] The federal statute expressly said that it did not preempt state law tort suits. Thus, there was no conflict between Geier's state cause of action and any provision of the relevant federal law. Yet the Court nonetheless ruled in favor of Honda and deemed a state tort action to be preempted.

### *Lorillard Tobacco Co. v. Reilly*

In this case, the Court invalidated a Massachusetts law that prohibited outdoor advertising for cigarettes, such as billboards, within 1,000 feet of a playground or school.[21] The Supreme Court relied on the language of a federal law adopted in 1969 that proscribes any "requirement or prohibition based on smoking and health . . . imposed under State law with respect to the advertising or promotion of . . . cigarettes."[22] The Court reviewed the history of federal regulation of cigarette advertising and concluded: "In the 1969 amendments, Congress not only enhanced its scheme to warn the public about the hazards of cigarette smoking, but also sought to protect the public, including youth, from being inundated with images of cigarette smoking in advertising. In pursuit of the latter goal, Congress banned electronic media advertising of cigarettes. And to the extent that Congress contemplated additional targeted regulation of cigarette advertising, it vested that authority in the FTC [Federal Trade Commission]."[23]

Justice Stevens, in a dissenting opinion, argued that the state law was not preempted because it regulated the location and not the content of cigarette advertisements.[24] The majority, however, rejected this distinction and declared: "But the content/location distinction cannot be squared with the language of the pre-emption provision, which reaches all 'requirements' and 'prohibitions' 'imposed under State law.' A distinction between the content of advertising and the location of advertising in the FCLAA [*Federal Cigarette Labeling and Advertising Act*] also cannot be reconciled with Congress' own location-based restriction, which bans advertising in electronic media, but not elsewhere."[25]

Again, this case can be understood only if it is seen as putting a presumption in favor of preemption.[26] The federal law was designed to limit cigarette advertising so as to protect children. The federal preemption provision was meant to keep states from adopting conflicting requirements for warning labels on cigarette packages. There is nothing in the law that says or implies that all state regulation of cigarette advertising is preempted by federal law. Indeed, the Massachusetts law advances the goals of the federal statute by protecting children from tobacco ads. The federal statute has nothing to do with whether there can be billboards near schools or whether ads in stores need to be a certain level above the floor. These, as the dissent points out, go entirely to placement, an issue not addressed by the federal law. Nonetheless, the Court protected the tobacco industry and invalidated the Massachusetts statute.

### Crosby v. National Foreign Trade Council[27]

Massachusetts adopted a law that prohibited the state and its agencies from purchasing goods or services from companies that do business with Burma (Myanmar). The state adopted this law because of human rights violations in that nation. The Supreme Court unanimously found that federal law preempted the state law. Justice Souter, writing for the Court, explained that Congress had enacted a sanctions law against Burma. He found that this preempted states from imposing their own sanctions.

Justice Souter rejected the State's argument that its policy furthered the federal objective of imposing sanctions on a nation that violated basic norms of human rights. Justice Souter wrote: "The conflicts are not rendered irrelevant by the State's argument that there is no real conflict between the statutes because they share the same goals and because some companies may comply with both sets of restrictions. The fact of a common end hardly neutralizes conflicting means."[28] Justice Souter said that the existence of the state law "undermines the President's capacity . . . for effective diplomacy. It is not merely that the differences between the state and federal Acts in scope and type of sanctions threaten to complicate discussions; they compromise the very capacity of the President to speak for the nation with one voice in dealing with other governments."[29]

The decision, though unanimous, again must be seen as putting a presumption in favor of preemption. Congress had not expressed or implied any intent to preempt states from imposing sanctions and the state law was not inconsistent with the federal law. There was no conflict between the Massachusetts law and anything done by the President. The state was simply choosing how it would spend its taxpayers' money and whom it would do business with. Likewise, many state and local governments adopted similar laws refusing to contract with companies doing business in South Africa at the time of apartheid. Nonetheless, the Court found preemption.

### American Insurance Association v. Garamendi

California's *Holocaust Victim Insurance Relief Act of 1999* ("HVIRA") required any insurer doing business in the state to disclose information about all policies that company sold in Europe between 1920 and 1945. As Justice Ginsburg noted in her dissent:

> For insurance policies issued in Germany and other countries under Nazi control, historical evidence bears out, the combined forces of the German Government and the

insurance industry engaged in larcenous takings of gigantic proportions. For example, insurance policies covered many of the Jewish homes and businesses destroyed in the state-sponsored pogrom known as Kristallnacht. By order of the Nazi regime, claims arising out of the officially enabled destruction were made payable not to the insured parties, but to the State. In what one historian called a "charade concocted by insurers and ministerial officials," insurers satisfied property loss claims by paying the State only a fraction of their full value.[30]

Despite some efforts by the federal government, insurance companies had been largely successful in stonewalling and not disclosing their Holocaust-era policies. To remedy this, and to protect its many residents who are Holocaust survivors or their descendants, California enacted a law that declared that "[i]nsurance companies doing business in the State of California have a responsibility to ensure that any involvement they or their related companies may have had with insurance policies of Holocaust victims [is] disclosed to the state."[31] The Act required insurance companies doing business in California to disclose information concerning insurance policies they or their affiliates sold in Europe between 1920 and 1945, and directed California's Insurance Commissioner to store the information in a publicly accessible "Holocaust Era Insurance Registry."[32] The Commissioner was further directed to suspend the license of any insurer that failed to comply with the Act's reporting requirements.[33] These measures, the Act declared, were "necessary to protect the claims and interests of California residents, as well as to encourage the development of a resolution to these issues through the international process or through direct action by the State of California, as necessary."[34]

The Supreme Court, in a five-to-four decision, found that the California law was preempted by federal law. The Court said that the statute interfered with the President's conduct of the nation's foreign policy and was therefore preempted. The Court focused on executive agreements that the President had negotiated with Germany, France, and Austria.[35] However, the problem with this argument is that the California law did not conflict with any executive agreement and as Justice Souter, writing for the majority, admitted, "petitioners and the United States as amicus curiae both have to acknowledge that the agreements include no preemption clause."[36]

The Court relied on its prior decision in *Zschernig v. Miller*, which created a dormant foreign affairs power of the President.[37] In *Zschernig*, the Court declared unconstitutional an Oregon probate statute that prohibited inheritance by a nonresident alien, absent showings that the foreign heir would take the property "without confiscation" by his home country and that American citizens would enjoy reciprocal rights of inheritance there. As Justice Souter explained in his majority opinion in *Garamendi*, the Court in *Zschernig* found "that state action with more than incidental effect on foreign affairs is preempted, even absent any affirmative federal activity in the subject area of the state law, and hence without any showing of conflict."[38]

Even though no later decision had relied on *Zschernig*, the Court said that the case provided a basis for invalidating California's law. The Court stressed that the California disclosure statute limited what the President might do in some hypothetical future negotiations. Moreover, Justice Souter said: "If any doubt about the clarity of the conflict remained, however, it would have to be resolved in the National Government's favor, given the weakness of the State's interest, against the backdrop of traditional state legislative subject matter, in regulating disclosure of European Holocaust-era insurance policies in the manner of HVIRA."[39]

At the very least, one can understand *Garamendi* as creating an enormous presumption in favor of federal preemption of state laws in cases where state law has international implications. In the absence of any express preemption or any conflict with federal law, the Court nonetheless found preemption simply because the California statute was seen as touching on an issue of foreign policy. The California law, of course, regulated businesses operating within its borders and did not directly deal with foreign nations. Nonetheless, the Court found that a broad "dormant foreign affairs power" of the President was sufficient to preclude the state law protecting California's residents. It is hard to imagine a stronger presumption in favor of preemption.

## WHAT'S WRONG WITH THE COURT'S APPROACH TO PREEMPTION?

The prior section attempted to show that many important recent preemption cases conflict with the Supreme Court's oft-stated principle that federalism requires a presumption against preemption. The decisions, of course, also seem inconsistent with a Court committed to protecting states' rights and federalism. In each case, the Court invalidated a significant choice of a state government.

Yet this does not go far enough from a normative perspective in explaining why the Court was wrong in these cases. The underlying question must be, why have a presumption against preemption?[40] The answer must begin with an assessment of why federalism and concern about states matter. Ironically, the Supreme Court decisions and academic writings defending the use of federalism to invalidate federal laws provide the best explanation of these values and show why the recent preemption decisions are undesirable.

The Supreme Court has identified many values of federalism. For example, it often is emphasized that states are closer to the people and thus more likely to be responsive to public needs and concerns. Professor David Shapiro clearly summarizes this argument when he writes: "[O]ne of the stronger arguments for a decentralized political structure is that, to the extent the electorate is small, and elected representatives are thus more immediately accountable to individuals and their concerns, government is brought closer to the people, and democratic ideals are more fully realized."[41]

Also, the Court has often spoken of the need to protect federalism so that states can serve as laboratories for experimentation. Justice Brandeis apparently first articulated this idea when he declared: "To stay experimentation in things social and economic is a grave responsibility. Denial of the right to experiment might be fraught with serious consequences to the Nation. It is one of the happy incidents of the federal system that a single courageous State may, if its citizens choose, serve as a laboratory; and try novel social and economic experiments without risk to the rest of the country."[42]

More recent federalism decisions, too, have invoked this notion. Justice Powell, dissenting in *Garcia v. San Antonio Metropolitan Transit Authority*, lamented that "the Court does not explain how leaving the States virtually at the mercy of the Federal Government, without recourse to judicial review, will enhance their opportunities to experiment and serve as 'laboratories.'"[43] Likewise, Justice O'Connor, dissenting in *Federal Energy Regulatory Commission v. Mississippi*, stated that the "Court's decision undermines the most valuable aspects of our federalism. Courts and commentators frequently have recognized that the 50 [s]tates serve as laboratories for the development of new social, economic, and political ideas."[44]

Another frequently advanced justification for federalism is that the division of power between federal and state governments advances liberty. For example, Chief Justice Rehnquist wrote: "This constitutionally mandated division of authority "was adopted by the Framers to ensure protection of our fundamental liberties.'"[45] Similarly, Justice Scalia declared: "The separation of the two spheres is one of the Constitution's protections of liberty."[46] Justice O'Connor likewise wrote: "Just as the separation and independence of the coordinate branches of the Federal Government serve to prevent the accumulation of excessive power in any one branch, a healthy balance of power between the States and the Federal Government will reduce the risk of tyranny and abuse from either front."[47]

Although the relationship between these values and the Supreme Court's decisions invalidating federal laws can be questioned,[48] these considerations offer clear reasons for having a presumption against preemption. Preempting state laws limits the ability of states to make choices that are responsive to their residents' desires, to experiment, and to advance liberty and freedom within their boundaries. Simply put, a broad vision of inferred preemption invalidates beneficial state laws.

This can be seen by looking at the cases described above. In *Geier*, a state choice to allow injured citizens to recover was preempted, notwithstanding a federal law expressly preserving state causes of action. The benefits of liability, in terms of compensating injured people and deterring harmful products, are lost. In *Lorillard*, the Court preempted a state law intended to protect children from tobacco advertising. Putting aside the First Amendment issue and focusing just on preemption, there can be no doubt that decreasing cigarette consumption among children is a compelling state interest. The Supreme Court frustrated the ability of states to respond to the desire of their residents to restrict cigarette advertising to children and stopped states from experimenting with new ways of accomplishing this. In *Crosby*, the Court denied Massachusetts the ability to decide how it wanted to spend its taxpayers' money. The state law in *Crosby* provided that the state would not contract with companies doing business in Burma. The state was not making foreign policy for the United States, but rather a choice as to how Massachusetts' dollars would be spent. In *Garamendi*, the Court denied California the ability to help its many residents who were survivors of the Holocaust or descendants of survivors. The state was frustrated in its regulation of businesses within California, a traditional prerogative of state governments. Also, the country lost the benefit of seeing how California's experiment with this type of regulation would work.

To be clear, I am not arguing that Congress lacked the authority to preempt state laws in these areas. Rather, my point is that in each of these cases desirable state laws were lost because of the Court's abandoning the presumption against preemption. The laws were desirable because of what they sought to achieve: protecting injured consumers, decreasing tobacco consumption among children, protecting human rights, and protecting Holocaust survivors. The state laws also were desirable in terms of the underlying values of federalism, which the presumption in favor of preemption compromised in each case.

It is striking that in each of these four recent cases the Supreme Court ruled in favor of business interests and against state regulations. The four cases ruled, respectively, in favor of the automobile industry, cigarette manufacturers, companies doing business in Burma, and insurance companies. When these cases are juxtaposed with the Supreme Court's federalism decisions limiting federal power from the last decade, a clear hierarchy of the Rehnquist Court's values becomes clear. Two principles explain the vast majority of these rulings:[49]

(1)  If there is a state challenge to a federal civil rights law, the state wins and the federal interests lose.[50]

(2)  If there is a business challenge to a state regulatory law, the state loses.

As to the first point, many of the Supreme Court's decisions limiting congressional power in the name of federalism have invalidated laws expanding civil rights. For example, in *United States v. Morrison*, the Court struck down the civil damages provision of the *Violence Against Women Act*, a law that allowed women to sue under federal law for gender-motivated violence, as exceeding the scope of Congress's powers under the Commerce Clause. In *City of Boerne v. Flores*, the Court struck down the Religious Freedom Restoration Act, which sought by statute to expand religious freedom to what previously had been protected under the Constitution. In *Kimel v. Florida Board of Regents*, and in *Board of Trustees of the University of Alabama v. Garrett*,[51] the Court said that states could not be sued for employment discrimination against the elderly under the *Age Discrimination in Employment Act* or against people with disabilities under Title I of the *Americans with Disabilities Act*.[52] It is striking that in each of these cases, the Court limited Congress's powers to enforce and expand the protection of civil rights.

This comparison undermines the view that concern for states' rights or the application of a neutral methodology animate the Rehnquist Court's decisions limiting federal power. Instead, the decisions reflect traditional conservative value choices to limit civil rights and to protect business. The preemption cases show us that this Emperor really has no clothes; federalism is used, as it has been so often throughout American history, to cloak politicized substantive value choices in a seemingly more neutral and palatable garb.

## A DIFFERENT VIEW OF FEDERALISM AND PREEMPTION

For much of American history, and especially in recent years, courts and scholars have discussed federalism primarily in terms of limiting federal power so as to protect state sovereignty. For example, during the first third of this century, dual federalism was entirely about restricting the authority of Congress by narrowly defining its powers under Article One of the Constitution and by reserving a zone of activities to the states.[53] Under the Burger Court, federalism was used to restrict federal court authority. The Court invoked "Our Federalism" in *Younger v. Harris*, for example, which held that federal courts must abstain from decisions that would interfere with ongoing state court proceedings.[54] Most recently, in the 1990s, in cases such as *New York v. United States*, *United States v. Lopez*, and *Seminole Tribe of Florida v. Florida*,[55] the Court has invoked federalism to protect states from federal laws and federal courts. The preemption decisions are also about limiting power, although the traditional dynamic is reversed. As described in the first section of this chapter, the Supreme Court's preemption decisions have used federalism as a limit on state power, and as explained in the following section, the limits have frustrated desirable state policy choices. As argued above, these rulings undermine the underlying values of federalism.

There is another, dramatically different way of looking at federalism: seeing its function as empowering government, not merely imposing limits. As we enter the twenty-first century, American government faces, and will continue to face, enormous social problems with which it must deal. In this regard, federalism can make a crucial difference. The value of having multiple levels of government lies in having many institutions capable of acting to solve social problems. From this perspective, federalism should be viewed as not being about limits on any level of government, but empowering each to act to solve difficult social issues.[56]

Seeing federalism as furthering empowerment would mean broadly defining the scope of federal powers under the Commerce Clause and Section Five of the Fourteenth Amendment, as the Supreme Court did between 1937 and the 1990s. The Tenth Amendment, which reserves to the states or to the people the powers not delegated to the United States, would not be regarded as a limit on Congress, except as a reminder that Congress can legislate only if it had express or implied powers.[57] Sovereign immunity would be abolished as a limit on the ability to enforce federal laws against state governments.[58] Defending all of this is, of course, beyond the scope of this chapter.

However, my specific focus here is on preemption and what federalism as empowerment would mean in this particular regard. A key way of empowering state and local governments is by reducing the circumstances under which there is preemption by federal law. I propose that preemption should be found only in two circumstances: where a federal law expressly preempts state law, and where federal and state laws are mutually exclusive. This would preserve the ability of Congress to preempt state law whenever it deemed that to be in the nation's interest. It also would preserve the supremacy of federal law by ensuring that any conflict between the levels of government would be resolved in favor of federal power. But it would dramatically limit the ability of federal courts to find preemption based on inferences concerning congressional intent or because of a dormant power of the federal government. This approach to preemption would have produced the opposite results in *Geier*, *Lorillard*, *Crosby*, and *Garamendi*.

For example, in *Geier*, not only was there no express preemption or conflict with federal law, but a federal statutory provision expressly preserved state law claims. In *Lorillard*, too, there was nothing in the federal law that limited the ability of states to regulate the location of tobacco advertisements and no conflict between the Massachusetts law and federal law. In *Crosby* and *Garamendi*, the federal government certainly could act to prevent such state laws; but it never did. No federal statute expressly limited the ability of states to decide the businesses they would contract with or to require insurance companies to disclose information. Nor do these requirements conflict with any federal statute. A narrower view of preemption, as I urge, would have found preemption in none of these cases.

This, of course, would not resolve all preemption issues. As evidenced by the countless cases concerning preemption under ERISA [the *Employee Retirement Security Act*],[59] even explicit preemption provisions require interpretation as to their scope and application. Similarly, the issue of whether a state law conflicts with a federal law is often disputed and the determination depends on how the purpose of each is conceptualized. But limiting preemption in this way would go a long way toward empowering state and local governments to have more authority to reflect the choices of their residents, to experiment, and most important, to advance liberty and freedom.

An important example of this is the events surrounding the decision in *ACLU of New Jersey v. County of Hudson*.[60] After September 11, 2001, the federal government detained a large number of individuals, many in state prisons and jails. Many were held in New Jersey's prisons. Although the federal government refused to disclose the number held or their identities, the American Civil Liberties Union sued under New Jersey law to gain information. Specifically, it sued counties, who held detainees for the Immigration and Naturalization Service ("INS") in their jails, to disclose information on detainees pursuant to New Jersey's Right-to-Know Law and Jailkeeper's Law. The Jailkeeper's Law, which is meant to prevent secret detentions, provides:

> The keeper of every jail or other penal or reformatory institution supported by public moneys of any county or municipality, shall keep a book provided by the board of freeholders in the county where the institution shall be, in which he shall set forth the date of entry, date of discharge, the description, age, birthplace and such other

> information as he may be able to obtain as to the inmates committed to his care, which book shall be exposed in a conspicuous place in the institution and shall be open to public inspection.[61]

The Superior Court ruled in favor of the plaintiffs. But the General Counsel of the INS directed the county jails to refuse to answer such requests for information. Also, the United States intervened in the litigation. The INS promulgated a new regulation directing state and local authorities to keep secret information concerning detainees, even when state or local law requires disclosure.[62]

The New Jersey Court of Appeals then found that this regulation preempted New Jersey laws and required that information concerning the detainees be kept secret. The New Jersey court found that the new regulation was within the scope of Congress's powers: "[W]e conclude that the regulation was promulgated within the scope of the Commissioner's delegated authority. The judgment of the Commissioner that information concerning INS detainees should not be divulged falls well within the discretion afforded him by the INA (*Immigration and Nationality Act*)."[63] The court concluded that New Jersey law was preempted by federal law:

> The issues before us do not concern merely the ministerial functioning of State officials under State law, or the State's choice to house federal prisoners. Rather, they involve the nature and scope of information that must be made available to the public concerning INS detainees. The power to regulate matters relating to immigration and naturalization resides exclusively in the federal government. The State simply has no constitutionally recognized role in this area. Thus, while the State possesses sovereign authority over the operation of its jails, it may not operate them, in respect of INS detainees, in any way that derogates the federal government's exclusive and expressed interest in regulating aliens.[64]

What is troubling about this ruling is that preemption was found even though no federal statute expressly or implicitly preempted state law. Moreover, the New Jersey court admitted that there was no conflict between federal law and state law. Nonetheless, preemption was found. A narrower view of preemption, such as I argue for, would have come to an opposite conclusion. If Congress wants to preempt such state laws, it may do so. But until then, states should be accorded the power to act. Rejecting preemption would have better served the goals of federalism: advancing liberty, preventing a power—secret detentions—that runs the risk of tyrannical government action, and allowing states to be laboratories for experimentation.

## CONCLUSION

Federalism is often misdefined as synonymous with states' rights. A better view of federalism conceives of its purpose as the proper allocation of authority between the federal and state governments. The structure of government is not an end in itself, but rather a means to the end of effective government that minimizes the possibility of tyrannical rule, provides for the related goal of greater accountability, and sets the stage for vigorous experimentation. The Supreme Court's federalism decisions of the last decade—both those limiting Congress's powers and finding preemption of state law—are unrelated to, and indeed inconsistent with, the underlying values of federalism.

In this chapter, I have focused on the Supreme Court's preemption decisions and argued that they conflict with the presumption against preemption and that they have frustrated desirable social policy. I argue for an alternative vision that would greatly narrow preemption and focus instead on empowering government at all levels to deal with social problems.

Power, of course, can be used for good or for ill. States might use their greater authority not to protect consumers and advance individual freedom, but for more pernicious objectives. Empowering government can be bad. But I do not argue for unlimited state power; Congress still could preempt state actions and courts, of course, could invalidate laws that conflict with the Constitution and federal law. At the same time, desirable federal laws advancing freedom—such as the *Violence Against Women Act* and the *Religious Freedom Restoration Act*—would be preserved. Simply put, it is time to replace a formalistic view of "federalism as limits" with a functional approach to federalism as a means of empowerment.

## Notes

1. See, for e.g., *United States v. Lopez*, 514 U.S. 549 (1995) (invalidating the *Gun Free School Zone Act* as exceeding the scope of Congress's power to legislate under the Commerce Clause); *United States v. Morrison*, 529 U.S. 598 (2000) (invalidating the civil damages provision in the *Violence Against Women Act*); *City of Boerne v. Flores*, 521 U.S. 507 (1997) (invalidating the *Religious Freedom Restoration Act* as exceeding the scope of the power conferred on Congress by Section Five of the Fourteenth Amendment to enforce the Fourteenth Amendment's guarantees).

2. See, for e.g., *New York v. United States*, 505 U.S. 144 (1992) (invalidating provisions of the *Low-Level Radioactive Waste Act* as violating the Tenth Amendment); *Printz v. United States*, 521 U.S. 898 (1997) (invalidating the *Brady Handgun Control Act* as violating the Tenth Amendment).

3. See, for e.g., *Seminole Tribe of Florida v. Florida*, 517 U.S. 44 (1996); *Florida Prepaid Postsecondary Education Expense Board v. College Savings Bank*, 527 U.S. 627 (1999) (limiting Congress's power to authorize suits against state governments).

4. *Geier v. American Honda Motor Co.*, 529 U.S. 861 (2000).

5. Ibid., 868 (quoting *U.S. Code 15*, sec. 1397(k) (1988)).

6. *Lorillard Tobacco Co. v. Reilly*, 533 U.S. 525 (2001).

7. *Crosby v. National Foreign Trade Council*, 530 U.S. 363 (2000).

8. *American Insurance Association v. Garamendi*, 539 U.S. 396 (2003).

9. *Medtronic, Inc. v. Lohr*, 518 U.S. 468, 485 (1996) (quoting *Rice v. Santa Fe Elevator Corp.*, 331 U.S. 218, 230 (1947), and *Hillsborough County v. Automated Medical Laboratories, Inc.*, 471 U.S. 707, 715 (1985)).

10. For an argument against the presumption against preemption, see Viet D. Dinh, "Reassessing the Law of Preemption," *Georgetown Law Journal* 88 (2000): 2085–2118.

11. See *Gade v. National Solid Wastes Management Association*, 505 U.S. 88, 108 (1992) (deriving preemption from the supremacy clause); but see Stephen A. Gardbaum, "The Nature of Preemption," *Cornell Law Review* 79 (1994): 767–815; S. Candice Hoke, "Transcending Conventional Supremacy: A Reconstruction of the Supremacy Clause," *Connecticut Law Review* 24 (1992): 829–891 (arguing that only some preemption should be based on the supremacy clause).

12. *Gade v. National Solid Wastes Management Association*, 1084 (internal quotations and citations omitted). In *Gibbons v. Ogden*, 22 U.S. 1, 211 (1824), Chief Justice John Marshall said: "[A]cts of the State Legislatures . . . [that] interfere with, or are contrary to the laws of Congress [are to be invalidated because] [i]n every such case, the act of Congress . . . is supreme; and the law of State, though enacted in the exercise of powers not controverted, must yield to it."

13. *Gade v. National Solid Waste Management Association*, 98 (internal quotations and citations omitted). In an earlier case, *Pennsylvania v. Nelson*, 350 U.S. 497 (1956), the Supreme Court identified three situations where preemption could be found:

> First, the scheme of federal regulation is so pervasive as to make reasonable the inference that Congress left no room for the states to supplement it. . . . Second, the federal statutes touch a field in which the federal interest is so dominant that the federal system must be assumed to preclude enforcement of state laws on the same subject. . . . Third, [where] enforcement of state . . . acts presents a serious danger of conflict with the administration of the federal program.

Ibid., 502–505 (internal quotations and citations omitted).

14. *Hines v. Davidowitz*, 312 U.S. 52, 67 (1941).

15. *New York State Department of Social Services v. Dublino*, 413 U.S. 405, 413 (1973) (citation omitted).

16. *Medtronic, Inc. v. Lohr*, 485 (citing *Hillsborough County v. Automated Medical Laboratories, Inc.*, 715).

17. Ibid., 867 (quoting *U.S. Code 15*, sec. 1397(k) (1988)).

18. Ibid., 869–870.

19. Ibid.

20. The dissent by Justice Stevens forcefully makes this point. See ibid., 907 (J. Stevens, dissenting); see also Susan Raeker-Jordan, "A Study in Judicial Sleight of Hand: Did *Geier v. American Honda Motor Co.* Eradicate the Presumption against Preemption?" *Brigham Young University Journal of Public Law* 17 (2002): 1–44.

21. The Court found that the Massachusetts law was preempted in its regulation of advertising of cigarettes. As for the regulation of advertising of cigars and smokeless tobacco, which are not the subject of federal regulation, the Court found that the law violated the First Amendment.

22. *Lorillard Tobacco Co. v. Reilly*, 537 (quoting *Federal Cigarette Labeling and Advertising Act, U.S. Code 15*, sec. 1334(b)).

23. Ibid., 547–548.

24. Ibid., 592–594 (J. Stevens, dissenting).

25. Ibid., 548–549.

26. My focus here is only the preemption issue and not whether the Massachusetts law violates the First Amendment.

27. 530 U.S. 363 (2000).

28. Ibid., 379.

29. Ibid., 380.

30. Ibid., 430–431 (J. Ginsburg, dissenting) (citations omitted).

31. Ibid., 434 (J. Ginsburg, dissenting) (quoting *Holocaust Victim Insurance Relief Act of 1999, California Insurance Code*, sec. 13801(e)).

32. Ibid. (J. Ginsburg, dissenting) (citing *California Insurance Code*, sec. 13803).

33. Ibid. (J. Ginsburg, dissenting) (citing *California Insurance Code*, sec. 13806).

34. *American Insurance Association v. Garamendi*, 434 (J. Ginsburg, dissenting) (quoting *California Insurance Code* sec. 13801(f)).

35. Ibid., 408.

36. Ibid., 417.

37. *Zschernig v. Miller*, 389 U.S. 429 (1968).

38. *American Insurance Association v. Garamendi*, 418.

39. Ibid., 425.

40. See Viet D. Dinh, "Reassessing the Law of Preemption," *Georgetown Law Journal* 88 (2000): 2085–2118 (arguing that there should not be a presumption against preemption).

41. David L. Shapiro, *Federalism: A Dialogue* (Evanston, IL: Northwestern University Press, 1995), 91–92.

42. *New State Ice Co. v. Liebmann*, 285 U.S. 262, 311 (1932) (J. Brandeis, dissenting).

43. *Garcia v. San Antonio Metropolitan Transit Authority*, 469 U.S. 528, 567–68 n.13 (J. Powell, dissenting).

44. *Federal Energy Regulatory Commission v. Mississippi*, 456 U.S. 742, 787–788 (1982) (J. O'Connor, dissenting).

45. *United States v. Lopez*, 552.

46. *Printz v. United States*, 921.

47. *Gregory v. Ashcroft*, 501 U.S. 452, 458 (1991).

48. See Erwin Chemerinsky, "Does Federalism Advance Liberty?" *Wayne Law Review* 47 (2002): 911–930; Erwin Chemerinsky, "The Values of Federalism," *Florida Law Review* 47 (1995): 499–540.

49. See David L. Shapiro, "Mr. Justice Rehnquist: A Preliminary View," *Harvard Law Review* 90 (1976): 293–357.

50. See *United States v. Morrison; City of Boerne v. Flores; Kimel v. Florida Board of Regents*, 528 U.S. 62 (2000); *Cedar Rapids Community School District. v. Garrett*, 526 U.S. 66 (1999); but see *Nevada Department of Human Resources v. Hibbs*, 538 U.S. 721 (2003).

51. *Board of Trustees of the University of Alabama v. Garrett*, 531 U.S. 356 (2001).

52. However, it should be noted that in *Nevada Department of Human Resources v. Hibbs*, the Court held that state governments may be sued for violating the family leave provisions of the *Family and Medical Leave Act*, and in *Tennessee v. Lane*, 541 U.S. 509 (2004), the Court ruled that state governments may be sued under Title II of the *Americans with Disabilities Act* when the fundamental right of access to the courts is implicated.

53. See, for e.g., *Carter v. Carter Coal Co.*, 298 U.S. 238 (1936); *Hammer v. Dagenhart* (The Child Labor Case), 247 U.S. 251 (1918); *United States v. E. C. Knight Co.*, 156

U.S. 1 (1895) (invalidating federal laws as exceeding the scope of Congress's commerce clause authority or as violating the Tenth Amendment).

54. *Younger v. Harris*, 401 U.S. 37 (1971). See also *Fair Assessment in Real Estate Association v. McNary*, 454 U.S. 100 (1981) (using federalism as a basis for precluding federal court review of the constitutionality of state taxes); *Rizzo v. Goode*, 423 U.S. 362 (1976) (using federalism as a basis for precluding federal court review of systematic police abuse).

55. *New York v. United States* (declaring unconstitutional a federal law as violating the Tenth Amendment because it coerced state legislative and regulatory activity); *United States v. Lopez* (declaring unconstitutional the federal *Gun Free School Zones Act* as exceeding the scope of Congress' commerce clause authority); *Seminole Tribe of Florida v. Florida* (holding that Congress may not override the Eleventh Amendment except if acting under Section Five of the Fourteenth Amendment and that state officers may not be sued pursuant to federal laws that contain a comprehensive enforcement mechanism).

56. For an argument that this conception of federalism is in accord with the design of the Constitution and is historically supported, see Deborah J. Merritt, "Federalism as Empowerment," *Florida Law Review* 47 (1995): 541–556.

57. *United States v. Darby*, 12 U.S. 100 (1941).

58. I defend this proposition in Erwin Chemerinsky, "Against Sovereign Immunity," *Stanford Law Review* 53 (2001): 1201–1224.

59. For a discussion of this issue, see Chemerinsky, "Does Federalism Advance Liberty?" *Wayne Law Review* 47 (2002): 911–930; Erwin Chemerinsky, "Against Sovereign Immunity," *Stanford Law Review* 53 (2001): 1201–1224; Erwin Chemerinsky, "Formalism and Functionalism in Federalism Analysis," *Georgia State University Law Review* 13 (1997): 959–984.

60. *ACLU of New Jersey v. County of Hudson*, 799 A.2d 629 (2002).

61. *N.J. Statutes Annotated* sec. 30:8–16 (West 2002).

62. Interim Rule, *Release of Information Regarding Immigration and Naturalization Service Detainees in Non-Federal Facilities, Federal Register* 67, 19,508 (April 22, 2002), as confirmed at *Federal Register* 68, 4364 (January 29, 2003) (codified at *Code of Federal Regulations* 8 sec. 236.6).

63. *ACLU of New Jersey v. County of Hudson*, 650.

64. Ibid., 654.

# Converse § 1983 Suits in Which States Police Federal Agents: An Idea Whose Time Has Arrived

Vikram David Amar

## INTRODUCTION: THE RANGE OF LOCAL OPPOSITION TO FEDERAL ACTIONS

A key question for the country today is: What role, if any, can state and local governments play in shaping the way America prosecutes its war on terror and its wars against those countries—like Iraq—that are alleged to be breeding grounds for terrorists? This fundamental question lies at the core of a movement that has swept across America recently.

State and local governmental opposition to the federal government's decisions in the war on international terror has taken many forms. Often, state and local entities simply disagree with the policy advisability of the international course pursued by the federal government, and want to register their dissent. For example, in February 2003, the Los Angeles City Council voted to "oppose unilateral war in Iraq." Although Los Angeles was the biggest city to have taken such a stance, it was far from alone. Close to 100 other American cities and towns, including San Francisco, Chicago, Detroit, and Philadelphia, had already passed similar resolutions condemning any U.S. invasion unsupported by the United Nations and most large allies.[1]

In other instances, local governments have questioned the wisdom of domestic legislative enactments and executive rules. For example, a huge number of local governments have denounced the USA PATRIOT Act—the law Congress passed in the wake of 9/11 to enhance antiterrorism law enforcement. Towns like Oakland, Berkeley, and Boulder (Colorado), in addition to the larger cities of San Francisco and Detroit, have approved such measures.[2] Most of these resolutions harshly criticize the policies of Congress and the Bush Administration.[3]

But local entities seem concerned with more than just whether federal decisions are wise and effective; many cities and states have registered concerns that federal decisions have violated or will inevitably violate the constitutionally guaranteed liberties of Americans and those non-Americans who may be affected by the exercise of American power.[4] It is for this reason that many local proposals go so far as to call upon local agencies to decline to provide any aid to federal authorities in investigations and enforcement actions that might jeopardize civil liberties.[5] All of these measures have had to overcome, among other things, the deep-seated notion that state and local lawmakers have no business meddling in national and international affairs. On this view, locals should stick to the truly day-to-day narrow issues on which they campaigned and were put in office.

On the surface, at least, this intuition—that state and local government should stick to state and regional affairs—appears to have its roots in our Constitution itself. As commentators have observed, "[I]t may [at first] seem incongruous that states [and their subdivisions] would enjoy any role in foreign affairs. The Constitution, after all, was designed to ensure that the federal government had sufficient authority to check state foreign relations activities."[6] That is why many people welcome Supreme Court rulings that "help put an end to state and local efforts to make foreign policy."[7]

It is true that federal law—both the Constitution itself and laws Congress enacts under it—does impose some limits on what states can do in the international realm, even as globalization has drawn the local and international spheres much closer together. But, federal law does not, and cannot, cut state and local government out of the picture altogether. States certainly have the power—and perhaps the duty—to speak out on international matters, and to regulate their own citizenries in ways the federal government may disfavor, so long as state regulation is not preempted by valid federal laws. The Constitution itself sometimes shields state authority from federal interference. And, as we shall see, state governments may use the Constitution as more than a shield for themselves; they may use it to affirmatively shield the citizens from federal laws that trample not on states' rights, but rather on individuals' rights. The converse § 1983 device that I will explain and discuss at length in the second half of this chapter provides one useful example of how states can act offensively to counter federal abuses.

## DEFENSIVE FEDERALISM—THE DOCTRINES AS THEY EXIST TODAY

### Preemption

Before we turn to proactive steps states can take against federal overreaching, let us first consider some doctrines that are supposed to—but do not always— insulate state governments from federal interference. First let us look briefly at preemption, a topic Professor Erwin Chemerinsky takes up in earnest in this volume.[8] An example of federal preemption in this area—and perhaps a good illustration of interpreting the powers of states more narrowly than is appropriate—can be found in an important Supreme Court case from a few years back, *Crosby v. National Foreign Trade Council*.[9] In that case, the Court invalidated a Massachusetts statute that had directed state agencies not to purchase goods and services from any companies doing business in Burma, a nation with a notoriously bad human rights record.

In support of its result, the Supreme Court reasoned that Congress's own sanctions imposed on Burma through a federal statute represented Congress's considered choice about how much, and in what ways, Burma should be induced to change its evil ways. The federal government, the Court pointed out, had acted affirmatively in this area by imposing particular sanctions. And, the Court believed, commercial activity by Massachusetts might have interfered with the commercial system of incentives Congress sought to establish.[10]

I think the Court may well have decided *Crosby* wrongly. It ought to be clear that the people of a state, acting collectively through their state legislature, can speak their consciences, even as to matters of foreign affairs. One can plausibly argue that declining to spend money is simply one form of collective local expression. But even assuming that Congress does have the power to regulate the choices that a state makes when it acts—as Massachusetts did there—in its capacity as a conscientious consumer (as opposed to its capacity as a sovereign regulator of private consumers), I think the evidence is fairly thin that the Massachusetts policy frustrated congressional will.

After all, the federal law implemented by President Clinton in 1997 was itself anti-Burma—sending a message that America wanted the human rights violations to end.[11] Because the Massachusetts policy reinforced rather than undermined this overall American goal, I do not see the clear conflict that the Court did. In the preemption realm states typically have the power to go further than federal law, but in the same direction; for instance, their antidiscrimination laws can be more protective than federal ones.[12] Had Massachusetts in its purchasing policies favored companies that did business in Burma, a finding of conflict would have been more plausible. But since Congress did not provide any clear statement in its law that the judiciary should infer preemption, I think respect for federalism should have counseled the Court to come out the other way.

Additionally, it bears noting that the Massachusetts law existed when Congress acted (and indeed might have helped put the issue on Congress's agenda).[13] But Congress did not say anything negative about the Massachusetts law when it enacted the federal measures; no member of Congress voiced opposition to what Massachusetts had done. Moreover, the federal policy in effect when Massachusetts acted—a policy that had been formed during the 1980s when cities like Berkeley wanted to divest of holdings in companies operating in South Africa—clearly allowed states and cities to vote with their dollars. Indeed, President Clinton and Secretary of State Albright had publicly lauded such local policies in the years before the Court decided *Crosby*. It was against this backdrop that the U.S.

Solicitor General's office under Seth Waxman seemed to change the rules without clear guidance from Congress and against the settled expectations of the states. Given these circumstances, the Court's invalidation of the Massachusetts law seems somewhat dubious.

Some of the same criticisms apply to the Court's decision to strike down, by a five-to-four vote, a California law that regulated insurance companies doing business within the state in an attempt to force them to disclose information about the industry's treatment of Holocaust victims over fifty years ago.[14] The Court held that California's attempt conflicted with the policy the President had been pursuing, which was less coercive. Reading presidential actions broadly, the Court reasoned that because the Constitution gives to the federal government, and in particular the President, the power (which he had exercised) to negotiate with foreign countries and foreign companies, California's law could not stand.[15]

Regardless of whether these two preemption decisions were right, they do not resolve the issue of the states and localities expressing their views on Iraq and the war on terrorism. That is because in these rulings the Court stopped short of holding that state regulation of foreign affairs is invalid even in the absence of some affirmative preemptive action by Congress or the President. This is not to say, of course, that the Constitution itself would never impose limits on state and local attempts to affect international affairs. For example, suppose New Jersey enacted a statute saying that "any company that makes arms that the U.S. government may use in any upcoming war cannot incorporate or sell to any customers in our state." Such a law would clearly burden interstate and international commerce, not to mention Congress's ability to raise and support troops, and would thus be preempted by the Constitution itself. The Constitution gives Congress the authority to regulate such commerce and the military,[16] and in doing so, displaces much state legislation on the topic.

## Anti-Commandeering

What about those local resolutions passed after 9/11, like San Francisco's, which direct local agencies not to assist the federal government? Do states and localities have latitude to opt out of cooperation with federal agencies? I think they do—at least to some extent.

As Professor Ann Althouse discusses in much more detail in this book,[17] the Supreme Court, in a series of cases from the mid-1990s, has made clear that state and local governments cannot be required to implement a federal law or program on behalf of the national government if they do not want to. For example, the Court ruled in *Printz v. United States* that Congress could not simply direct local sheriffs to conduct the prepurchase background checks called for in the *Brady Act* gun control law.[18]

If Congress wants such background checks performed, the Court opined, it can certainly employ federal personnel to conduct them, or it can induce states to cooperate by threatening to preempt states from the field or providing them generous federal funding conditioned upon their help. But the federal government cannot simply tell unwilling state personnel to enforce federal law. The idea that the federal government cannot "commandeer" or "conscript" states to do federal bidding, the Court said, is central to the structure of our system of federalism.[19]

How that plays out in the context of laws like the USA PATRIOT Act and related executive decisions could get interesting. I think the federal government cannot require (although it can effectively bribe) state and local authorities to help surveil persons suspected of violating federal immigration and other laws. But other questions remain: Can Congress require a locality to provide to the federal government information already in the locality's control that concerns people within its jurisdiction? Can it require local agencies to compile and gather information that might not yet exist? These may be other matters.

### The Bigger Federalism Picture

Much of the ambiguity described in the preceding section stems from a very basic but unresolved question: What is the vision of federalism that leads us to prevent the federal government from commandeering the states really all about? Why, exactly, is commandeering bad? Justices O'Connor and Scalia—the authors of the major opinions in the area—have talked about "accountability" problems that arise when the federal government coerces the states.[20] Suppose, for instance, that federal legislation forces states to implement a federal policy of tracking down and interrogating aliens from Middle Eastern countries. Suppose further that the public does not like such policies. The accountability concern arises because the populace may blame the state implementers, rather than the federal policymakers who, after all, are really the ones who should take the heat.

I have never entirely agreed with this reasoning. In the end, I think American federalism—with its marbled layers of government, from fire districts to water boards, to cities, to counties, to states, to federal agencies—is not really designed to make it easy for people to figure who is to blame for bad policy decisions. So being a stickler on the accountability issue in this one instance, when accountability is largely ignored in the constitutional framework, seems to me somewhat odd.

For example, the Supreme Court allows Congress easily to condition federal funds on state assistance in the enforcement of federal programs.[21] When states administer such federal programs, are people really aware that the only reason states are doing what they are doing may be the desire, or need, for federal funding for other projects? I doubt it. If we really wanted to facilitate clear accountability to voters, we probably would not have as many overlapping levels of government as we do. Indeed, we might not have a federal system, in which federal and state activities and jurisdictions inevitably coincide, in the first place.

Nevertheless, I think federal commandeering—and overly broad preemption, for that matter—may be bad for other reasons, ones that have little to do with accountability. For instance, in the worst case, federal commandeering of state legislatures may allow the federal government to hijack state governmental agendas. If the state lawmaking bodies have to spend all their time administering federal programs (on the theory that if Congress can commandeer a little, presumably it could commandeer a lot), theoretically states may never have the time or opportunity to define their own messages and legislative identities. That is a problem because the value of federalism lies, to my mind, largely in making sure that there are multiple legislative philosophies and identities out there to help the American people figure out what is best.[22]

In this sense, then, our federal system sets up a healthy competition—between one state and another, and between states and the federal government—to win over American hearts and minds on what is the best way to administer democratic self-governance. It hardly seems like a fair match if one participant in a competition (the federal government) can consume all the resources of its competitors (the states). The vision of federalism I suggest values states not just for the particular policies they may adopt, but also, more generally, for the alternative vision of good government that they may define and advance. In a real sense, a state government—through its legislative decisions and agenda—expresses a philosophical message that is different from the messages that other states and the federal government may express.[23]

Fine and good, some may say—but not when it comes to foreign affairs, which is precisely the arena where we cannot tolerate multiple messages. In that arena, the argument would run, we need to "speak in one voice." I do not think that is true. As others have pointed out,

> [t]aken literally, [the one voice argument] offends the very basis of our system of government. Americans emphatically do not speak with one voice. Individual Americans are free to [speak out on foreign affairs]. States, too, must be free to speak out. This vital point was established early in American history, when the Virginia and Kentucky legislatures famously spoke out [in words written by James Madison and Thomas Jefferson, respectively] in 1798 against federal policies penalizing France.[24]

The Alien and Sedition Acts of the late eighteenth century (to which the Virginia and Kentucky Resolutions were responses) are prime examples in which state and local government served as the point of organization for those critical of federal policies. But these are far from the only instances. Before the Civil War, abolitionist forces used local governmental bodies to voice their criticisms of southern states, as well as of federal laws that helped support the institution of slavery.

In some ways, state and local governments are natural places for dissidents to organize and speak. Individual protestors, acting alone, often face societal pressure and ostracism. For precisely this reason, the Constitution goes out of its way to create and protect institutions where individuals who may not be able to act by themselves can come together with others to associate, organize, and have their voices be heard. These "mediating" institutions—so called because they stand between the federal government and the People—include juries, churches, the militia, civic associations, and perhaps most importantly, state and local governments.[25]

I thus believe states can speak out, refuse to cooperate, and regulate private people unless preempted by a valid and clear federal law. But what about the local fears that the federal government will, in executing its policies, violate the constitutional rights of the citizens of the several states? Besides declining to participate in such injustice and railing and lobbying against it, is there anything states can do? I think there is. In particular, states can affirmatively and offensively develop legal vehicles to redress and deter such transgressions. I shall take up that idea next.

## FROM HERE, WHERE? CONVERSE § 1983 SUITS

The specific legal vehicle that I use is one my older brother, Akhil Reed Amar, first floated fifteen years ago—the notion of "converse § 1983" laws.[26] I was a law student at Yale when my brother first ran the idea by me in a draft of an article. I remember vividly spending countless hours discussing with him the possibilities the notion raised. I was excited then and fifteen years later the concept intrigues me even more.

The term "converse-1983" describes a proposed type of state law designed to provide a remedy or cause of action for violations of federal constitutional rights committed by federal officials:

> Whereas 42 U.S.C. §1983 provides a federal law remedy/cause of action for federal constitutional violations perpetrated by state officials, a converse-1983 law would provide a state law remedy/cause of action for federal constitutional violations perpetrated by federal officials. Such a converse-1983 law would both invoke and invert the logic and language of §1983, and might read something like this: Every person who, under color of any statute, ordinance, regulation, custom, or usage, of the United States, subjects or causes to be subjected, any citizen of this state or other person within the jurisdiction thereof to the deprivation of any rights, privileges, or immunities secured by the [United States] Constitution, shall be liable to the party injured in an action at law, suit in equity, or other proper proceeding for redress.[27]

Practically speaking, a new state converse-1983 norm could emerge in any of three ways. First, it could become part of the state constitution via initiative, referendum, convention, or special legislative action. Second, a state legislature by a simple majority could enact converse-1983 language as an ordinary state statute. Third, state judges have power to fashion legal norms—such as converse-1983—as part of the common law process. Such common law norms, like the norm against trespass developed by state courts and invoked in the nineteenth century against federal agents who violated privacy rights,[28] can be, and for over 200 years have been, invoked against federal officials. In essence, the converse-1983 idea builds upon the tradition of state courts policing Fourth Amendment privacy violations by federal officials using state tort law until the 1970s,[29] and extends that tradition to cover federal violations of all federal constitutional rights, not just those under the Fourth Amendment.

Valid congressional removal statutes might allow many federal officials, if they so choose, to remove damage actions from state court to a lower federal court. Thus, as a practical matter, a very high percentage of converse-1983 causes of action might end up being tried in federal district courts.[30] But whether pursued in state or federal court, a converse-1983 action, unlike a *Bivens*[31] claim created by the federal courts, cannot be abolished by the federal courts if their attitude about inferring causes of action changes. Moreover, and more important, a converse-1983 cause of action need not be saddled with the "qualified immunity" doctrines that courts have read into Section 1983 and the *Bivens* creation.[32] And as I will explain below, Congress has no power to require courts to afford qualified immunity if states have decided not to provide it.

The time has never been as ripe as it is today for one or more states to enact such a converse-1983 device. First, as already noted, states and localities are concerned about federal lawlessness as never before in recent memory. These changes in the political environment make experimentation very timely and potentially politically feasible. Second, the Supreme Court over the past decade and a half has confirmed (or established, depending upon how one views things) the essential soundness of the intellectual foundations upon which the converse-1983 idea rests. Third, academics are beginning to see the light as well—but they (apparently) still need a bit more guidance. The following subsections address the latter two points.

### Friendly Legal Developments

#### *The Importance of the Theory of Vertical Competition*

As important as changes in the political environment described above are, changes in the legal environment—particularly the evolution of the Supreme Court's attitudes—may be even more helpful. In short, the doctrinal habitat created by the High Court seems as hospitable today as it has in generations to the development and survival of the converse-1983 animal.

To begin with, let us look at the larger landscape that has emerged over the past ten to fifteen years. The point to be made here is not simply that the Court today takes seriously the concept of federalism and the idea that state institutions and state law deserve to be treated with respect—although surely it does that. Instead, the key notion is that the particular results the Court has reached in the "new federalism" arena are completely compatible with, indeed perhaps best explained by, the theory of vertical competition I adverted to earlier—Madison's notion that a "double security arises to the rights of the people . . . [when] different governments will control each other, at the same time that each is controlled by itself."[33] And it is this theory of vertical competition that gives rise to the converse-1983 vision.

Consider, in this regard, the two most important recent cases construing Congress's powers under the Commerce Clause: *United States v. Lopez* and *United States v. Morrison.*[34] In each case, the Court invalidated a congressional enactment—in *Lopez* the *Gun Free Schools Zone Act* and in *Morrison* the *Violence Against Women Act*—on the key ground that the activity regulated by the statute was not "economic" or "commercial" in nature at all and therefore was not a permissible use of Congress's power to regulate under the Commerce Clause.

Critics, both on and off the Court, have questioned this line between economic activity and noneconomic activity as artificial, if not completely arbitrary. For instance, in his dissent in *Morrison,* Justice Breyer asks: "[W]hy should we give critical constitutional importance to the economic, or noneconomic, nature of an interstate-commerce-affecting cause? If chemical emanations through indirect environmental change cause identical, severe, commercial harm outside a State, why should it matter whether local factories or home fireplaces release them?"[35] Justice Souter echoes this critique: "What difference should it make whether the causes of effects are themselves commercial? . . . The [majority's] answer is that it makes a difference to federalism, and the legitimacy of the Court's new judicially derived federalism is the crux of our disagreement."[36]

There is clearly something to this criticism. The Court never does explain why the economic nature of the activity matters, only that it does matter. In response to Justice Souter's implicit charge of activism (by his use of the term "judicially derived"), the majority could, I suppose, point to the text of the Constitution. The language of Article I of the Constitution, after all, does give Congress power to regulate not "activities" or "things" generically, but rather "commerce" itself.[37] As a matter of text, then, "commercial" things that affect commerce may be more naturally regulable than noncommercial things that affect commerce to an equal degree.

But I think the Court's real response to Breyer and Souter is not textual but rather practical—the majority clings to an arbitrary line because some line is needed. If the dissent's view were correct, Congress could always point to the Commerce Clause as a basis for its actions, and the notion of limited, enumerated, federal powers would be gutted entirely.

That raises the crucial, if underexplored, questions: Why do we need a line? And what would be so bad about gutting the notion of limited, enumerated, federal powers? Among the possible answers, I think the most attractive and the most plausible is the one that focuses on vertical competition, and the resulting requirement that states have available to them some space in which to operate. If there were no line circumscribing federal power, then the federal government could preempt everything a state may want to do to create its own competitive identity. There would be, in other words, no guarantee of any room for states to stake out a competing vision, an alternative agenda. Competition is meaningless if one competitor can, theoretically, prevent the other from ever leaving the locker room to get out onto the field. This is why, I think, Justice Kennedy, who provides the crucial fifth vote in *Lopez*, writes an important, if cryptic, explanation in his concurring opinion where he observes that the two sovereigns "hold each other in check by competing for the affections of the people."[38]

The other most prominent line of recent federalism cases is also best understood to be about facilitating vertically competitive agendas. I am speaking here of the so-called anti-commandeering cases mentioned earlier. In *New York v. United States*, and then again in *Printz v. United States*, the Court held that Congress could not directly commandeer state legislatures or state executive officials to administer federal policies and programs.[39] But in reaching these results, the Court acknowledged that Congress could preempt state action in these areas and induce states to cooperate by threatening to preempt all state regulation in the field. When I think and teach about these cases, the difficult questions have always come down to the distinction between preemption and commandeering. If Congress can keep states out of a field, why can't Congress make them toil in it?

The Court, as noted above, tried to explain the anti-commandeering rule in accountability terms. But wouldn't field preemption (or bribing the states through the spending power, for that matter) create even more accountability problems? If states are not dealing with the nuclear waste problem (at issue in *New York*) because Congress has prevented them from entering the area, or because Congress has conditioned needed federal funds on a promise to stay out, and if people are disappointed by the lack of regulation, how many voters would know to blame Congress and not the locals? To be blunt, accountability is, I think, a very weak rationale for justifying the *New York v. United States* rule.

But vertical competition is a fair explanation. If the federal government can commandeer a little, then it can commandeer a lot. And if the state lawmaking bodies have to spend all their resources administering federal programs, they never have the time or opportunity to define their own message and legislative identity. Unlike preemption, which we know—after *Lopez* and *Morrison*—has theoretical limits, commandeering, if permitted, is a federal power that has no logical limits or stopping points. And again, if one competitor can prevent the other from ever beginning its warm-ups, let alone its routine, there is not much real competition.

### More Specific Things the Justices Have Said Bearing on Converse-1983 Actions

Let us move beyond the general backdrop of the recent cases to more specific things the Justices have said and done. What one sees here is a renewed receptivity to a crucial premise of the converse-1983 device: the notion that state laws regulating federal activities are not preempted when the federal activities themselves are beyond the bounds of the Constitution. This is the central doctrinal point my brother, Akhil, made when discussing the most obvious criticism of the converse-1983 device—that it would run afoul of the Supremacy Clause as understood in the seminal case of *McCulloch v. Maryland*.[40]

In *McCulloch*, Maryland believed that the Second Federal Bank was unconstitutional; that Congress had no enumerated power to create such a bank; and that the bank's federal charter was thus unlawful. Maryland therefore attempted to impose upon the bank a tax, and when the bank officials refused to pay, Maryland brought suit in its own state courts against a bank official, asking for a fine against him for his failure to comply with the Maryland law. On appeal, the U.S. Supreme Court reversed. As Akhil observed,

[T]he Supreme Court nowhere denied the legitimacy of the jurisdiction exercised by the state court below in an action for damages, of sorts, against a federal official alleged to be part of an unconstitutional federal operation. Note also how the Supreme Court structured its analysis in *McCulloch*. The first question, said the Court, was whether the bank was in fact constitutional. Only after assuring itself that the bank was indeed consistent with the federal Constitution—"necessary and proper"—did the Court address what it labeled as the second question in the case: whether the state of Maryland could nonetheless impose its tax. The structure of the Court's analysis and several passages in the opinion plainly imply that if the bank had indeed been unconstitutional, perhaps state law could impose liability on the bank official, Mr. McCulloch. If anything, all this suggests that when federal officials are acting in violation of the federal Constitution, state law-created liability may well be appropriate at times. Of course, if a state converse-1983 law were to provide for liability far in excess of making a plaintiff whole, and far in excess of the quantum of damages for other state causes of action, this punitive converse-1983 law might offend the spirit of *McCulloch*. Imagine, for example, a converse-1983 law that provided for one million dollars of presumed damages for any Fourth Amendment violation by federal officials, however technical the violation and however minimal the actual harm to Fourth Amendment values of property, personhood, and privacy. This presumed damage rule could well be seen as a tax masquerading as a remedy, and thus violative of *McCulloch*'s spirit.[41]

This centrality of the first part of *McCulloch*—that the bank is constitutional—in reaching the result in the second part—that the tax is unconstitutional—has itself been realized and commented upon by members of the Court over the last decade. Most directly, in *U.S. Term Limits, Inc. v. Thornton*,[42] Justice Thomas, in arguing in favor of a state's ability to regulate federal officials—in that case the power of a state to prescribe qualifications for persons from the state to be elected to Congress—observed that the "structure" of *McCulloch*'s analysis was set up such that

[t]he question before the Court was whether the State of Maryland could tax the Bank of the United States, which Congress had created in an effort to accomplish objects entrusted to it by the Constitution. Chief Justice Marshall's opinion began by upholding the federal statute incorporating the bank. It then held that the Constitution affirmatively prohibited Maryland's tax on the bank created by this statute. The Court relied principally on concepts deemed inherent in the Supremacy Clause of Article VI, which declares that "this Constitution, and the Laws of the United States which shall be made in Pursuance thereof, . . . shall be supreme Law of the Land. . . ."[43]

As Justice Thomas went on to explain, it was the *McCulloch* Court's view that "when a power has been 'delegated to the United States by the Constitution,' . . . the Supremacy Clause forbids a State to 'retard, impede, burden, or in any manner control, the operations of constitutional laws enacted by Congress.'"[44] Thus, according to Justice Thomas, Maryland's lack of power turned on the existence of federal power to enact the policy in question.

This seemingly simple point has not been appreciated deeply enough, even though it underlies all of federal preemption doctrine, not just the cases dealing with so-called intergovernmental immunity—that is, cases involving laws by one governmental entity regulating another. For example, when we decide whether federal policy preempts a state law regulating private businesses or private citizens, we ask first whether the federal policy is constitutional. If not, then there is no federal policy to do any preempting. Even in the field of foreign affairs preemption, where the Court wrongly thinks states have little role to play, the Court first asks in each case whether the allegedly preempting federal decision to regulate is itself a valid exercise of the federal government's powers.[45]

Indeed, in *Thornton* Justice Thomas indicates that his reading of *McCulloch*—as a species of preemption doctrine more generally—has been embraced by the Court for over 175 years. For instance, he describes the *Osborn*[46] case with the following parenthetical reference to *McCulloch*: "reaffirming *McCulloch*'s conclusion that by operation of the Supremacy Clause, the federal statute incorporating the bank impliedly pre-empted state laws attempting to tax the bank's operations."[47]

And it makes perfect sense to think of *McCulloch* as just one example of preemption more broadly. Most of the time federal preemption is asserted, the question presented is whether state laws are regulating private persons in a way different than that preferred by Congress. But whether states regulate private persons in a way that the federal government does not like, or whether the states regulate the federal regulators themselves in a way that bothers the federal government, federal objectives are equally frustrated in both settings. Federal instrumentalities—be they statutes, banks, legislators, or executive officers—exist under our democratic theory only to pursue federal policies on behalf of the national populace; they are means to various ends, not ends in themselves. If we do not preempt state regulation of private parties that is inconsistent with congressional desires except when those congressional desires are themselves constitutionally permissible—and we do not—then we should not preempt state regulation of federal entities when those entities are engaged in constitutionally impermissible activities. Since it is the "operations of the constitutional laws enacted by Congress"[48] (the phrase *McCulloch* uses) that is the thing to be protected, the rules should be the same whether the state frustrates that "operation" by interfering with the "operators" (the federal agents), or by interfering with those on whom the federal law purports to "operate" (the citizens).

For example, in *Lopez*, if, prior to the Supreme Court's ruling, a state had told citizens that they were obliged to possess guns near schools—indeed, if a state had written its laws to provide explicitly that "those persons who are subject to the federal Gun Free School Zone Act's prohibitions, as they are written in the United States Code, are required to possess guns near schools"—we would not find the state law preempted. Because the federal policy that the state legislation frustrated would itself have been unconstitutional, there would be no preemption, as there would be no valid preempting federal action. States remain free to frustrate the federal government's objectives—by regulating the federal government or by targeting the citizens the federal government is trying to regulate—when the federal objectives themselves are not within federal power.

One may assert a couple of possible responses against the foregoing analysis. First is the observation that Justice Thomas' analysis in *Thornton* commanded the support of only four dissenting Justices, suggesting that the majority must have a different conception in mind. Second is the related idea that there is a difference between regulating the regulator and regulating the regulated, and the Court's opinions in *New York* and *Printz* demonstrate this. I shall address each of these suggestions in turn.

### Justice Stevens's Opinion in "Thornton"

As for the majority analysis in *Thornton*, it is true that Justice Stevens does purport to rest the Court's holding that Arkansas could not impose qualifications on members of Congress on two "independent" ideas:[49] first, that states lack that power in the first place because no power over federal institutions is "reserved" within the meaning of the Tenth Amendment; and second, the Constitution affirmatively divests states of any power over the newly created congressional offices.

There are a number of observations that need be made about this, only some of which—remarkably enough—were made in the opinions in the case itself or commentary since. To begin, even Justice Stevens concedes that his first holding is not necessary to the case. In Justice Stevens's mind, the second "divesting" theory is "independent" enough to sustain on its own the result in the case.

In fact, this second (and quite correct, I might add)[50] "divesting" theory must do all the work, because the first reason Stevens advances is quite weak. Justice Stevens tries to argue that states cannot regulate congresspersons because power to regulate them is not "reserved" to states within the meaning of the Tenth Amendment[51] for the simple reason that the federal institutions did not predate the Constitution and you cannot "reserve" what you never had. As Stevens, quoting Joseph Story, writes: "No state can say that it has reserved, what it never possessed."[52]

This (to my mind somewhat facile) argument clearly fails. For starters, as Justice Thomas points out, the word "reserved" does not necessarily mean "preexisting."[53] Thomas's textual argument would have been even stronger had he contrasted the word "reserved" in the Tenth Amendment with the word "preserved" in the Seventh Amendment.[54] "Preserved" does tend to focus on that which existed before, much more so than "reserved."

Moreover, and more important as a textual matter, there is no text in the Constitution that says: "States have only those powers that were 'reserved' within the meaning of the Tenth Amendment and that were not taken away by the Constitution." Justice Stevens' first argument in *Thornton*, which he says is "independent" of the second divesting theory, reads such a clause into the Constitution, even though there is no reason to, and even though it would not make sense under founding theory. Thus, whether the power to regulate federal entities is "reserved" does not answer the only question that matters, namely, whether such a power exists.[55]

Imagine, for example, that at the time of the founding, most state constitutions gave state governments no power over, say, the raising of horses. Indeed, assume that most state constitutions explicitly said: "The state shall have no power over raising horses." Assume that the federal Constitution contains no provision to regulate horse raising that could be read to displace any state power that might exist. Can't the people of each state, after 1787, give their governments the power to regulate horse raising? No one would say that state laws concerning horse raising today violate the federal Constitution simply because state power over horses did not exist in 1787 and thus was not "reserved." Instead, the only federal question we would ask (and the Supreme Court gets to ask only federal questions) is: Is there anything in the text or structure of the federal Constitution that prevents states from regulating horses? This more precise question is akin to the second "divesting" question Stevens asks in *Thornton*.

Even the language from John Marshall that Justice Stevens quotes in *Thornton* illustrates this. Marshall points out that the exercise of power by state government, where it has not been affirmatively foreclosed by the federal constitution, is not a federal concern, but rather a matter between the state government and the people of that state—the source of all legitimate power in that state, save what has been given up to the federal government or the federal populace: "These [state] powers proceed, not from the people of America, but from the people of the several States; and remain, after the adoption of the constitution, what they were before, except so far as they may be abridged by that instrument."[56] But what "they were before" is subject to expansion by the people of the states themselves.

Indeed, even Justice Stevens must realize this. He does not want to call into question the application of all state law to any federal institution, even though the federal institution by definition did not predate 1787. For instance, states have power to require federal officials to obey some local traffic rules,[57] and I doubt Justice Stevens would want to call that into question. And if Justice Stevens' response were to invoke the principle of generality—if he were to argue that states had power in 1787 to regulate traffic more generally and that is what gives them the power to regulate, say, federal postal vehicles—then I would say, with regard to converse-1983s, states have all along had the power to regulate "illegality" more generally.

In a similar vein, in *Adarand Constructors v. Pena*[58] the Supreme Court—in rejecting the notion that Section Five of the Fourteenth Amendment gives Congress a remedial power that states lack altogether—effectively realized that states have authority to remedy Thirteenth and Fourteenth Amendment violations on terms similar to those enjoyed by the federal government, even though the Thirteenth and Fourteenth Amendments postdate the "reserved powers."[59] Regardless of whether states enjoy the power to remedy constitutional violations because it was delegated to them in the Supremacy Clause itself—which tells states as well as the federal government to "support" the Constitution[60] —or simply because states are free to exercise this power so long as the people of a state want to, whether such power did or did not exist before 1787 seems to be of no moment.

If there is any lingering question whether Justice Stevens's temporal argument applies to the realm of unconstitutional federal conduct, let me point out that in *Thornton* the Court did not address a situation where Arkansas was regulating congresspersons to try to keep them in compliance with the Constitution. No matter how laudable Arkansas's goals may have been, not even Arkansas argued that term limits were required under the federal Constitution. Justice Stevens's observations, then, do not have much force at all in a context, like converse-1983s, where states regulate not federal policy, but federal unconstitutionality. Indeed, Justice Kennedy's concurrence in *Thornton* limits Justice Stevens's majority opinion, and Justice Kennedy explicitly and carefully addresses Justice Stevens's temporal argument and the meaning of *McCulloch*, in the following terms: "The states have no power, reserved or otherwise, over the exercise of federal authority within its proper sphere."[61] In a converse-1983 setting, by definition, federal authority has exceeded its proper scope. Also, Joseph Story, on whose words Justice Stevens builds his argument, says explicitly in a part of his Commentaries not mentioned by Justice Stevens that the rightly decided *McCulloch* ruling (and a similar ruling that held invalid state efforts to interfere with federal bonds) "turn upon the point that no state can have the authority to tax an instrument of the United States, or thereby to diminish the means of the United States, used in the exercise of powers confided to it."[62]

### *Intergovernmental Respect and Immunity*

It seems clear, then, that state remedies against federal lawlessness are not prohibited merely on the ground that states as a general matter lack such remedial power. If there is a problem with such a remedy, it must be because the Constitution's structure affirmatively forbids the states from exercising remedial power against federal agents. As indicated above, *McCulloch* does not support that position. But *McCulloch* is not, of course, the Court's last word on the limits that the Constitution places on the ability of one level of government to directly regulate another. There are many decisions of the last decade or so that address this issue.

In particular, some may read *New York* and *Printz* to say that one participant in this vertical competition cannot target and discriminate against the other. I do not understand these cases to stand for such a broad principle at all. Instead, as I noted earlier, they are cases about accountability or more plausibly the dangers of one government hijacking the agenda of the other. Needless to say, because converse-1983 actions would target only behavior unlawful under a federal standard, there are no accountability or agenda-hijacking concerns in a converse-1983 setting.[63]

Indeed, even as nothing in *Printz*'s general rule and its justification call into question converse-1983, an exception to the *Printz* rule supports the converse-1983 idea. In *Printz* itself, Justice Scalia's opinion for the Court noted that an early Congress had conscripted state executive officials in one particular setting—to comply with the Constitution's extradition requirements. Justice Scalia explained away this episode as not inconsistent with the rest of his opinion on the ground that this early federal statute was "in direct implementation ... of the Extradition Clause of the Constitution itself."[64] Thus, unlike the *Brady Act*, the *Extradition Act* was a permissible kind commandeering because it was designed to enforce the Constitution itself rather than simply some statutory goal. Whatever the scope of the anti-commandeering principle protecting states, then, it does not apply when the Constitution itself is being enforced. Converse-1983 statutes, of course, are "a direct implementation of the entire Constitution itself."

This distinction between federal statutory enforcement and federal constitutional enforcement also explains why, under the Court's jurisprudence concerning Section Five of the Fourteenth Amendment, which gives Congress the power to implement the provisions of that Amendment, the federal government can regulate the states directly and indeed impose upon them monetary liability that may interfere with their ability to structure their own identities and agendas. In cases like the recently decided *Nevada Department of Human Resources v. Hibbs*,[65] Congress is allowed, under the new federalism, to discriminate against states and even subject them to unique monetary liability, when states have been violating federal constitutional rights,[66] even though Congress cannot impose such liability on states merely for violating ordinary federal statutes.[67]

### Academic Developments

In addition to these political and doctrinal developments, constitutional scholars seem more interested in and somewhat more receptive to the idea of a converse-1983 device than they were a decade ago. To begin with, the "vertical competition" premise behind the idea is at least part of the mainstream federalism dialogue now in a way that it was not ten years back.[68] Second, the particular idea of a converse-1983 device is at least being acknowledged much more in the literature. During the first six years after Akhil first floated the idea, not a single citation to the device was made in any law review article picked up by the legal databases, Westlaw or Lexis. In the last six years, the idea has at least been cited, if not discussed, over thirty times.

And some people are devoting a lot of thought to the idea, and internalizing its basics—sort of. The most important, prominent, and recent academic treatment of the converse-1983 device comes in a recent essay by former Solicitor General,

Seth Waxman, and Trevor Morrison (who worked for Solicitor General Waxman and who now teaches law) on federal immunities from state law recently published in the *Yale Law Journal*.[69]

First, the good news: Solicitor General Waxman and Professor Morrison say they are "inclined to agree that at least some kinds of converse-1983 laws are constitutional" and not barred entirely by federal Supremacy principles because Akhil "convincingly points out that converse-1983 statutes in fact would enforce the Supremacy Clause by ensuring that federal action complies with the Constitution."[70] (Supremacy of the federal Constitution over inconsistent federal governmental action is, after all, the basis of *Marbury*.) They also apparently find quite important the fact—documented by my brother Akhil—that in the nineteenth century, the Supreme Court applied and thus implicitly upheld state law causes of action brought against federal officials to redress conduct that violated the federal Constitution.[71]

Now the bad news: I do not think Solicitor General Waxman and Professor Morrison completely understand the converse-1983 theory. I say this because they part company with the converse-1983 device at a most crucial point—whether such a device can strip federal officials of the qualified immunity they now enjoy under *Bivens* actions.[72] I think it is helpful to explain exactly how and why they—to my mind—get it wrong, because I fear that their instincts are all too common.

At the outset, they make what I view as a bit of a false start. They begin with the question of whether a remedy that contains qualified immunity itself violates the Constitution, and they conclude (quite sensibly) that it cannot, else *Bivens* and Section 1983 would themselves be unconstitutional. But in a converse-1983 case, the question is not whether a federal court or Congress must abolish immunity in remedies that it creates, but rather whether federal law necessarily forecloses a state's decision to abolish immunity in a remedy that the state creates. That a federal court or Congress could rationally choose to include immunities in remedies that it fashions does not mean that the federal government can override a state's decision not to include immunities in its own causes of action.[73] So, the only question is whether the Constitution or a congressional statute can operate to preempt a state's decision in this regard. Solicitor General Waxman and Professor Morrison ultimately see this as the $64,000 question, but their detour concerning whether the Constitution requires all remedies to remove immunity takes us away from the central inquiry.

Moreover, their reasoning on the key question of whether Congress could pass a law reinstating immunity—they say Congress could—is to my mind underexplanatory and unpersuasive.[74] They assert that Congress could validly pass a law reinstating qualified immunity in order to vindicate the interest in vigorous federal law enforcement. The idea—commonly invoked in immunity circles—is that if the agents know they are personally liable for crossing a line, they may not approach the line at all, to the detriment of vigorous enforcement. The need for "breathing room" in law enforcement, they suggest, is a valid federal concern.[75] I have some problems with that.

First, they never explain why, if (as they suggest) the existing broad array of federal statutes reflect this interest in breathing room, the Supreme Court declined in the nineteenth century to displace state causes of action that lacked immunity. They acknowledge cases in which state causes of action unencumbered by immunity doctrines imposed liability on federal agents for federal constitutional misdeeds. Indeed, Solicitor General Waxman and Professor Morrison cite to such cases to explain why they are "inclined to agree" that converse-1983s are not impermissible per se. And yet they do not explain how those cases could exist—or where the opposing cases are—if existing federal interests reflected in existing federal statutes are preemptive.

Second, and more crucially, they never ask or explain why such federal interests—and the statutes that implement them—would be "proper" within the meaning of the Sweeping Clause, also known as the "Necessary and Proper Clause."[76] Again, their argument on behalf of Congress would proceed along the following lines: "We need to violate the Constitution so that we can enforce the laws that don't violate the Constitution." But that is another way of arguing that the constitutionally permissible ends justify some unconstitutional means. That is exactly what Justice Marshall in the first part of *McCulloch* said Congress could not do: "Let the end be legitimate, let it be within the scope of the [C]onstitution, and all means which are appropriate, which are plainly adapted to that end, which are not prohibited, but consist with the letter and spirit of the constitution, are constitutional."[77]

The Constitution itself draws lines—identifies impermissible means—so that the federal government cannot argue, for instance, we need to deny persons "due process" in order to better and more efficiently regulate immigration. There are many things a government might have a sincere and laudable reason for wanting to do; the Constitution tells us not only what the federal government can want to do, but also how the government can go about doing it.

Of course, many constitutional provisions take account of exigencies of the day. For instance, what constitutes an "unreasonable" search may depend upon whether there is a war. And whether the federal government has a valid claim to operate in an area may also depend upon the foreign affairs context—the theory of delegated enumerated powers may not be as applicable in the arena of federal control of foreign relations as it is in the domestic affairs realm.[78] But even in the area of international affairs, federal power is not absolute, and is limited by particular provisions of the Constitution, including some that create individual rights[79] enforceable under a converse-1983 statute. Once we say something is unconstitutional—and converse-1983s impose liability only if there is a substantive violation of the Constitution—then the federal government has no "proper" or valid interest in using an impermissible means.

My point may also be seen, I think, by imagining an injunctive action rather than a damage claim against a federal officer. Damages and injunctive relief are designed to do the same thing—to restore or maintain the position plaintiff would be in if there were no illegal action by the defendant[80] —and the only reason we cannot get an injunction for everything is there is never a court around at the instant you need one.[81] Imagine we knew that federal agents were about to violate the Fourth Amendment, say, by impermissibly taking into account the race of the searched persons. Suppose further that we were about to go to a court to seek an injunction against the impermissible use of race in the minds of the INS (Immigration and Naturalization Service) agents deciding whom to search. Now imagine that Congress had passed a law saying: "Courts can issue no injunctions against the use of race by INS agents, because even if the use of race is unconstitutional, when INS agents are worried about whether they can have race on the mind, they may worry too much and forget about other relevant and permissible things. In other words, any injunction, no matter how narrowly drafted, may induce, because of the fear of a contempt citation, a timidity that we think would hinder aggressive enforcement of valid laws."[82]

Could this concern over federal "gun-shyness" be genuine by Congress? Sure. Is it rational for Congress to think that agents would more vigorously enforce laws if there were no injunctions and thus no possibility of contempt? Yes.[83] Would a court still issue the injunction? I think so. And the only basis on which a court could and would disregard the congressional statute would be that it is not constitutional, because it is not constitutionally "proper." Unless the court were to find Congress's law unconstitutional, it could not prefer the Fourth and Fifth Amendments to the congressional statute; unless constitutionally improper, the federal statute would be entitled to supremacy under *Marbury* just as much as the Constitution would. Indeed, it is the constitutional supremacy ideal that Solicitor General Waxman and Professor Morrison acknowledge that makes the converse-1983 device defensible in the first place. And yet they seem to forget their own premises when they say that a congressional law designed to facilitate violations of the constitution—albeit with a good motive—is supreme and thus can displace state law.

Waxman and Morrison themselves seem to intuit that their reasoning is a bit shaky, so they say that in situations where the officer "by any reasonable standard . . . clearly act[ed] ultra vires," then perhaps congressional immunity would be unavailable.[84] Where does that standard come from? It is literally made up. The Constitution itself tells us what is "ultra vires"—namely, those things done in violation of the Constitution. By definition an action is not within lawful power if unconstitutional, as would be the case for any conduct targeted by a converse-1983 law. There are no degrees of "ultra vires"—that concept is digital; either something is "beyond the powers" (the Latin translation of "ultra vires") or it is not. For my part, I will stay with the lines the Constitution draws.


## CONCLUSION: WILL STATE LEGISLATURES, STATE COURTS, AND FEDERAL COURTS LISTEN?

Who knows whether state legislatures or courts will seize the current opportunity. States may understandably fear federal reprisals in funding and other areas if they were to act aggressively to rein in federal abuses. Funding to cities will likely remain a key point of contention in the war on terror. As for the reaction of the federal judiciary, there remains a persistent asymmetrical federalism instinct out there. No one, for instance, targets federal sovereign immunity even though some Justices argue that state sovereign immunity under the Eleventh Amendment makes no sense and runs counter to our founding ideals. Courage and consistency are not always easy to come by. But the time is as ripe as ever for states to test the soul of this new federalism.

## Notes

1. See Vikram David Amar, "Is It Appropriate, Under the Constitution, for State and Local Governments to Weigh in on the War on Terror and a Possible War with Iraq?" *Find Law's Writ*, March 7, 2003, http:// writ.news.findlaw.com/amar/20030307.html.

2. Ibid.

3. Ibid.

4. Ibid.

5. Ibid. Perhaps the best-known illustration of a local community's reluctance, at least until its concerns were addressed, to assist the federal government involved the city of Detroit, Michigan. See, for e.g., Fox Butterfield, "A Police Force Rebuffs F.B.I. on Querying Mideast Men," A Nation Challenged: The Interviews, *New York Times*, November 21, 2001 (late edition); Jodi Wilgoren, "University of Michigan Won't Cooperate in Federal Canvass," A Nation Challenged: The Interviews, *New York Times*, December 1, 2001 (late edition).

6. See Jack Goldsmith, "State Foreign Policies After the Burma Case," *Find Law's Writ*, June 26, 2000, http://writ.news.findlaw.com/commentary/20000626_goldsmith.html.

7. Ibid.

8. Erwin Chemerinsky, "Empowering States When It Matters: A Different Approach to Preemption" (in this book).

9. *Crosby v. National Foreign Trade Council*, 530 U.S. 363 (2000).

10. Ibid., 373–387.

11. See *Foreign Operations, Export Financing, and Related Programs Appropriations Act of 1997*, 104 Public Law 104-208, sec. 570, *U.S. Statutes at Large 110* (1997): 3009-121, 3009-166 to 3009-167 (enacted by the *Omnibus Consolidated Appropriations Act of 1997*, 104 Public Law 104-208, sec. 101[c], *U.S. Statutes at Large 110* (1997): 3009).

12. California's *Fair Employment and Housing Act* in some respects goes farther than does the federal Title VII or Title VIII, dealing, respectively, with employment and housing. Compare *Fair Employment and Housing Act, California Government Code* secs. 12900 to 12940 (West 1992 & Suppl. 2004), with *Civil Rights Act of 1964, U.S. Code 42* (1964) secs. 2000e to 2000e–17 ("Title VII"), and *Fair Housing Act, U.S. Code 42* secs. 3601 to 3619, 3631 ("Title VIII").

13. See *Crosby v. National Foreign Trade Council*, 367.

14. *American Insurance Association v. Garamendi*, 539 U.S. 396 (2003). The *Garamendi* case may be less susceptible to my criticism here than *Crosby* because in *Garamendi*, California was not deciding how to spend its own money, but rather deciding how to regulate private insurance companies. Constitutional preemption doctrine has always given states

more leeway when they are deciding how their monies should be spent, as, for example, in the so-called "market participant exception" to dormant Commerce Clause principles.

15. Ibid., 413–428.

16. See U.S. Constitution Art. I, sec. 8.

17. Ann Althouse, "The Vigor of Anti-Commandeering Doctrine in Times of Terror" (in this book).

18. *Printz v. United States*, 521 U.S. 898 (1997).

19. Ibid., 919–922.

20. See *Printz v. United States*; *New York v. United States*, 505 U.S. 144 (1992).

21. See, for e.g., *South Dakota v. Dole*, 483 U.S. 203 (1987) (allowing Congress to deny funding to states that had a minimum drinking age below twenty-one).

22. See generally, Todd Pettys, "Competing for the People's Affection: Federalism's Forgotten Marketplace, *Vanderbilt Law Review* 56 (2003): 329–394 (hereinafter as "Competing for the People's Affection").

23. Ibid.

24. See Akhil Reed Amar, "A State's Right, A Government's Wrong," *Washington Post,* March 19, 2000 (final edition).

25. See generally Jason Mazzone, "Freedom's Associations," *Washington Law Review* 77 (2002): 639–768.

26. See Akhil Reed Amar, "Of Sovereignty and Federalism," *Yale Law Journal* 96 (1987): 1512–1519.

27. Akhil Reed Amar, "Using State Law to Protect Federal Constitutional Rights: Some Questions and Answers about Converse-1983," *University of Colorado Law Review* 64 (1993): 160 (emphasis in original) (hereinafter as "Using State Law").

28. Ibid., 161–163; see also Akhil Reed Amar, "Five Views of Federalism: 'Converse-1983' in Context," *Vanderbilt Law Review* 47 (1994): 1229–1250.

29. See Amar, "Using State Law," 161–162.

30. Ibid., 165.

31. See *Bivens v. Six Unknown Named Agents of Federal Bureau of Narcotics*, 403 U.S. 388 (1971), where the Supreme Court decided to create a cause of action against federal officers who violate constitutional rights, parallel to the actions against state officers authorized by Section 1983.

32. See, for e.g., *Harlow v. Fitzgerald*, 457 U.S. 800 (1982).

33. James Madison, *The Federalist No. 51*.

34. *United States v. Lopez*, 514 U.S. 549 (1995); *United States v. Morrison*, 529 U.S. 598 (2000).

35. *United States v. Morrison*, 657 (J. Breyer, dissenting) (emphasis in original).

36. Ibid., 643 n.13 (J. Souter, dissenting).

37. U.S. Constitution, Art. I, sec. 8, cl. 3.

38. *United States v. Lopez*, 576 (J. Kennedy, concurring).

39. *New York v. United States*; *Printz v. United States*.

40. *McCulloch v. Maryland*, 17 U.S. 316 (1819). See also Akhil Reed Amar, "Of Sovereignty and Federalism," *Yale Law Journal* 96 (1987): 1513–1514.

41. Amar, "Using State Law," 168.

42. *U.S. Term Limits, Inc. v. Thornton*, 514 U.S. 779 (1995).

43. Ibid., 853–854 (J. Thomas, dissenting) (emphasis added) (citations omitted).

44. Ibid., 854 (emphasis added) (quoting U.S. Constitution amend. X and *McCulloch v. Maryland*, 436).

45. See, for e.g., *American Insurance Association v. Garamendi*, 539 U.S. 396, 413–414 (2003). Note that under the theory of inherent federal powers in some areas, the federal power need only be valid, not necessarily enumerated. (See, for e.g., *United States v. Curtiss-Wright Export Corp.*, 299 U.S. 304 (1936)).

46. *Osborn v. Bank of the United States*, 22 U.S. 783, 859–868 (1824).

47. *U.S. Term Limits, Inc. v. Thornton*, 854 (J. Thomas, dissenting).

48. *McCulloch v. Maryland*, 436 (emphasis added).

49. *U.S. Term Limits, Inc. v. Thornton*, 800.

50. I think it is quite clear that the people of each State were affirmatively deprived of any control over federal legislators. See generally, Vikram David Amar, "The People Made Me Do It: Can the People of the States Instruct and Coerce Their State Legislatures in the Article v. Amendment Process?" *William & Mary Law Review* 41 (2000): 1049–1053, 1090–1091.

51. U.S. Constitution, amend. X.

52. *U.S. Term Limits, Inc. v. Thornton*, 802 (quoting Joseph Story, *1 Commentaries on the Constitution of the United States sec. 627* (3d ed. 1858)).

53. *U.S. Term Limits, Inc. v. Thornton*, 851 (J. Thomas, concurring).

54. U.S. Constitution, amend. VII.

55. To say that Stevens is wrong in styling his first argument as "independent" is not to say that the question of whether states had "reserved" powers to regulate federal entities is irrelevant to the case. If such powers were assumed to exist in 1787, then such assumptions may bear on the second (and to my mind, key) question—whether any such powers are foreclosed by the Constitution's words, structure, and history.

56. *U.S. Term Limits, Inc. v. Thornton*, 801 (quoting *Sturges v. Crowninshield*, 17 U.S. 122, 193 (1819)).

57. See, for e.g., *Johnson v. Maryland*, 254 U.S. 51 (1920): "[A]n employee of the United States does not secure a general immunity from state law while acting in the course of his employment . . . [W]hen the United States has not spoken, the subjection to local law would extend to general rules that might affect incidentally the mode of carrying out the employment—as, for instance, a statute or ordinance regulating the mode of turning at the corners of streets." (Ibid., 56).

58. *Adarand Constructors, Inc. v. Pena*, 515 U.S. 200 (1995).

59. There may be other good reasons to afford the federal government more latitude to use race-conscious laws, but the mere existence of Section Five is not necessarily one of them.

60. See U.S. Constitution, Art. VI, sec. 3. As David Currie has pointed out, Congress itself relied on the Supremacy Clause to enact oath laws and fugitive slave laws. See, for e.g., David P. Currie, "The Constitution in Congress: The First Congress and the Structure of Government, 1789–1791," *University of Chicago Law School Roundtable* 2 (1995): 171. If the Supremacy Clause is itself a delegation of authority to the federal government to make appropriate laws to enforce the Constitution, its language would indicate that states—who are equally bound to support the Constitution—would have the same power. If this is true, though, one might ask, why were Section Two of the Thirteenth Amendment and Section Five of the Fourteenth Amendment needed? Perhaps to remove all doubt on the question. (See generally, Akhil Reed Amar, "Constitutional Redundancies and Clarifying Clauses," *Valparaiso University Law Review* 33 (1998): 1–21.)

61. *U.S. Term Limits, Inc. v. Thornton*, 841 (J. Kennedy, concurring) (emphasis added). Indeed, Kennedy argues in his next breath that Arkansas must be kept from interfering with

valid federal policies for the same reason that the federal government must be kept within its bounds, making clear his overarching concern with policing the Constitution's substantive limits.

62. Joseph Story, *1 Commentaries on the Constitution of the United States* sec. 503 (1833) (emphasis added).

63. Moreover, a converse-1983 law that a state enacted that applied to state officers as well as federal officers would not "discriminate" against the federal government in any event. Such laws may, however, be less likely to pass than ones that target federal misdeeds, and I, like my brother, Akhil Reed Amar, do not think such a nondiscrimination requirement exists in this setting.

64. *Printz v. United States*, 909.

65. *Nevada Department of Human Resources v. Hibbs*, 538 U.S. 721 (2003).

66. Ibid. Indeed, Congress can even act prophylactically. Perhaps under a converse-1983, a state could try to be prophylactic too—targeting not just unconstitutional federal conduct but rather conduct that includes, yet extends beyond, unconstitutional actions by federal officials. Query whether states should enjoy the same license to be prophylactic that Congress enjoys, even assuming the state remedy in question were "congruent and proportional" to federal violations.

67. Cf. *Seminole Tribe of Florida v. Florida*, 517 U.S. 44 (1996) (distinguishing between constitutional violations by states and violations of federal laws that do not enforce the Constitution but rather simply are consistent with Congress' enumerated powers).

68. See, for e.g., *Competing for the People's Affection*, 22.

69. Seth P. Waxman & Trevor W. Morrison, "What Kind of Immunity? Federal Officers, State Criminal Law, and the Supremacy Clause," *Yale Law Journal* 112 (2003): 2195–2260 (hereinafter as "What Kind of Immunity?")

70. Ibid., 2246–2247.

71. Ibid.

72. Ibid., 2248.

73. Congress didn't have to provide a Section 1983 remedy at all, so Congress can be underinclusive if it wants to. And certainly judicial caution could lead a federal court to move incrementally in the remedies it creates. As Akhil has put the point:

> Why might the Supreme Court allow state law to be more generous towards citizen victims [on either the immunity issue, or possibly on the issue of quantum of damages] than the Court itself has been under *Bivens*? Perhaps because the Court itself has been dubious of the legitimacy of *Bivens* and has chosen to tread very carefully and gingerly. Even though *Bivens* is not a species of the *Swift v. Tyson* type of "general" federal common law condemned in *Erie*, but is rather a prime example of what Judge Friendly labeled the "new" federal common law, it was condemned as illegitimate by several dissenters in *Bivens*, including Justice Black. But however controversial federal common law—"new" or old—fashioned by federal judges may be, no one disputes the common law role of state judges. Thus, Justice Black went out of his way in his *Bivens* dissent to concede that he would cheerfully enforce a cause of action against lawless federal officials if either "Congress [] or the State of New York" had created such a cause of action. (Amar, "Using State Law," 174–175.)

74. If a state passed a converse-1983 law, and Congress had to explain why it was preempting part of it, at least there would be political costs to pay.

75.  Solicitor General Waxman and Professor Morrison note that:

[The federal government's] interest is not just in keeping the letter of federal law free from state interference, but also in affording federal officers enough leeway to implement federal law and policy effectively. The integrity of federal law depends on its sound execution, which, in turn, depends on the actions of federal officers. Thus, as we have explained, the policy aim of qualified immunity—protecting against the "risk that fear of personal . . . liability and harassing litigation will unduly inhibit officials in the discharge of their duties"—also describes the federal interest at stake in Supremacy Clause immunity. (Waxman & Morrison, "What Kind of Immunity?" 2251.)

76.  U.S. Constitution, Art. I, sec. 8, cl. 18.

77.  *McCulloch v. Maryland*, 421 (emphasis added).

78.  See, for e.g., *United States v. Curtiss-Wright Export Corp.*, 299 U.S. 304, 321 (1936).

79.  See, for e.g., *Reid v. Covert*, 354 U.S. 1, 6 (1957).

80.  See generally, Douglas Laycock, *Modern American Remedies: Cases and Materials* (New York: Aspen Law & Business, 3d ed., 2002).

81.  This timing problem drives the mootness and ripeness doctrines. See, for e.g., *Los Angeles v. Lyons*, 461 U.S. 95, 101 (1983).

82.  Such a law would not strip courts of jurisdiction. Cf. *Ex Parte McCardle*, 74 U.S. 506 (1868). Nor would it direct who wins or loses on the merits. Cf. *U.S. v. Klein*, 80 U.S. 128, 146 (1871). Rather, it would simply regulate remedies the courts could give. Cf. *Federal Rule of Civil Procedure* 65.

83.  That is why, if converse-1983s came into being, Congress would naturally indemnify its agents.

84.  Waxman & Morrison, "What Kind of Immunity?" 2255.

# The Roots of *Printz*: Proslavery Constitutionalism, National Law Enforcement, Federalism, and Local Cooperation

## Paul Finkelman*

## INTRODUCTION

The USA PATRIOT Act[1] and the creation of a cabinet level Department of Homeland Security signaled a new chapter in the tension between civil liberties and national security. How secure can we be, and at what cost to our personal liberty and personal privacy will that security come? A concomitant issue is the role that the States can play, or must, play in implementing the plans of the national government. The leading case on this issue is *Printz v. United States*.[2] Here the Supreme Court struck down the portion of the Brady Act[3] that required the Chief Law Enforcement Officer (CLEO) in each county to administer the law. One of the tasks of the CLEO under the Brady Act was to conduct a background check on prospective gun purchasers. The statute also provided a penalty of up to a year in jail for anyone who refused to comply with the law. Presumably this penalty was applicable to a CLEO who failed or refused to conduct a background check on a prospective gun purchaser. In overturning this provision of the law, Justice Scalia argued that the Act breached the wall of separation created by federalism. He characterized the law as "conscripting state officers."[4] While the majority opinion did not use the term "unfunded mandates," this was also part of the debate.[5] Oddly, none of the opinions in this case mentioned the first Supreme Court case to deal with these issues, *Prigg v. Pennsylvania*.[6]

---

* The author thanks Susan Herman, Jason Mazzone, and Stephanie J. Wilhelm for their comments and suggestions on this chapter.

In *Printz* both the Solicitor General of the United States (Walter Dellinger), arguing for the constitutionality of the provision, and Justice Scalia, finding the law unconstitutional, invoked the Fugitive Slave Law of 1793.[7] The use of this statute was unusual. Modern courts rarely discuss our constitutional heritage of slavery, and when they do mention slavery, it is usually to attack a statute, earlier decision, or the opinion of another justice.[8] For example, a frustrated Justice Scalia compared the majority opinion in *Planned Parenthood of Southeastern Pennsylvania v. Casey* to the *Dred Scott* decision.[9] Similarly, Justice Brennan compared the majority opinion in *McKleskey v. Kemp* to *Dred Scott*.[10] In his heroic opposition to the constitutionalization of segregation in *Plessy v. Ferguson*, Justice John Marshall Harlan chastised the Court for writing an opinion that he correctly predicted would "prove to be quite as pernicious as the decision made by this tribunal in the *Dred Scott* case."[11] Given the usual propensity of justices to use slavery only to attack modern opinions that they dislike, it is startling to see both the attorney for the United States and the Court itself invoke a proslavery statute in support of a legal proposition. It is particularly odd to imagine that the Solicitor General would turn to the Fugitive Slave Law of 1793 as a viable precedent for upholding a modern statute. Perhaps even more peculiar than the resurrection of this law is the fact that neither the Solicitor General nor Justice Scalia seemed to get it right.

In his majority opinion Justice Scalia wrote that some early statutes "apparently or at least arguably required state courts to perform functions unrelated to naturalization, such as . . . hearing the claims of slave owners who had apprehended fugitive slaves and issuing certificates authorizing the slave's forced removal to the State from which he had fled. . . . " He noted that the Solicitor General had mentioned this statute as one in which the United States had required state officials to enforce a federal law. In response to this claim, Justice Scalia wrote: "These early laws establish, at most, that the Constitution was originally understood to permit imposition of an obligation on state *judges* to enforce federal prescriptions, insofar as those prescriptions related to matters appropriate for the judicial power." After a brief discussion of these laws, Scalia concluded: "For these reasons, we do not think the early statutes imposing obligations on state courts imply a power of Congress to impress the state executive into its service."[12]

Both Justice Scalia and Solicitor General Dellinger ignored the history of the 1793 law, including Justice Joseph Story's opinion upholding its constitutionality in *Prigg*.[13] In upholding this law Justice Story had concluded that the federal government could not force state officials to implement the law. Oddly, Justice Scalia did not use this point in his opinion. He also failed to note that Justice Story developed an argument against "unfunded mandates" that was similar to argument used in *Printz*. Neither the Justices nor Solicitor General Dellinger considered whether the obligation to perform government functions imposed by the 1793 law was similar to that imposed by the Brady Act.

Even if we think that *Printz* might have been wrongly decided, a careful examination of the 1793 law and its history can tell us a great deal about why we must be skeptical of statutes that conscript state officials. The lessons of the 1793 law and opinion of Justice Story in *Prigg* also illustrate why, if Congress wants to or needs to recruit state officials to enforce federal law, it should be required to use carrots rather than sticks to accomplish its goals.

This chapter offers a brief history of the Fugitive Slave Law of 1793 and the Court's decision in *Prigg v. Pennsylvania*, in order to illustrate the pitfalls of relying on state officials to implement and enforce federal policy. The Fugitive Slave Law of 1793 was one of the first attempts by the national government to have a law enforcement policy that could reach into local communities on a regular basis. The Congress assumed that state officials would willingly enforce this law. In fact, throughout the North there was hostility to the law and the policy behind it. As a result, states passed their own laws, known as personal liberty laws, that undermined the federal law. These state laws were ostensibly passed to protect free blacks from wrongful seizure. However, many northerners also hoped these laws might shield fugitive slaves from being returned to bondage. The second section of this chapter describes the Fugitive Slave Law of 1793. The third section examines the state personal liberty laws that undermined the effectiveness of that law. The fourth section analyses *Prigg v. Pennsylvania*, and the development of the doctrine of "unfunded mandates." *Prigg* illustrates the problem of "conscripting" state officials to implement federal policy. The fifth section shows how Justice Story's opinion in *Prigg* set the stage for federal enforcement of the fugitive slave law, and how this might be a model for implementing national policy in our modern age of terrorism. Finally, the sixth section of this chapter offers some policy arguments in support of federal enforcement of federal laws. These arguments are based on the experiences of the nation with the Fugitive Slave Laws of 1793 and 1850 as well as the Court's decisions in both *Prigg* and *Printz*.

## THE FUGITIVE SLAVE LAW OF 1793 AND STATE ENFORCEMENT

The Fugitive Slave Law of 1793 authorized a master or his agent to seize an alleged fugitive slave and bring that person before a federal judge, a state judge, or "any magistrate of a county, city, or town corporate" where the arrest was made. The statute provided that upon "proof to the satisfaction of the judge or magistrate" that the person arrested was a fugitive slave, "it shall be the duty of such judge or magistrate to give a certificate" to allow the claimant to remove the fugitive. This law seemed to *require* that judges enforce and implement the law, although the term "duty" is unclear. The law provided no penalty for a judge or magistrate who did not do his "duty." Nor did the law set any standard process for appeal of the decision of a judge who found the claimant's evidence unpersuasive. The law did provide a penalty of $500 for anyone who "shall knowingly and willingly obstruct or hinder such claimant."[14] However, this provision does not seem to have applied to judges who might refuse to hear such a case. Thus it is hard to know exactly how Congress intended "duty" to apply to a state judge or magistrate.

There appears to have been no immediate remedy if a state judge refused to take jurisdiction in a fugitive slave case. Similarly there was no remedy if a judge arbitrarily ruled against the claimant. For example, the abolitionist newspaper, *The Liberator*, discussed an 1807 Vermont case, in which Justice Theophilus Harrington, speaking for a unanimous Vermont Supreme Court, allegedly refused to return a fugitive slave to his owner, declaring, "If the master could show a bill of sale, or grant, from the Almighty, then his title to him would be complete: otherwise it would not."[15] Although perhaps apocryphal, this unreported decision was viewed by abolitionists as an example of how judges ought to deal with the Fugitive Slave Law.

The abolitionist argument implied by the opinion attributed to Justice Harrington raised the issue of a judge's "duty" to a new level. If a state judge refused to take a case or took a case and then refused to issue a certificate of removal, what could a claimant do? The claimant might have gone to a federal judge to ask for a certificate of removal. In theory the claimant could have also asked for a writ of mandamus to force the state judge to act. If the claimant was able to actually find a federal judge, he would not need a mandamus to be directed at the local or state judge, since he could get his certificate of removal directly from the federal judge. However, at this time there were relatively few federal judges in the nation—most of the northern states had only one or two federal district judges before 1850. Thus, actually finding a federal judge in a timely manner was problematic, especially if the fugitive slave was discovered outside of a major city. Alternatively, if one state judge refused to act under the 1793 law, there was nothing to prevent the claimant from finding another state judge or magistrate to help him. This would not even have been an appeal, since the first judge's refusal to act under the law would not have produced an opinion, or anything else, to appeal. But all these alternatives would have been expensive and time-consuming and might not have led to the removal of the fugitive slave. While the claimant was seeking a second forum under the 1793 Law, the slave would have been free to leave the region, since the claimant would have had no legal authority to hold a black person against his or her will, especially after a magistrate had in effect declared that there was not enough evidence to hold the person as a fugitive slave. Alerted to what was happening, the alleged slave would probably have moved away, gone into hiding, or left the country. Thus, whatever the term "duty" meant in the 1793 law, it does not appear to have had a practical effect on northern judges beyond setting out what they *ought* to do. The term clearly did not set out what they *had* to do.

## PERSONAL LIBERTY LAWS

Initially the northern states cooperated with the fugitive slave law. Most northern jurists who heard cases under the law made good faith attempts to enforce it. For example, in 1819, Pennsylvania's Chief Justice, William Tilghman, enforced the federal law while denying that a fugitive slave had the right to a jury trial.[16]

Similarly, in 1823 Chief Justice Isaac Parker of Massachusetts also upheld the 1793 law but limited his analysis to "a single point, whether the statute of the United States giving power to seize a slave without a warrant is constitutional."[17] Parker upheld this warrantless seizure because "slaves are not parties to the constitution, and the [Fourth] [A]mendment has [no] [sic] relation the parties." Parker noted, without any citation or actual reference to the Constitution that "[t]he [C]onstitution does not prescribe the mode of reclaiming a slave, but leaves it to be determined by Congress."[18] Thus, despite the story of Justice Harrington in Vermont, there were no mass revolts against the law by northern judges.

The northern states did, however, pass a number of laws to provide procedural protections for people claimed as fugitive slaves. In the 1820s Maine, New Jersey, New York, and Pennsylvania passed laws to protect the personal liberty of their black residents. Known as "personal liberty laws," these Acts were designed to protect free blacks from kidnapping, while at the same time providing some mechanism for the state to comply with the federal obligation to return fugitive slaves to their owners.[19] In order to prevent fraud, kidnapping, and the wrongful seizure of free blacks, these laws required a stronger evidentiary basis for the removal of a black from a free state to a slave state than did the federal law of 1793. The 1793 law allowed a master to seize a fugitive slave and bring that slave before any state or federal judge, who would then issue a certificate of removal for the black. The federal law had a very lax standard for determining if the person seized was indeed a fugitive slave, requiring only proof "either by oral testimony or affidavit taken before and certified by a magistrate" in the state where the claimant resided that the claimant actually owned a slave as described in the affidavit or testimony.[20] Under the federal law, anyone willing to commit perjury might easily kidnap a free black by giving false oral testimony claiming the person was a fugitive slave.

The personal liberty laws were aimed at preventing such frauds. Typical of these laws was Pennsylvania's Act of 1826, which required that anyone removing a black person from the state must first obtain a warrant from a Pennsylvania judge, who would then direct the sheriff to arrest the alleged fugitive. In order to obtain the warrant, the claimant had to prove a prima facie ownership through "oath, or affirmation" while also producing "the affidavit of the claimant of the fugitive, taken before and certified by a justice of the peace or other magistrate authorized to administer oaths in the state or territory in which such claimant shall reside, and accompanied by the certificate of the authority of such justice or other magistrate to administer oaths, signed by the clerk or prothonotary, and authenticated by the seal of a court of record, in such state or territory, which affidavit shall state the said claimant's title to the service of such fugitive, and also the name, age, and description of the person of such fugitive."[21]

Once this was done, the sheriff could arrest the alleged fugitive and bring him or her back to the judge for a hearing on whether to issue a certificate of removal. The law allowed for removal of the fugitive "upon proof to the satisfaction of such judge" that the person arrested was a fugitive slave owned by the claimant.

However, at this stage the statute provided that "the oath of the owner or owners, or other person interested, shall in no case be received in evidence before the judge on the hearing of the case."[22] Thus, the claimant needed some proof of ownership, such as a bill of sale, eyewitness testimony from a disinterested third party, or some sort of certified record from a lower court.

These standards required far more evidence than the federal law. They were also more likely to lead to adverse results for a claimant. The state judges had the power to actually consider evidence before sending a black back to the South. The 1826 law also provided that state judges who refused to hear fugitive slave cases could be fined. Thus, unlike the "duty" provision of the federal law, the Pennsylvania law actually backed up the "duty" requirement with an enforcement mechanism. Northerners saw these laws as good faith attempts to balance the needs of the free states to prevent kidnapping with the rights of slave owners under the Constitution.

Only after reviewing the status of an alleged fugitive slave under the state law, could a Pennsylvania judge or magistrate comply with the "duty" imposed by the federal law. The juxtaposition of these two laws shows that while Pennsylvania recognized it had a "duty" to enforce the federal law, it would only do so under its own rules. This condition clearly had the potential to wreak havoc on national law enforcement by setting the stage for each state to create its own rules for implementing a federal law. It is hard to imagine a more chaotic scheme for law enforcement. Moreover, southern claimants would have found such a system intolerable. How could they hope to vindicate a right, created by the Constitution and enforced by a federal statute, if they could not be certain that courts would uniformly interpret and apply the law? How could a master know what the rules would be in each state? Against this background the Court decided *Prigg v. Pennsylvania*.

### *PRIGG V. PENNSYLVANIA* AND THE DEVELOPMENT OF THE DOCTRINE OF UNFUNDED MANDATES

In 1837, Edward Prigg, Nathan Bemis, and two other Marylanders traveled to York County, Pennsylvania, where they obtained a warrant from a Pennsylvania justice of the peace to arrest Margaret Morgan and her family. Prigg and his associates asserted that Morgan was a fugitive slave owned by Margaret Ashmore, who was Bemis's mother-in-law. Mrs. Ashmore was the widow of a small farmer named John Ashmore who had lived in Harford County, Maryland. John Ashmore had owned Margaret Morgan's parents (whose names are unknown), but shortly after the War of 1812 he allowed them to live as free people. Margaret was raised in this environment and always considered herself to be free. Sometime in the mid-1820s Margaret married a free black man from Pennsylvania named Jerry Morgan. The Morgans lived in Harford County, Maryland, where the 1830 census recorded them and their two children as "free black" persons.[23] Clearly, the county sheriff, who took the federal census, believed Margaret and her children were free. In 1832 the Morgans moved to Pennsylvania and in 1837 Margaret Ashmore sent Nathan S. Bemis, her son-in-law, to bring Margaret back to Maryland as a fugitive slave. Bemis brought three neighbors to help him, including Edward Prigg.

The four Marylanders seized Margaret and her family under a warrant issued by Justice of the Peace Thomas Henderson. But, when the Morgans were brought before Henderson he refused to give Bemis and Prigg the authority to remove them from the state. Acting under the state law, rather than the federal law, Henderson concluded that the Morgans were not slaves. Jerry Morgan was clearly a free black born in Pennsylvania and one or two of their children had been born in Pennsylvania and were thus born free under Pennsylvania law. Margaret's parents were once slaves but she had never been considered a slave. Justice of the Peace Henderson clearly thought she was free.

Henderson released the Morgans. Bemis and his cohorts politely offered to take them back to their home but once in their wagon they forcibly restrained Margaret and her children—but not the free-born Jerry—and took them to Maryland. The four Marylanders were indicted for kidnapping and after two years of negotiations between the governors of the two states, Maryland agreed to allow only one of the indicted men, Edward Prigg, to be extradited to Pennsylvania for prosecution. The agreement between the two governors provided that if Prigg was convicted he would not be incarcerated until the U.S. Supreme Court heard his appeal. As expected, a jury in York County convicted Prigg for violating the 1826 Act, and the Pennsylvania Supreme Court quickly upheld the conviction without an opinion. In 1842 the case went to the Supreme Court.[24]

Speaking for an eight-to-one majority, Justice Joseph Story overturned Edward Prigg's conviction for kidnapping Margaret Morgan and her children. In his opinion, Justice Story reached five major conclusions: (1) that the federal Fugitive Slave Law of 1793 was constitutional; (2) that no state could enforce any law that added additional requirements to the federal law or impeded the return of fugitive slaves; (3) that claimants (masters or their agents) had a constitutionally protected common law right of recaption, or "self-help," which allowed a claimant to seize any fugitive slave anywhere and bring that slave back to the South without complying with the provisions of the Fugitive Slave Law of 1793; (4) that a captured fugitive slave was entitled to only a summary proceeding to determine if he was the person described in the papers provided by the claimant; and (5) that state officials should, but could not be required to, enforce the Fugitive Slave Law.[25] In his opinion, Story wrote:

> We hold the [1793] Act to be clearly constitutional in all its leading provisions, and, indeed, with the exception of that part which confers authority upon state magistrates, to be free from reasonable doubt and difficulty upon the grounds already stated. As to the authority so conferred upon state magistrates, while a difference of opinion has existed, and may exist still on the point, in different states, whether state magistrates

are bound to act under it; none is entertained by this Court that state magistrates may, if they choose, exercise that authority, unless prohibited by state legislation.[26]

Story, in fact, suggested that Congress did not have the power, under the Constitution, to require state officials to enforce the fugitive slave law, noting:

> The states cannot, therefore, be compelled to enforce them; and it might well be deemed an unconstitutional exercise of the power of interpretation, to insist that the states are bound to provide means to carry into effect the duties of the national government, nowhere delegated or intrusted to them by the Constitution. On the contrary, the natural, if not the necessary conclusion is, that the national government, in the absence of all positive provisions to the contrary, is bound, through its own proper departments, legislative, judicial, or executive, as the case may require, to carry into effect all the rights and duties imposed upon it by the Constitution. The remark of Mr. Madison, in the *Federalist* (No. 43) would seem in such cases to apply with peculiar force. "A right (says he) implies a remedy; and where else would the remedy be deposited, than where it is deposited by the Constitution?" meaning, as the context shows, in the government of the United States.[27]

Thus, in 1842, in a case dealing with slavery, the Supreme Court for the first time addressed the constitutionality of "conscripting" state officials. Story's opinion is perhaps less clear than one would have liked, and perhaps even less clear than one might find in a modern case. He does not exactly tell us if Congress can *force* a state official to act; rather, consistent with nineteenth century respect for federalism, he allows that the States might prevent officials from acting. Nevertheless, despite its antique ring, the opinion in *Prigg* comes down against what today we call unfunded mandates. Despite his professed commitment to "originalism" and history, Justice Scalia did not cite *Prigg* to bolster his contention that the law at issue in *Printz* was unconstitutional, even though he could have mustered the intellectual support of Justice Story. Perhaps Justice Scalia did not do so because he would have been citing a case that otherwise supported slavery and was indeed, next to *Dred Scott*, the most important judicial support for slavery in our constitutional jurisprudence.

## THE EFFECT OF *PRIGG* ON THE FEDERAL-STATE BALANCE

*Prigg*, and the issue of fugitive slaves in general, illustrates one of the major problems of "conscripting" state officials: a state official is elected or appointed to enforce state laws and state policy. State policy may be at odds with federal policy. Thus, the conscripted state official might be forced to choose between his oath to the state and the mandates of the federal government. Furthermore, state officials are the servants of a local or statewide electorate. State and local sentiments may be at odds with national policy. Thus, compelling state officials to enforce national policy can be counterproductive. The political reality of enforcement could lead to a destruction of the very policy that the national government is seeking to implement. If state officials are forced to implement a policy that they oppose, then they will do a poor job; they may undermine the federal policy by their lack of serious enforcement. The image of Judge Harrington is real. In the years after *Prigg* a number of northern judges simply refused to enforce the Fugitive Slave Law of 1793, even though under *Prigg* they were legally free to do so, and in Story's eyes had a constitutional or even moral obligation to do so.[28] Southern masters complained (even before *Prigg*) that northern officials were unhelpful in returning fugitive slaves. This problem was finally solved by the Fugitive Slave Law of 1850,[29] which federalized enforcement of the Fugitive Slave Clause of the U.S. Constitution. In passing this statute, Congress understood that conscripting state officials to do the work of the federal government was a bad idea because, as experience had shown, it may not work. Thus, Congress thought it better to simply have the federal government enforce its own laws, or to pay (rather than conscript) state officials to be part of the enforcement process.

In his opinion, Story suggested that states could, if they chose, refuse to allow their officials to enforce the federal law. A number of states followed Story's "hint"—if that is what it can be called—and prohibited their judges from hearing cases under the Federal Fugitive Slave Law of 1793.[30] In 1851 Story's son, William Wetmore Story, claimed that his father intended his decision in *Prigg* to undermine the enforcement of the Fugitive Slave Law of 1793. According to William Wetmore Story, Justice Story "repeatedly and earnestly spoke" of his *Prigg* opinion as a "triumph of freedom."[31] The evidence for this is weak. Indeed, except for his son's published statements *after* Story's death, there is no evidence at all that the justice ever took this position. He did not make this claim in any of his private letters and no other friend, ally, or colleague of the Justice ever supported it. The very fact that William Wetmore Story's statement was made after his father's death, seems suspicious. Unlike his father, the younger Story was a committed opponent of slavery, and he seems to have wanted to paint his father in the best light. Indeed, it would have been entirely out of character, and completely inconsistent with his entire life's work, for Justice Story to have secretly attempted to undermine the authority of the national government or the U.S. Constitution.[32] In reality, Justice Story's goal in *Prigg* was not to weaken slavery, but to strengthen federal power. By removing state judges from the process, Story in effect forced Congress to assume a more aggressive role in the return of fugitive slaves. Story's own actions illustrate this.

In 1842, shortly before the decision in *Prigg* was announced, Story sent a private letter to Senator John Macpherson Berrien of North Carolina, urging a recodification of all federal criminal law and the extension of the common law to all federal admiralty jurisdiction. This was consistent with his lifelong attempts to expand federal powers and federal jurisdiction in criminal and civil matters.[33] It also comports with his opinion in *Swift v. Tyson*,[34] delivered the same month as *Prigg*.

Shortly after the Court decided *Prigg*, Story again wrote to Senator Berrien about various legislative matters. The letter began with a discussion of their collaboration on legislation involving federal criminal law and bankruptcy. This evidence suggests the close relationship Story had with the slaveholding North Carolina senator, and thus makes his next suggestion even more important. Story began to discuss the draft bill on federal jurisdiction that he had sent to Berrien. He reminded Berrien that in that draft legislation he had suggested

> that *in all cases*, where by the Laws of the U[nited] States, powers were conferred on State Magistrates, the same powers might be exercised by Commissioners appointed by the Circuit Courts. I was induced to make the provision thus general, because State Magistrates now generally refuse to act, & cannot be compelled to act; and the Act of 1793 respecting fugitive slaves confers the power on State Magistrates to act in delivering up Slaves. You saw in the case of Prigg . . . how the duty was evaded, or declined. In conversing with several of my Brethren on the Supreme Court, we all thought that it would be a great improvement, & would tend much to facilitate the recapture of Slaves, if Commissioners of the Circuit Court were clothed with like powers.[35]

Essentially, Story presented Senator Berrien with the solution to the debate over federal exclusivity and the role of the States in enforcing the Fugitive Slave Law of 1793. Through the appointment of commissioners, the federal government would supply the enforcement mechanism so that enforcement would be uniform throughout the nation. The fundamental problem with this idea was how to enact it in a Congress where Northerners, who were at least somewhat opposed to slavery, controlled the House of Representatives. Story, the Justice, had the answer for Berrien, the politician:

> This might be done without creating the slightest sensation in Congress, if the provision were made general. . . . It would then pass without observation. The Courts would appoint commissioners in every county, & thus meet the practical difficulty now presented by the refusal of State Magistrates. It might be unwise to provoke debate to insert a Special clause in this first section, referring to the fugitive Slave Act of 1793. Suppose you add at the end of the first section: "& shall & may exercise all the powers, that any State judge, Magistrate, or Justice of the Peace may exercise under any other Law or Laws of the United States."[36]

This was not the letter of a man hoping that *Prigg* would be transformed into a "triumph of freedom." This was the letter of a Justice committed to the return of fugitive slaves and to the aggrandizement of federal power. Here he could have both. In effect, Story was arguing that the national government, not the states, should be in the business of enforcing federal law.

In 1850 Congress followed the outlines of this strategy when it passed the Fugitive Slave Law of 1850. That law created United States commissioners in every county, whose powers included hearing and deciding fugitive slave cases. Many of these commissioners were local lawyers, and some were even state officeholders or state judicial officials. For example, in Boston one of the commissioners was a probate judge.[37]

In the 1850 law Congress did what it did not do in the Brady Act. In the 1850 law Congress provided its own enforcement mechanisms for its own laws. The 1850 law is correctly seen as a draconian, punitive, and unfair statute that denied alleged slaves the most basic procedural protections. Its enforcement mechanism, however, was remarkably rational and respectful of federalism. Through the creation of local commissioners, Congress provided for federal enforcement of a federal law. This made for more efficient and predictable enforcement than what had existed under the 1793 law, when claimants had, for the most part, to rely on local law judges and magistrates who were often opposed to the law. By allowing for the appointment of local officials as commissioners, Congress provided a mechanism for taking advantage of local expertise and manpower, but yet at the same time did not dragoon local officials into acting against their own interests and own political and law enforcement needs. One need not endorse the substance of the 1850 law—which was truly an affront to justice and fairness—to appreciate the value of its enforcement apparatus.

## CONCLUSION

As we face the prospect of additional demands that the states enforce federal antiterrorism or immigration laws, there are lessons from *Prigg*, *Printz*, and the Fugitive Slave Law of 1850 that we can learn.

First, it is clear that local officials may not always support federal law or wish to enforce it. Sheriff Jay Printz did not want to enforce the Brady Bill. It ran counter to his own political views and presumably to the desires of the constituency he served. Many of the people who elected him, and who paid him with their taxes, opposed the law. Printz did not want to be the servant of the national government in regulating firearms ownership. Had he been required to enforce it, Printz would have done so grudgingly, and perhaps not done a very good job. Similarly, many northern judges were loath to become complicit in returning fugitive slaves to their owners. Many states adamantly resisted a federal law that seemed to facilitate kidnapping. Ultimately, however, it mattered little whether the claimant seized a bona fide fugitive slave, or was attempting to legally kidnap a free person, or had seized someone, like Margaret Morgan, whose status was truly in doubt. Whatever the substantive issue, Northerners in general were unlikely to want to aid in the return of fugitive slaves.

Likewise, we can certainly imagine under present circumstances that at least some state and local law enforcement officers will be reluctant to assist in implementing a federal law against people in their community who may be remotely connected to terrorists—or utterly unconnected to terrorism. In the Detroit area for example, local law enforcement officials were unwilling to interrogate large numbers of their constituents, merely because those constituents were Muslims or of Arab or Middle Eastern backgrounds.[38] Efficient law enforcement may not be possible if the national government has to rely on state officials. Because of differentials in training, sophistication, and experience, it is also possible that local law enforcement will do an inadequate job of enforcing federal law, even when the local leadership supports the law.

Second, it also seems obvious that if the national government cannot rely on the states, it must expand its own enforcement machinery. In his dissent in *Printz*, Justice John Paul Stevens noted:

> Perversely, the majority's rule seems more likely to damage than to preserve the safeguards against tyranny provided by the existence of vital state governments. By limiting the ability of the Federal Government to enlist state officials in the implementation of its programs, the Court creates incentives for the National Government to aggrandize itself. In the name of State's rights, the majority would have the Federal Government create vast national bureaucracies to implement its policies. This is exactly the sort of thing that the early Federalists promised would not occur, in part as a result of the National Government's ability to rely on the magistracy of the States.[39]

In a footnote to the paragraph, Stevens notes:

> The Court raises the specter that the National Government seeks the authority "to impress into its service...the police officers of the 50 States." But it is difficult to see how state sovereignty and individual liberty are more seriously threatened by federal reliance on state police officers to fulfill this minimal request than by the aggrandizement of a national police force. The Court's alarmist hypothetical is no more persuasive than the likelihood that Congress would actually enact any such program.[40]

This is exactly what happened with the Fugitive Slave Law of 1850. Federal enforcement made the law more efficient, although it never worked well.[41] We can imagine that this would also happen with laws like the one at issue in *Printz*, assuming Congress ever passes such a law, or with the USA PATRIOT Act.

But it is not at all clear that Justice Stevens is correct in his implication that federal enforcement will be a greater threat to civil liberties than state enforcement. Police corruption scandals in Los Angeles, Chicago, New York City, Philadelphia, and many other places suggest one danger of local law enforcement. The failure of local or state law enforcement to implement state and federal civil rights laws in the deep South was notorious until very recently. The violations of civil rights by police in New York City, Los Angeles, and elsewhere further underscore the misplaced faith Justice Stevens may have in local enforcement.

The historical example of the situation during World War I also illustrates this point. During World War I local authorities were often far more repressive than the national government.[42] The willingness of states to oppress religious and ethnic minorities[43] is well-known. Furthermore, the training of local law enforcement is often less rigorous and less successful than the training of federal officers. Anyone who has traveled through airports has realized that the federally trained and monitored security staffs at most airports are generally far more polite, efficient, and competent than the security personnel were before the system was federalized. Moreover, the implementation of policies and rules is far more consistent and predictable under federalized airport security than it was when security was under local control. The federalization of airport security is perhaps similar to the model Congress created in the Fugitive Slave Law of 1850. The Fugitive Slave Law of 1850 of course did not protect the civil liberties of alleged fugitive slaves or their allies. On the contrary, it was one of the most draconian laws ever passed by Congress. It was passed to implement a proslavery Constitution,[44] and the law reflected the pre-Civil War Constitution. At least two states tried to limit the reach of the law, although with little success.[45]

The purpose of looking at the Fugitive Slave Law of 1850 is emphatically *not* to use its substantive procedures as a model for modern legislation. Rather, it is to illustrate two points about federal law enforcement and federalism.

First, if Congress chooses to implement a law enforcement policy, the only sure way to make that policy work is for the national government to fund and direct that implementation. Northerners resisted complying with the Fugitive Slave Law of 1793 because they hated it and thought it was immoral and wrong. Furthermore, they hated the policies behind it. In 1864, responding to a changed political atmosphere—and the secession of eleven slave states—Congress would repeal both the 1793 and 1850 Fugitive Slave Laws. A year later a constitutional amendment would radically change the policies behind the Fugitive Slave Laws.[46] But, in the meantime, if Congress wanted to enforce the Fugitive Slave Clause of the Constitution, it had to do it with a federal enforcement apparatus. The same thing is true with the Brady handgun bill. The response to local resistance cannot be to *force* local sheriffs to implement the law; rather it is to use federal money and statutes to create a mechanism for implementation. My point here is not to praise the fugitive slave laws as models of civil liberties. Rather, the point is to show that the history of this law illustrates the problem of expecting the states to implement federal law.

The second point is that local law enforcement in the end cannot work to achieve the policy goals Congress desires. The Fugitive Slave Law of 1793 did not work because free state officials simply would not implement it. Thus under the proslavery Constitution, in a government dominated by slaveholders and their northern "doughface"[47] allies, Congress passed the law to implement the Constitution's Fugitive Slave Clause.[48] Similarly, the nation cannot rely on local sheriffs to implement the Brady Handgun bill or expect that local law enforcement officials would necessarily be in sympathy with the government's dragnet approach to investigations after the September 11 attack on the nation.

The lesson of the Fugitive Slave Law of 1793 and Story's decision in *Prigg* is that instead of conscripting state officials like Printz, Congress might simply create some modern equivalent of the commissioners or other law enforcement officials who would be able to implement federal policy. This would have the advantage of involving local people in federal investigations and enforcement, but only because they were hired or volunteered, rather than being conscripted. At the same time, these local people would be subject to federal rules and federal standards.

Finally, federal enforcement is by its nature limited. The nation is too big, and the enforcement field too vast, for the federal government to simply sweep across the nation. The kind of petty bullying that local law enforcement can easily do is less likely under a federalized regime. There are of course problems with federal law enforcement. The FBI (The Federal Bureau of Investigation), DEA (Drug Enforcement Administration), ATF (The Bureau of Alcohol, Tobacco, Firearms and Explosives), INS (Immigration and Naturalization Service), IRS (Internal Revenue Service), and a host of other agencies have sometimes been heavy-handed in their approach to law enforcement. Although the FBI is unlikely to be run by another J. Edgar Hoover, there is no reason to believe that law enforcement abuses will never be a problem in the future. However, it is somewhat easier to monitor the actions of the federal government than it is to monitor the actions of the states. The national media can more easily focus on abuses by federal officials than those committed by state and local officials.

Moreover, as the example of the Fugitive Slave Law suggests, if the States are not part of the federal law enforcement process, they can sometimes protect their own citizens from arbitrary federal power. Similarly, if States violate the civil rights of individuals, then the federal government can become the watchdog. In the age of "homeland security" it is not unthinkable that a state will step over the line of constitutional propriety, and that the federal courts might intervene to protect basic liberty, or the FBI and Justice Department might also investigate violations of constitutional rights. But, again, as the fugitive slave experience shows, if the states become *part* of the federal law enforcement, then the States cannot monitor the federal government. Conversely, the federal government could not monitor the States. Indeed, the genius—if we can call it that—of American federalism is that in times of crisis the States can be a check on the national government and the national government can also be a check on the States. But, if the States become a mere adjunct of the federal government, then there will be no checking possibilities, and the potential for the violation of rights will be that much greater.

## Notes

1. *Uniting and Strengthening America by Providing Appropriate Tools Required to Intercept and Obstruct Terrorism Act of 2001*, Public Law No. 107-156, *U.S. Statutes at Large* 115 (2001): 272 (hereinafter "USA PATRIOT Act").

2. *Printz v. United States*, 521 U.S. 898 (1997).

3. *Brady Handgun Violence Prevention Act*, Public Law No. 103-159, *U.S. Statutes at Large* 107 (1993): 1536 (codified as amended in scattered sections of 18 U.S.C.) (hereinafter "Brady Act").

4. *Printz v. United States*, 925.

5. Ibid., 957 (J. Stevens, dissenting).

6. *Prigg v. Pennsylvania*, 41 U.S. 539 (1842).

7. *Act of February 12, 1793*, 2d Cong., ch. 7, *U.S. Statutes at Large* 1 (1783): 302 (law setting out procedures for the return of fugitive slaves).

8. For a discussion of the constitutional history of slavery, see Paul Finkelman, "Teaching Slavery in American Constitutional Law," *Akron Law Review* 34 (2000): 261–282, and Paul Finkelman, *Slavery and the Founders: Race and Liberty in the Age of Jefferson*, 2d ed. (Armonk, NY: M. E. Sharpe, 2001) (hereinafter as "*Slavery and the Founders*"). On the use of slavery by the Court, see Paul Finkelman, *Dred Scott v. Sandford: A Brief History with Documents* (Boston, MA: Bedford Books, 1997), 5–6.

9. *Planned Parenthood of Southeastern Pennsylvania v. Casey*, 505 U.S. 833, 984 (1992) (J. Scalia, concurring in part, dissenting in part); *Dred Scott v. Sandford*, 60 U.S. 393 (1857).

10. *McKleskey v. Kemp*, 481 U.S. 279, 343–344 (1987).

11. *Plessy v. Ferguson*, 163 U.S. 537, 559 (1896).

12. *Printz v. United States*, 906–907.

13. *Prigg v. Pennsylvania*.

14. *Act of February 12, 1793*, ch. 7, sec. 3, *U.S. Statutes at Large* 1 (1793): 302–305 (respecting fugitives from justice, and persons escaping from the service of their masters).

15. Samuel E. Sewell, "Harrington's Decision," *The Liberator*, January 6, 1843, 1.

16. *Wright v. Deacon*, 5 Serg. & Rawle 62 (Pa. 1819).

17. *Commonwealth v. Griffith*, 19 Mass. 11, 18 (1823).

18. Ibid., 19.

19. For a general history of these laws, see Thomas D. Morris, *Free Men All: The Personal Liberty Laws of the North, 1780–1861* (Baltimore, MD: Johns Hopkins University Press, 1974) (hereinafter as "*Free Men All*").

20. *Act of February 12, 1793*, 2d Cong., ch. 7, *U.S. Statutes at Large* 1 (1793): 303–305.

21. *Act of March 25, 1826*, ch. 50, 1826 Pa. Laws 150 (giving effect to the provisions of the Constitution of the United States relative to fugitives from labor, for the protection of free people of color, and to prevent kidnapping), quoted in *Prigg v. Pennsylvania*, 41 U.S. 539 (1842), quoted in sec. IV.

22. Ibid., sec. VI.

23. U.S. Census Bureau, 1830 Census: Manuscript Census for Harford County, Maryland, 394.

24. For a discussion of these facts, see Paul Finkelman, "Story Telling on the Supreme Court: *Prigg v. Pennsylvania* and Justice Joseph Story's Judicial Nationalism" (hereinafter as "Story Telling on the Supreme Court"). *Supreme Court Review 1994* (1995): 247–294; and Paul Finkelman, "Sorting Out *Prigg v. Pennsylvania*," *Rutgers Law Journal* 24 (1993): 605–666.

25. *Prigg v. Pennsylvania*, 41 U.S. 539, 536-542 (1842). For a fuller discussion of Story's opinion, see Finkelman, "Story Telling on the Supreme Court."

26. Ibid., 622.

27. Ibid., 615–616. This was not an example of the Court holding a federal law unconstitutional, because the law did not *require* that state officials act, and the Court did not hold that state officials had no power to act.

28. For a discussion of judges who refused to enforce the law, see Paul Finkelman, "*Prigg v. Pennsylvania* and Northern State Courts: Anti-Slavery Use of a Pro-Slavery Decision," C*ivil War History* 25 (1979) 5–35 (hereinafter as "*Prigg v. Pennsylvania* and Northern State Courts").

29. *Act Respecting Fugitives from Justice, and Persons Escaping from the Service of Their Masters*, 31st Cong., ch 60, *U.S. Statutes at Large* 9 (1850): 462 (hereinafter "Fugitive Slave Act").

30. *Act of March 24, 1843, to Further Protect Personal Liberty*, 1843 Mass. Acts 33; *Act for the Protection of Personal Liberty*, 1844 Conn. Pub. Acts; *Act for the Protection of Personal Liberty*, 1843 Vt. Acts & Resolves; *Act for the Further Protection of Personal Liberty*, 1846 N.H. Laws; *Act to Prevent Kidnapping, Preserve the Public Peace, Prohibit the Exercise of Certain Powers Heretofore Exercised by Judges, Justice of the Peace, Aldermen and Jailors in This Commonwealth, and to Repeal Certain Slave Laws*, 1847 Pa. Laws 206-208. See generally Morris, *Free Men All*; Finkelman "*Prigg v. Pennsylvania* and Northern State Courts."

31. William Wetmore Story, ed., *Life and Letters of Joseph Story, Associate Justice of the Supreme Court of the United States, and Dane Professor of Law at Harvard University* (Boston, MA: Charles C. Little and James Brown, 1851), 2: 392 (hereinafter as "*Life and Letters of Story*").

32. See Finkelman, "Story Telling on the Supreme Court," 282–294.

33. *Life and Letters of Story*, 402–403 (letter from Joseph Story to Senator John Macpherson Berrien (February 8, 1842)); and Finkelman, "Story Telling on the Supreme Court," 282–294.

34. *Swift v. Tyson*, 41 U.S. 1 (1842).

35. James McClellan, *Joseph Story and the American Constitution: A Study in Political and Legal Thought* (Norman, OK: University of Oklahoma Press, 1971), 262 n.94 (letter from Joseph Story to Senator John Macpherson Berrien (April 29, 1842)) (citing John Macpherson Berrien Papers, Southern Historical Collection, University of North Carolina).

36. Ibid., 262–263 n.94.

37. Paul Finkelman, "Legal Ethics and Fugitive Slaves: The Anthony Burns Case, Judge Loring, and Abolitionist Attorneys," *Cardozo Law Review* 17 (1996): 1793, 1810.

38. See, for e.g., Fox Butterfield, "Police Force Rebuffs F.B.I. on Querying Mideast Men," A Nation Challenged: The Interviews, *New York Times*, November 21, 2001 (final edition) B7; Jodi Wilgoren, "University of Michigan Won't Cooperate in Federal Canvass," *New York Times*, December 1, 2001 (final edition).

39. *Printz v. United States*, 959 (J. Stevens, dissenting).

40. Ibid., 959 n.21 (citation omitted).

41. In the eleven years that the Act was in force, fewer than 375 fugitive slaves were returned to the South. Stanley W. Campbell, *The Slave Catchers: Enforcement of the Fugitive Slave Law, 1850–1860* (Chapel Hill, NC: University of North Carolina Press, 1968), 199–207 tbls. Based on fugitives reported in the 1850 census, at least 10,000 slaves escaped in that period, and probably another 10 to 20,000 fugitives were already living in the North. Thus, the law did little to actually facilitate the return of runaway slaves.

42. See Paul L. Murphy, *World War I and the Origin of Civil Liberties in the United States* (New York: Norton, 1979).

43. See *Meyer v. Nebraska*, 262 U.S. 390 (1923), which vindicated the rights of Americans to teach foreign languages to their children in the face of xenophobic laws in

Nebraska and elsewhere that were designed to prohibit immigrants, especially German-speaking immigrants, from teaching their native languages to their children. For more on this case see Paul Finkelman, "German Victims and American Oppressors: The Cultural Background and Legacy of *Meyer v. Nebraska*," in *Law and the Great Plains: Essays on the Legal History of the Heartland*, ed., John Wunder (Westport, CT: Greenwood Press, 1996), 33. For a full history of this persecution throughout the nation, see also William G. Ross, *Forging New Freedoms: Nativism, Education, and the Constitution*, 1917–1927 (Lincoln, NE: University of Nebraska Press, 1994). A similar sort of persecution was directed at Jehovah's Witnesses. For Supreme Court cases dealing with this problem, see *Cantwell v. Connecticut*, 310 U.S. 296 (1940); *Minersville School District v. Gobitis et al.*, 310 U.S. 586 (1940); *West Virginia State Board of Education v. Barnette*, 319 U.S. 624 (1943). For a good summary of this persecution of Jehovah's Witnesses see, Renee C. Redman, "Jehovah's Witnesses," in *Religion and American Law: An Encyclopedia*, ed., Paul Finkelman (New York: Garland Publishers, 2000), 245–253; and Paul Finkelman, "The Flag Salute Cases," in *Religion and American Law: An Encyclopedia*, 186–190.

44.  See Finkelman, *Slavery and the Founders*, 3–36.

45.  Wisconsin challenged the law by approving a writ of habeas corpus to release the abolitionist Sherman Booth who had helped a slave escape the custody of U.S. Marshal Stephen Ableman. The Supreme Court rejected this attempt by Wisconsin to interfere with the law in *Ableman v. Booth*, 62 U.S. 506 (1859). For a complete history of this case see H. Robert Baker, *The Rescue of Joshua Glover: A Fugitive Slave, the Constitution, and the Coming of the Civil War* (Athens, OH: Ohio University Press, 2007). Ohio flirted with going down this road after the Oberlin-Wellington Rescue, but the Ohio Supreme Court, by a one-vote majority, refused to issue a writ of habeas corpus directed against a federal marshal. See *Ex parte Bushnell, Ex parte Langston*, 9 Ohio St. 77 (1859).

46.  U.S. Constitution, amend. 13.

47.  "Doughface" was a term of derision for proslavery Northerners or Northerners who worked closely with Southerners. The term evolved because it was said that these Northern politicians had faces of "dough," which the Southerners could shape any way they wanted. Classic doughfaces included the last three antebellum presidents, Millard Fillmore, Franklin Pierce, and James Buchanan. Fillmore signed the 1850 fugitive slave bill into law while Pierce and Buchanan vigorously enforced it.

48.  U.S. Constitution, Art. IV, sec. 2, par. 3.

# The Security Constitution

**Jason Mazzone**

The war on terrorism, begun following the attacks on American cities on September 11, 2001, is fought at home and abroad. Abroad, the nation's military—regulars, Reserves, and National Guardsmen—do the fighting. At home, the soldiers in the war are the personnel of state—and especially local—government. Police, firefighters, city transport officials, public health officers, and other state and local employees are the men and women who guard the tunnels and bridges, monitor ports and harbors, protect transportation systems, secure public events, test for radiation and biological agents, and prepare responses to potential attacks. They are also the first responders should an attack occur.

Securing the homeland is not cheap. The U.S. Conference of Mayors estimates that in the fifteen months after September 11, cities spent $2.6 billion on increased homeland security costs.[1] According to another estimate, each time the Department of Homeland Security raises the national terror alert level from yellow (elevated threat) to orange (high threat), the enhanced security measures implemented nationwide amount to as much as $1 billion per week.[2] Operation Atlas, New York City's counterterrorism program, costs $5 million per week, much of which represents overtime for police and other city personnel.[3]

In our federal system of government, who is responsible for homeland security? Though it deploys some federal personnel (like FBI agents) for domestic security, the executive branch relies largely on state and local officials for the necessary manpower. Although Congress has made available to states and cities billions of dollars in funding for overtime and equipment, it has not assumed responsibility for covering all of the security costs incurred locally.[4] Mayors and governors complain about the unfairness of asking them to shoulder the burden of preventing terrorist attacks that would affect the entire nation, pointing to the inherent risk of refusing states and cities the resources they require. Vulnerable locales also object to funding allocations that fail to adhere strictly to actual security needs. Meanwhile, the residents of states and cities less vulnerable to attack have expressed reluctance to contribute to the high costs of necessary security efforts in places like New York City and Washington, DC, and have insisted on receiving a share of any national funding.

Ratified in an age of insecurity, the Constitution, in a largely forgotten clause of Article IV, Section 4, which I call for ease of reference the Protection Clause, provides clear guidance on the issue of responsibility for homeland security. Article IV, Section 4, states in full: "The United States shall guarantee to every State in this Union a Republican Form of Government, and shall protect each of them against Invasion; and on Application of the Legislature, or of the Executive (when the Legislature cannot be convened) against domestic Violence." In addition to guaranteeing republican government within the states, the provision requires the national government to *protect* the states from invasion and domestic violence.

This Protection Clause was a central component of the 1789 Constitution. The Clause reflects the ratifying generation's understanding of, and response to, the very problem the war on terrorism presents today: Security represents a collective-action dilemma because each state is reluctant to contribute to the costs of defending other states although the cost of an attack is not geographically confined. The ratifying generation understood that without a constitutional mechanism to overcome this dilemma, vulnerable states and cities would not receive adequate defense, leaving the whole nation at risk. Governors and mayors therefore stand on strong constitutional ground when they argue today that the national government should bear the burdens of homeland security—either by providing the necessary security itself or by paying for security measures implemented locally. The Protection Clause once maintained a prominent role in guiding federal efforts in fortifying coastal towns, securing the frontiers, and responding to invasions and domestic insurrections. Examining how the Protection Clause governed early conceptions of national security—as well as early implementation of security efforts—unlocks a constitution designed expressly to address many of the logistical concerns now raised by the war on terrorism. In clause after clause, the Constitution represents a blueprint for safeguarding states and their cities. At its core, the document is a security constitution.

In fulfilling its security obligations under the Protection Clause, the national government may enlist the assistance of state and local personnel so long as Congress pays the costs of their efforts. In the past, those personnel were militiamen who, under the Constitution's several Militia Clauses, could be (and often were) relied on by the federal government for security purposes. The Supreme Court's anti-commandeering doctrine, based on the Tenth Amendment, should not limit the national government's ability to deploy for counterterrorism work modern state and local security personnel like law enforcement. Indeed, the Constitution specifically provides for—and encourages—this type of commandeering as a way to protect citizens from the alternative of the national military taking over towns and cities. In sum, the national government is obligated to protect states and their cities in the war on terrorism, but in doing so it may delegate (with payment) the work to state and local personnel.

The first part of this chapter examines the ratifying generation's experience with the problem of homeland security and the origin of the Protection Clause as a response to the collective-action barriers to securing vulnerable states and cities. The second part turns to the mechanisms available to the national government to protect the states: by deploying national personnel and by delegating the work to state and local personnel. The third part traces the early history of Congress in fulfilling its protection mandate. The final part applies the Protection Clause to the war on terrorism and the modern issue of homeland security.

## THE PROTECTION CLAUSE

### Invasions and Insurrections

With more than two centuries of national government behind us, it is easy to forget that in the early years following the Revolutionary War, it was far from certain that the American experiment in independence would ultimately succeed. Eighteenth-century America was a precarious setting. Although they had defeated the British, Americans remained preoccupied with the notion that there were forces conspiring against their freedom. One threat was foreign invasion (a notion that included attacks from Indians). The proximity of British and Spanish settlements was a constant source of unease. Alexander Hamilton was not paranoid when he cautioned his fellow Americans against having "an excess of confidence or security," and against becoming "too sanguine in considering ourselves as entirely out of the reach of danger."[5] "On one side of us, and stretching far into our rear," Hamilton warned, "are growing settlements subject to the dominion of Britain." "On the other side, and extending to meet the British settlements, are colonies and establishments subject to the dominion of Spain," while "[t]he [Indian tribes] on our Western frontier . . . [are] our natural enemies."[6] Wars in other parts of the world, particularly Europe, might also spill over onto the American continent—"[P]eace or war," Hamilton admonished, "will not always be left to our option."[7]

In addition to external attacks, violence might erupt from within. Sleeper cells might seem a new evil, but eighteenth-century Americans took for granted that foreign sympathizers were living among them, biding their time for the right moment to strike or to stir up trouble. "Nova Scotia and New Brunswick," Francis Dana warned the Massachusetts Convention considering the proposed Constitution in 1788, "filled with tories and refugees, stand ready to attack and devour these states, one by one."[8] Representative Harrison Gray Otis of Massachusetts had this same mindset when he warned Congress how "an army of soldiers would not be so dangerous to the country, as an army of spies and incendiaries scattered through the Continent."[9] Foreign spies were not the only problem at home: Economic instability represented a constant source of internal disruption, with debtor revolts and other protests common occurrences. Disputes over trade and territory raised the threat of war between the new states.[10]

### Security as a Collective-Action Dilemma

The ratifying generation understood that in a federal system of government, providing the right level of domestic security is a persistent problem. Left to their own devices, states are often unable or unwilling to deal sufficiently with sources of insecurity. Consider this scenario: State A is invaded or violence erupts there. Unable to deal with the problem itself, State A asks its neighbor, State B, for assistance. B will have an interest in helping A, but only to the extent that B itself is likely to suffer the effects of ongoing instability in A. States C, D, and E, farther away from A, will have less incentive to act. States F, G, and H, the states most remote and thus least affected by A's troubles, will pay little or no attention and certainly will not waste time or money to help out A. Conversely, if the effects of violence in State A are felt mostly in neighboring State B (for example, because insurgents conduct raids across the border), A is unlikely to deal with the problem sufficiently to secure B. Neither A nor B will do much if the effects are felt in C. And so on. Put simply, if the contribution to security reflects only what each state perceives to be in its own interest, the overall level of security is likely to be below what is needed to ensure ongoing stability in every state.

Likewise, in a federal system, decisions by the national government represent the collective preferences of the individual states. The collective-action dilemma is thereby replicated, because just as states are unlikely to send help to each other to ensure the optimal level of security, representatives of states in Congress are unlikely to vote in favor of national security measures that do not benefit their own constituents. As Alexander Hamilton stated at the New York ratifying convention: "While danger is distant, its impression is weak; and while it affects only our neighbors, we have few motives to provide against it."[11] This is true even though the sources and effects of insecurity rarely are confined neatly to a single state. Foreign invasions and domestic insurrections easily spill across geographical borders or otherwise end up affecting the nation as a whole. Accordingly, states often have an ultimate interest in the security of their neighbors beyond the level at which they are willing to contribute resources. Security represents, in modern terminology, a dilemma of collective action: No state wants to contribute fully to the collective effort even though each state is likely to be worse off as a result, and every state would be better off if each were to contribute its share.

When the Philadelphia Convention got under way in the summer of 1787, with delegate Edmund Randolph enumerating the defects in the Articles of Confederation and presenting the Virginia Plan, he therefore began not with the structures of government or with individual rights, but with the problem of maintaining security. Accordingly, Randolph's wish list for what the new government should accomplish also put security at the very top.[12]

Similarly, at the state ratifying conventions, the need for a coercive central authority to overcome the states' reluctance to contribute voluntarily to collective security efforts was a constant refrain. Alexander Hamilton and Robert Livingston pressed this theme at the New York Convention, focusing on how during the Revolutionary War New York had suffered from the inadequate contributions of other states.[13] In Connecticut, Oliver Ellsworth called for "[a] more energetic system" because "[t]he present is merely advisory. It has no coercive power," and given the experience of the Revolutionary War in which "[a] few states bore the burden, . . . a power in the general government to enforce the decrees of the Union is absolutely necessary."[14] In North Carolina, William Davie cautioned that "we cannot obtain any effectual protection from the present Confederation," calling it "universally acknowledged" that this was among the "greatest defects" of the Articles.[15] In Massachusetts, Francis Dana observed how "[t]he state oppressed must exert its whole power, and bear the whole charge of the defence; but common danger points out for common exertion; and this Constitution is excellently designed to make the danger equal. Why should one state expend its blood and treasure for the whole? Ought not a controlling authority to exist, to call forth, if necessary, the whole force and wealth of all the states?" [16]

*The Federalist* also explains at length the collective-action dilemma (although the essays do not use that term) underlying security. In *The Federalist No. 4*, John Jay writes how the states lack sufficient incentives to assist each other in times of war or insurrection even though it is unwise for them to refuse aid:

> Leave America divided into thirteen, or if you please into three or four independent Governments, what armies could they raise and pay, what fleets could they ever hope to have? If one was attacked would the other[s] fly to its succour, and spend their blood and money in its defence? Would there be no danger of their being flattered into neutrality by specious promises, or seduced by a too great fondness for peace to decline hazarding their tranquillity and present safety for the sake of neighbours, of whom perhaps they have been jealous, and whose importance they are content to see diminished? Altho' such conduct would not be wise it would nevertheless be natural.[17]

Moreover, Jay argued, even if states prove willing to come to the aid of another state under attack, they likely will be unable to mount a sufficient response because the states lack the means of, and experience with, military coordination.[18]

In *The Federalist No. 23*, Hamilton explains why only a strong national government with responsibility for defense can overcome the collective-action dilemma of states contributing security resources. Unlike the states, the national government will "make suitable provisions for the public defence" because it is the "center of information" and so "will best understand the extent and urgency of the dangers that threaten." The national government is the "representative of the whole," and so "will feel itself most deeply interested in the preservation of every part—which, from the responsibility implied in the duty assigned to it, will be most sensibly impressed with the necessity of proper exertions. . . . " Further, the national government, "by the extension of its authority throughout the States," is uniquely able to "establish uniformity and concert in the plans and measures by which the common safety is to be secured."[19]

In *The Federalist No. 25*, Hamilton delves further into the problem of relying on states to secure the Union, focusing on the ways in which differences and inequalities among the states undermine their contributions to collective defense. Making an argument that resonates with modern mayoral complaints about security funding in the war on terrorism, Hamilton observes how, in the absence of national coordination, individual states that are more vulnerable to attack will be forced to contribute disproportionately to defense, and how this unwisely leaves national security in the hands of a few states. Though the British and Spanish territories and the Indian lands "incircle the Union from Maine to Georgia," so that in one sense "[t]he danger is . . . common," and "the means of guarding against it ought in like manner to be the objects of common councils and of a common treasury," not all states require the same specific protections from these threats. "It happens that some States, from local situation, are more directly exposed. New York is of this class."[20] Similarly, in *The Federalist No. 41*, James Madison writes of the particular vulnerabilities of New York:

> If we except perhaps Virginia and Maryland, which are peculiarly vulnerable on their eastern frontiers, no part of the Union ought to feel more anxiety . . . than New-York. Her sea coast is extensive. The very important district of the state is an island. The state itself is penetrated by a large navigable river for more than fifty leagues. The great emporium of its commerce, the great reservoir of its wealth, lies every moment at the mercy of events, and may almost be regarded as a hostage, for ignominious compliances with the dictates of a foreign enemy, or even with the rapacious demands of pirates and barbarians.[21]

It is all there: the unique vulnerability of New York because of its coastline, the precariousness of Manhattan, and the temptation this commercial center represents to foreign enemies. The words could have been written yesterday.

Still, what exactly prevents vulnerable states like New York from putting in place sufficient security measures to defend themselves (and protect their wealth)? Madison explains that it is not that vulnerable states simply are lax, but that security is too difficult and expensive for one state to provide: "[I]f their single resources were equal to the task of fortifying themselves against the danger, the object to be protected would be almost consumed by the means of protecting them."[22]

Moreover, Hamilton cautions, other states should not *want* to leave vulnerable states to muster sufficient defenses to protect themselves from attack. Because attacks cannot easily be confined to a single state or region, "[t]he security of all would ... be subjected to the parsimony, improvidence or inability of a part."[23] Leaving the states to defend their own borders is therefore as unfair as it is unwise: "New-York would have to sustain the whole weight of the establishments requisite to her immediate safety, and to the mediate or ultimate protection of her neighbours. This would neither be equitable as it respected New-York, nor safe as it respected the other States."[24]

Hamilton also warns of a further consequence of asking a state like New York to create its own adequate defense apparatus: "If the resources of such part becoming more abundant and extensive, its provisions should be proportionally enlarged, the other States would quickly take the alarm at seeing the whole military force of the Union in the hands of two or three of its members; and those probably amongst the most powerful."[25] As if a New York War Department is not worrisome enough, consider, Hamilton suggests, the arms race that might result. "[M]ilitary establishments, nourished by mutual jealousy, would be apt to swell beyond their natural or proper size; and being at the separate disposal of the members, they would be engines for the abridgment, or demolition of the national authority."[26] In other words, ask New York to defend itself, and it may soon run the whole country. At the end of the day, depending on states to furnish security resources is, according to Hamilton, "[a] project oppressive to some States, dangerous to all, and baneful to the confederacy."[27]

## The Protection Solution

The Protection Clause of Article IV was the ratifying generation's solution to the problem of security. The Clause overcomes the barriers to collective action by taking the responsibility for security away from individual states and assigning it to the national government. Just as other collective-action dilemmas can be resolved by a coercive, coordinating force, so too is security accomplished when the national government takes charge. Moreover, by *requiring* the national government to provide security, the Protection Clause ensures that the dilemma of collective action is not simply replicated in the chambers of Congress. The national government is both empowered and obligated to protect the states.

While the impetus for constitutional provisions may often be hard to reconstruct, one event ensured that the Constitution would include a requirement that the national government protect the states. Shays' Rebellion, the farmer revolts that broke out in western Massachusetts in January 1787, made clear—if anyone had doubted it before—that the national government must have a security mandate. The events of the rebellion are well-known.[28] To pay off its debts, the state of Massachusetts levied high taxes in the period of economic hardship and currency shortages following the Revolutionary War, ignoring pleas for relief from farmers who feared foreclosure. Protests that began as town meetings and petitioning transformed into farmers blocking county courts in the fall of 1786 to prevent foreclosure proceedings. Despite deep concern over these events in Massachusetts, Congress lacked the authority under the Articles of Confederation (and as a practical matter lacked the manpower) to meet the governor's request for assistance. After violence escalated at the end of the year, a militia force assembled in the eastern part of the state and—financed by wealthy Boston creditors—moved westward to quell the riots. On January 25, 1787, before the eastern militia arrived, Daniel Shays, an officer in the Continental Army, led 1,500 men to seize the federal arsenal at Springfield. There, Shays and his men confronted a local militia force under the command of Major General William Shepard. Fearing that his troops might support their farmer neighbors, Shepard opened fire. Several of the insurgents were killed. The remainder fled—some to Vermont and New York, where despite requests to those states to turn them over, they continued periodic raids across the border. Shays and the other leaders of the revolts were sentenced to death (but later pardoned). Ultimately, the Massachusetts legislature caved, suspending taxes and exempting clothing, farm tools, and other household items from debt collection.

Though Massachusetts put down the farmer insurrections, the events of Shays' Rebellion heralded the risk of future disorder. Under the Articles of Confederation, the national government seemed powerless to guarantee security. Even assuming that Congress had the funds or the manpower (which it did not) to take action, nothing in the Articles provided explicit authority to Congress to intervene to quell a rebellion within a state (and Article II reserved to the states "every power, jurisdiction, and right" not "expressly delegated" to Congress). Though Article III bound the states "into a firm league of friendship with each other, for their common defence," by which they pledged to "assist each other, against all force offered to, or attacks made upon them, or any of them," this did not amount to much. Even assuming that the pledge extended to domestic revolt rather than just foreign attacks, there was no mechanism to enforce the requirement—in particular, there was no way to summon troops from other states to help. A pledge was just that. Moreover, states could not necessarily maintain security themselves. For one, a state dependent on militia forces might be rendered powerless. The sympathy that the farmers' plight evoked in the general population meant that the Massachusetts government could not fully rely on its own militia—particularly units within the western part of the state—to put down the revolts. And under the Sixth Article of Confederation, states (including Massachusetts) lacked their own large, professional armies.

Shays' Rebellion was very much on the minds of the delegates to the Philadelphia Convention in the summer of 1787. James Madison, in his April 1787 pamphlet, "Vices of the Political System of the United States," identified as vice number six the "want of Guaranty to the States of their Constitutions & laws against internal violence" and the problem that because "[t]he confederation is silent on this point... the hands of the federal authority are tied." Writing to Edmund Randolph that same month, Madison emphasized the need in the plan for a new government for "[a]n article... expressly [guaranteeing] the tranquility of the States [against] internal as well as external dangers," because "unless the Union be organized efficiently & on Republican Principles, innovations of a much more objectionable form may be [intruded]."[29]

At the convention on May 29, 1787, Randolph cited among the defects of the Articles that "the confederation produced no security against foreign invasion" and that "the federal government could not check the quarrels between states, nor a rebellion in any, not having constitutional power nor means to interpose according to the exigency."[30] Section 11 of Randolph's Virginia Plan therefore proposed: "a Republican Government [and] the territory of each State, except in the instance of a voluntary junction of Government [and] territory, ought to be guaranteed by the United States to each State."[31] When the convention delegates took up consideration of the proposal, on James Wilson's suggestion they changed it to read: "A Republican form of [Government] shall be guarantied to each State [and] that each State shall be protected [against] foreign [and] domestic violence."[32] Following some additional editing, including a clause inserted by the Committee of Detail for a state's application to trigger the national government's obligation to intervene to stop domestic violence,[33] the provision was sent in its now familiar form to the states for ratification as Section 4 of Article IV of the Constitution.[34]

### The Meaning of Protection

Focusing solely on the text for a moment, a few things can be said about the Protection Clause of Article IV, Section 4. There are two threats that the national government must protect the states from: invasion and domestic violence. The Clause treats the two differently. The national government's duty to protect a state from domestic violence is triggered when the state legislature (or governor if the legislature cannot convene) applies for protection. The national government's duty to protect the states from invasion exists without any further triggering action or event.

The use of "shall" in Article IV bears particular emphasis. In contrast to Congress's permissible Article I powers—powers that Congress may choose whether or not to exercise—the Protection Clause *requires* the national government to protect the states from invasion and domestic violence. Shall means must: Section 4 creates obligations. Viewed in the context of the Constitution as a whole, the reason for obligating the national government to protect the states is evident. Because preceding provisions of the Constitution disable the states from acting in their own defense, Article IV assigns the national government responsibility for securing the country.

In order to better understand the context of Article IV, consider what the first three Articles of the Constitution take away from the states. First, treaties: States cannot guard against attack by entering into treaties or military alliances with each other or with foreign nations or aggressors. Article I prohibits the states from "enter[ing] into any Treaty, Alliance, or Confederation" or from "enter[ing] into any Agreement or Compact with another State, or with a foreign Power." Article II gives the sole power to make treaties to the President, with the concurrence of two-thirds of the Senate. California cannot, therefore, send economic aid to Pyongyang in exchange for a promise that any missiles fired from North Korea will land in Arizona and Nevada. New York cannot prevent future terrorist attacks on Manhattan by allowing Al Qaeda to operate training camps in the Catskills. The Midwestern states cannot create their own mutual-defense treaty.

Second, waging war: Article I gives Congress the power to tax and spend for the common defense, to declare war, to raise and support armies, and to maintain a navy. Article II makes the President Commander in Chief. Article I denies the states a general power to maintain their own military forces and to wage war. States cannot, therefore, launch preemptive attacks, and they lack the means to do so in any event.

Third, the regulation of foreigners: One way to prevent attacks is to prevent the entry and movement of would-be attackers. But the states are disabled from regulating the entry of foreigners from abroad because the Constitution assigns the power exclusively to Congress.[35]

Fourth, trade: Because commercial disputes threaten war, a state might wish to favor commercial interests from powerful nations. However, the Constitution prohibits such efforts. Article I gives Congress authority to "regulate Commerce with foreign Nations," and it disallows states from imposing tariffs on imports or exports without Congress's consent.

In sum, because the states are not miniature sovereign nations with their own defensive capacities and full powers to deal with foreign states and their citizens, the national government must assume responsibility for protecting the states from attack. The meaning of the Protection Clause is clear. It obliges the national government to protect the states from invasions by external foes and from insurrections from within.

It is also no accident that Section 4 of Article IV contains both the requirement that the United States guarantee republican government within the states and protect the states—and that the two are linked by "and" rather than "or." These two obligations are closely related; security and republican government stand in Section 4 as constitutional bookends. While this is not the occasion for a full account of the elements of republican government, in very general terms it can be understood to mean self-rule: government by the people. Article IV, Section 4, containing both the Republican Guarantee Clause and the Protection Clause, implies that government based on self-rule is impossible to achieve and sustain without security. Conversely, security—protecting the states from attack—is a hollow achievement if its price is the loss of republican government itself. Section 4 therefore imposes dual obligations of republican government and security. Neither may be set aside to achieve the other.

## The Security Constitution

The Protection Clause is an important element of a constitution concerned as much with security as it is with governmental structures and individual rights. In clause after clause, the Constitution is a blueprint for domestic security. According to the Preamble, among the goals of "We the People" in "establish[ing] this Constitution" are to "insure domestic Tranquility, [and] provide for the common defence." Only then, the Preamble says, can we seek to "promote the general Welfare, and secure the Blessings of Liberty to ourselves and our Posterity."

Security also features prominently in the organization of the three branches of government under Articles I, II, and III of the Constitution. The opening clause of Article I, Section 8, empowers Congress "[t]o lay and collect Taxes, Duties, Imposts and Excises, to pay the Debts and provide for the common Defence . . . of the United States." Of the other seventeen clauses enumerating congressional powers in Section 8, by my count ten relate closely to security,[36] and an eleventh congressional power—to suspend habeas corpus in times of insecurity—can be inferred from Section 9.[37] Article I, as we have seen, also prohibits the states from exercising key security-related powers. Yet the Constitution does not make the states irrelevant to security. Under Article I, a state can fight back—"engage in war"—without waiting for federal authorization or a federal response if the state is "actually invaded" or in "imminent danger." The states determine when the national government will respond in cases of insurrection: the national obligation to protect the states from domestic insurrection is triggered by "Application" of the legislature (or governor). As the discussion in the next part of this chapter makes clear, the security provisions of the Constitution also take for granted the availability of state militiamen.

The first of the President's Article II powers is also for security. The President is "Commander in Chief of the Army and Navy of the United States, and of the Militia of the several States, when called into the actual Service of the United States. . . . " The second Article II power is to "make Treaties" with the concurrence of two-thirds of the Senate. Though courts are not often thought of as military actors, the security theme of the Constitution continues in one section of Article III: Section 3 contains the Constitution's single specification of a substantive criminal offense—treason.

Article IV, in addition to imposing the dual requirements that the national government protect and guarantee republican government to the states, contains three other security-related provisions. These are the Extradition Clause, the Fugitive Slave Clause, and a provision preserving state geography. Each seeks to harmonize relationships among the states by heading off three likely sources of war: harboring fugitives, harboring slaves, and altering state borders.

Over and over in the Constitution, security is thus taken up specifically or is never far from mind. Our modern characterization of the Constitution as one of government structures and individual rights pays insufficient attention to the Constitution as a document designed to prevent and respond to war and rebellion.

The Protection Clause, rather than a peripheral provision that deserves to be forgotten, in an important sense is the Constitution's key.

## OF ARMIES AND MILITIA

From this understanding of the purposes of and the reasons for the Constitution's Protection Clause, the discussion moves to practicalities. Requiring the United States to protect the states is all well and good, but the national government needs the right tools and sufficient resources to carry out the mandate. This part examines how the Constitution anticipates the national government will go about protecting the states and the reasons for the Constitution's particular design. As it turns out, the national government either can do the work of securing the states itself by sending in federal personnel, or it can pay the states, including by hiring their personnel, to carry out the task. Of these two options, the Constitution prefers (if a constitution can be said to have preferences) the second, because state personnel are more likely to respect and safeguard individual liberties. All of this is contained in the provisions of Articles I and II of the Constitution—provisions closely related to the Protection Clause of Article IV—that concern national employment of the principal state personnel of the eighteenth-century: the militia. The final section of this chapter will take up the issues of translating the Constitution from the age of the militia to today's war on terrorism, and the ways in which the early history of national security under the Protection Clause informs and resolves the problems of contemporary homeland security. For now, however, the task is to get straight the original story of how the national government is to provide security on the ground.

### Deployment and Employment

How does the federal government fulfill its obligation to protect the states? Here, too, the Constitution provides a clear answer. There are two mechanisms. The first is by the use of federal military personnel in accordance with the Article I authorization to Congress "[t]o raise and support Armies" and "[t]o provide and maintain a Navy," and the designation in Article II of the President as the "Commander in Chief of the Army and Navy of the United States. . . . " The second mechanism is by employing the militia of the states. Article I authorizes Congress to "provide for calling forth the Militia to execute the Laws of the Union, suppress Insurrections and repel Invasions," and Article II makes the President "Commander in Chief . . . of the Militia of the several States, when called into the actual Service of the United States." Therefore, though Article IV obligates the United States to provide protection, on the ground the actual work of providing security is split. The national government can deploy federal personnel or it can employ state personnel.

The Constitution envisages that the national government often will wish, and indeed will be required, to rely on state militia to respond to security threats. For that to happen, the militia must be trained and equipped properly. Hence, Congress has additional powers under Article I to "provide for organizing, arming, and disciplining, the Militia, and for governing such Part of them as may be employed in the Service of the United States," while "reserving to the States . . . the Appointment of the Officers, and the Authority of training the Militia according to the discipline prescribed by Congress." Although Congress is not required to outfit and organize the militia, as a practical matter it will need to do so if it wants to call forth an effective fighting force. Properly organized, armed, and disciplined, the militia can be employed and delegated by the national government, under the command of the President, to carry out the mandate of the Protection Clause.

## Security and Liberty

Military authority is normally thought to be indivisible. Consider, then, what the Constitution imagines in allowing the national government to fulfill its security obligation by employing militiamen in place of deploying federal personnel. Citizens of a state will be part of the state militia units. At certain times, the national government will call up those units, and they will serve under the authority of the President for the cause of national security. The militia will answer to the President as Commander in Chief, but the states will continue to train the militia and appoint their officers, albeit in a manner consistent with a plan the national government has devised.

An ingenious military strategy? Hardly. It is not difficult to see the potential problems in this scheme: state militiamen required during certain periods to obey federal officers, states conferring promotions on militiamen who might be deemed unworthy by the Commander in Chief, and militia units poorly trained to carry out the functions that the national government requires of them.

The division in the Constitution of the security function between a national military force and the militia, over which authority is further split, represented a compromise. Though it was clear to almost everyone in the period after the Revolutionary War that past security arrangements were inadequate, centralizing security presented its own problems. Chief among these to the ratifying generation was the threat nationalized security powers pose to liberty. For Americans of the 1780s, who knew all about abuses by Redcoats, the particular incarnation of the threat was the standing national army: professional soldiers, under the command of a national government, interfering with the rights of the people in the name of maintaining law and order. In contrast to the militia—members of the local community, operating under local control—security powers in the hands of a national government and its professional soldiers risked tyranny.

As a check, therefore, on the need for the federal government to create and maintain a large standing army, the Constitution authorizes the national government to call into periods of federal service the militia of the states, under the President's command. In meeting its constitutional mandate to protect the states from invasions and domestic violence, the national government can deploy the state militia—rather than resort to national troops. Militia troops from one state can be summoned to deal with security problems at home or to march into another state to deal with problems there. (Because militia units comprised ordinary citizens, even when deployed to other states under national command, the thinking went, the militia would never become an instrument of oppression.) The remainder of the time, states are free to use their militia for their own purposes. To ensure a dependable and effective force, the Constitution also authorizes Congress to decide how best to organize, arm, and train militia units, and to set the rules for governing militiamen in the service of the United States under the Commander in Chief. Overall, security is assured and freedom is protected.

## THE PROTECTION TRADITION

From the earliest days of the Republic, the national government took seriously its constitutional duty to protect the states. Congress and the Executive developed a strong protection tradition—putting in place the mechanisms for responding to threatened invasions and insurrections, fortifying coastal towns, and defending the frontiers.

In fulfilling its constitutional obligation, the national government depended frequently on the state militia. Militiamen were the nation's very first "first responders" to invasions and insurrections. However, while the militia existed as an alternative to the use of federal personnel for security purposes, the militia's availability did not alter the national government's underlying protection obligation. In particular, employing the militia was not a way for the national government to save the expenses that would be required to deploy national troops. Because the obligation of providing protection belonged to the national government, if it elected to rely upon the state militia to carry out security functions, Congress was responsible for the costs involved. Within a few months of its inception, Congress passed legislation to pay militiamen for their federal service. Thereafter, whenever the national government employed state militiamen for security, Congress footed the bill. To be sure, there were squabbles at times about how much militiamen were worth and which incidental expenses should be covered, but it was universally understood that the state militia did not work for the United States government for free. To be "employed in the Service of the United States,"[38] meant exactly that. The United States had to pay for services rendered.

The First Congress opened for business on March 4, 1789. In August 1789 Congress established the War Department, with an initial operating budget of $137,000.[39] The following month, Congress continued in service 700 troops raised by the Continental Congress and authorized the President to call into service such part of the militia as he judged necessary for "the purpose of protecting the inhabitants of . . . the United States from the hostile incursions of the Indians."[40] Congress knew that time was money: If called into service to protect against incursions, militiamen received the very same "pay and subsistence" as the federal troops.[41]

On May 2, 1792, Congress enacted the first general authorization for federal use of the militia, entitled "An act to provide for calling forth the Militia to execute the laws of the Union, suppress insurrections and repel invasions."[42] The Act authorized the President, in times of "imminent danger of invasion," "to call forth such number of the militia of the state or states most convenient to the place of danger or scene of action, as he may judge necessary to repel such invasion."[43] In the event of an insurrection, the Act authorized the President, upon application by the affected state, "to call forth such number of militia of any other state or states, as may be applied for, or as he may judge sufficient to suppress such insurrection."[44] The Act also authorized the President to deploy militiamen "whenever the laws of the United States shall be opposed, or the execution thereof obstructed, in any state, by combinations too powerful to be suppressed by the ordinary course of judicial proceedings, or by the powers vested in the [federal] marshals."[45] Before any federal deployment of the militia, the President was required to issue an order directing insurgents to disperse.[46] Federal service was limited to periods of three months per year, with militiamen paid at the same rate as regular troops.[47]

On May 8, 1792, Congress also passed "[a]n Act more effectually to provide for the National Defence by establishing an Uniform Militia throughout the United States."[48] This statute implemented Congress's powers to "provide for organizing, arming, and disciplining, the Militia."[49] For more than a century, this was the only federal statute under which the militia was organized. The Act enrolled every "free able-bodied white male citizen" between the ages of eighteen and forty-five in the militia company "within whose bounds such citizen shall reside."[50] The Act required militiamen to equip themselves with muskets, bayonets, and other gear.[51] Because the requirement that militiamen furnish their own arms and equipment proved impractical, Congress soon enacted programs for lending out arms, purchasing and reselling arms to the states for the use of their militiamen, and eventually equipped the militia itself.[52] The federal government, as we have seen, is not limited to using the militia. A series of early statutes therefore also provided for raising and deploying regular soldiers for security purposes.[53]

These statutes provided the framework through which the early national government carried out its constitutional duty to protect the states. Thus, in a massive show of force, the national government called into federal service 15,000 militiamen to quell the violence that broke out in western Pennsylvania in the early 1790s in opposition to the federal excise tax on distilled whiskey.[54] The national government's efficient response to the Whiskey Rebellion dramatically contrasted with the paralysis of the federal government during Shays' Rebellion just a few years earlier. So, too, the national government promptly dispatched militia forces to deal with the insurgency led by John Fries in southeastern Pennsylvania in the spring of 1799 in opposition to federal property taxes.[55] In addition to responding to security problems when they arose, the national government put in place specific preventive measures, including a massive program begun by Congress in 1794 to fortify the ports and harbors of coastal towns.[56]

In all of this, states at times complained that the early national government was not doing enough to protect them.[57] But, as confirmed by the constitutional text, the early statutes, and governing practices, it was universally understood that protection ultimately was the national government's obligation. The next part turns to some implications for homeland security in the war on terrorism.

## HOMELAND SECURITY AND THE WAR ON TERRORISM

The rediscovery of the national government's constitutional mandate to protect the states, and the mechanisms available to fulfill that mandate, has important implications for the war on terrorism. Securing the homeland is not a new problem: The nation's earliest security needs presented similar difficulties of coordination and similar federalism concerns as those that have arisen in the war on terrorism. The history of how the Protection Clause governed early conceptions of national security, and the early implementation of security efforts, informs and resolves analogous problems of homeland security today. The discussion begins with the most obvious implication: The Protection Clause requires the national government to protect states and their cities from terrorism either by putting in place the necessary security measures or by paying for security programs implemented locally. Next, it suggests that in the war on terrorism the national government is entitled to enlist police and other state and local security personnel to carry out counterterrorism programs so long as Congress pays for their services. The discussion then turns to whether states properly may refuse to comply with federal requests to carry out security programs.

### Protection and Terrorism

The 2004 report of the 9/11 Commission concludes that the United States was ill-prepared to defend itself against the terrorist attacks of September 11, 2001.[58] The Constitution did not leave such preparations to chance. Created in an age of war and instability by a people fresh from revolution, the Constitution at its core is about security. The ratifying generation thus put in place constitutional arrangements that, rather than act as a blueprint for governments free from threats, were designed for governing when threats abound. Today, like Americans of the late eighteenth century, we fear internal strikes launched by forces already within our borders. We worry about the secret aspirations of "aliens" among us, and we fear their connections to "enemies" abroad. We want the government to protect us, but we worry too about enhancing governmental authority in ways that might affect our own freedoms. To be sure, there are some important differences between the past and the present. The musket-wielding mobs and gunships off the coastline that concerned eighteenth-century Americans were different threats than the fuel-laden jets flown into skyscrapers or the lethal pathogens released in the subway that we worry about today. Moreover, few people nowadays imagine that the nation's very existence is in peril, a concern that was very real to Americans in the years immediately after the Revolutionary War. Yet in an important sense, the threat of terrorism opens a window into the late eighteenth century and the world of the generation that created the Constitution. In particular, the Americans who included in their Constitution (as plain as words could make it) the requirement that the United States government protect each of the states from attack, would surely recognize the terrible destruction of September 11 as the national government's failure and responsibility.

Rediscovering the Protection Clause, and how it resolved the nation's earliest security problems, leaves no room to doubt that the duty to secure states and their cities from acts of terrorism falls on the national government. The Protection Clause requires Congress to provide the means of defending each of the states and for the Executive to carry out the mandate. The national government can meet its protection obligations by putting in place the necessary counterterrorism measures itself, or by reimbursing the states for the costs of their security programs. As a practical matter, the best approach likely will be some combination of the two—an approach that brings together the specialized strengths of federal agencies and their ability to coordinate national responses with the particularized knowledge and experience of state actors within localized communities.

The Protection Clause requires Congress to pay for the security needs of the states. In the war on terrorism, Congress has treated homeland security funding programs as a form of general revenue spending rather than as fulfilling a constitutional obligation. Funds therefore have been spread around rather than concentrated where they are needed. Although Congress has followed many of the other recommendations of the 9/11 Commission, it has not fully adopted the Commission's strong recommendation to allocate homeland security funds solely on the basis of the security needs of individual states and cities.[59] With funds distributed not solely on the basis of actual security needs but in a way that ensures each state receives a share, Congress has reimbursed high-risk states and cities for only a portion of the costs of their counterterrorism programs.[60] Taking the Protection Clause seriously requires a new approach, one in which members of Congress understand homeland security as their duty to the states, and work to ensure that states receive assistance relative to the level of protection they require. Of course, there is room to debate what the needs of any particular state are, and this debate surely will be part of the process. However, identifying and meeting a state's needs requires recognizing first that homeland security, in contrast to virtually every other national governmental program, entails the performance of a constitutional obligation.

## The Commandeerer in Chief

The United States Supreme Court has ruled that under the Tenth Amendment to the Constitution, the federal government may not "commandeer" state legislatures or executive personnel to carry out federal programs. Under this doctrine, states cannot be forced to enact laws the federal government considers desirable or to provide the personnel and other resources to implement laws passed by Congress—in order to ensure it takes full responsibility for its choices and bears any resulting costs, the federal government has to carry out its own work.[61]

In the context of security, application of the anti-commandeering doctrine is misguided. As we have seen, the Constitution specifically authorizes the national government, in meeting its protection obligations, to commandeer state personnel, allowing militia to be called forth into federal service under the President's command for security purposes. Nothing about the Tenth Amendment suggests that, when it became part of the Constitution in 1791, it altered this power of the national government to call forth the militia to provide security. Even with the Tenth Amendment otherwise preventing commandeering, in the War on Terrorism, the federal government may commandeer state personnel for security work under the authority of the Commander in Chief.

Today, the states' security personnel are not militiamen, but principally are the members of local law enforcement—and the bulk of counterterrorism work will fall to them. Modern police forces are not equivalent to early militia units.[62] Yet the problems we face today of providing homeland security are analogous to those that were once resolved by federal deployment of state militiamen. If the Protection Clause is to resolve successfully the difficulties of coordinating security in the modern era, the national government should be entitled to deploy the states' modern security personnel for security purposes. In applying the Protection Clause, it makes sense to permit the federal government to delegate police officers to operate checkpoints at bridges and tunnels, patrol wharves and harbors, inspect cargo in trucks, test for noxious agents in subways, guard buildings and monuments, secure public events, and carry out all of the other tasks involved in securing the homeland from terrorism. Just as, notwithstanding the Tenth Amendment, the federal government regularly called forth the states' militiamen to provide security against invasions and insurrections, it should be allowed to enlist the states' police officers to prevent and respond to terrorism.

Beyond the application of the Constitution's Protection Clause, there are additional reasons to think differently about commandeering for security purposes. In the anti-commandeering cases, the Supreme Court has identified several federalism-related reasons for the doctrine. These include the burden to states and localities of having to carry out federal programs, and the interest citizens have in being able to identify—to hold accountable—the government actors behind a law or program. These concerns are less pressing in the context of the federal government commandeering local law enforcement for security purposes. With local law enforcement, several safeguards exist that are not necessarily present with respect to the general problem of commandeering the states. First, if commandeering is limited to local law enforcement for security purposes, the rest of the governmental apparatus of the states is free to pursue its own programs. Second, the requirement that Congress fund the national government's use of local law enforcement ensures that the national government will reflect upon and take proper account of the associated costs, and that the states and cities will not be stuck with the tab. Third, commandeering the part of the state apparatus made up of local law enforcement units contains some natural, built-in checks. Armed locals put under the command of the national government likely are better organized and better equipped to resist federal overreaching than are bureaucrats asked to implement more mundane federal regulatory programs. Security, therefore, highlights both a particular kind of dependence on local government, and the ways local government may uniquely safeguard the values of federalism.

When it comes to homeland security, a ban on commandeering is also likely bad for liberty. Allowing the federal government to commandeer state and local law enforcement and other personnel for security purposes can avoid the alternative of sending the national military into our towns and onto our streets. Given the choice between local militia units and professional soldiers, our predecessors always chose the militia. We should make an analogous choice and, in times of insecurity, opt for federal commandeering of state and local responders over the domestic deployment of military forces.

If the federal government chooses to rely on state and local personnel to do this security work, it must pay for their services. It is wrong, indeed constitutionally impermissible, for the national government to ask or expect police (and other employees of state and local government) to provide security against terrorism without covering the costs of their undertakings. There is room for negotiation and debate about how much those costs really are. The Protection Clause does not require Congress to write blank checks to the states—it would be unreasonable to expect payment without evidence supporting a state's claims. But these are details that can be worked out between the national government and the states. In the early years of the Republic, Congress and the War Department rapidly developed mechanisms to monitor expenses: advancing funds and preauthorizing spending, reviewing states' actual expenditures along the way, issuing warnings when they were excessive, requiring states seeking reimbursement to submit detailed evidence in support of their final costs, and conducting audits. Similar mechanisms are clearly within the competency of modern government. The starting point, though, must be understood. The security tab belongs to Congress. In providing states with homeland security funding, including paying for the work of local law enforcement, Congress is not doing the states any favors. It is fulfilling its constitutional obligation.

## State Resistance

Suppose that the national government wants to employ local law enforcement officers (or other state and local personnel) to carry out a security measure, but some of those officers refuse to assist. The scenario is not unimaginable. Local police might be too busy with other duties. They might think the work asked of them is too dangerous. Perhaps prior episodes in federal employ have been unpleasant or poorly compensated. Maybe local police disagree with or oppose what the federal government is seeking to accomplish or the means of going about it. Even if individuals are willing to comply with the federal government's request, the state or locality might refuse to have its employees used in a certain way (perhaps needing them at home or opposing a federal program).

Are such refusals proper? By placing so much emphasis on the role of the militia as a safeguard to liberties, the 1789 Constitution seems to take for granted that militiamen will, at some point when liberties are threatened, refuse to be called forth or refuse to do things asked of them, or that the states might refuse to lend their militia services. One conclusion is that this is exactly how it should be: Refusals of this nature serve to keep an overreaching national government in check, just as the Constitution intended, and the national government always has the alternative of sending in its own personnel (a factor that a reluctant militia or state will weigh in its own decision about whether to comply).

At the same time, it seems faithful to the Constitution's text and underlying values to recognize that the power of the militia—and of local law enforcement and other security personnel today—to refuse federal service is very limited. The Constitution allocates power to Congress to provide for calling forth the militia and puts militiamen under the authority of the President as Commander in Chief. There is no qualification, nothing requiring the states to agree with the deployment, no authorization for the states or their militia to decide whether and how Congress can exercise its calling-forth authority or to limit the President's command. Moreover, the militia's role in safeguarding liberties suggests only a limited right of refusal in the most serious of circumstances. Refusal is proper only when the request would entail oppression or abuse, the very things the militia units were meant to prevent.

Put differently, state and local personnel likely can refuse to comply with a federal request that exceeds the power of the federal government under the Constitution in the first place. One such scenario is when the request goes beyond using state or local personnel for the Article I purposes of repelling invasions, suppressing domestic insurrections, and dealing with opposition to federal laws. As a trivial example, state personnel, even if promised compensation, should be free to refuse to go to Washington for the purpose of raking leaves on the grounds of the White House. But if the call is for a purpose within the proper scope of the Constitution's authorization, then the states should comply.

A second scenario in which refusal seems proper is if the federal government asks the states and their personnel to do something that violates a protection of the Bill of Rights. If a federal program is unconstitutional on this basis, it surely makes sense that states can refuse a request to carry it out. In this regard, consider the role of local law enforcement in resisting federal overreaching in the war on terrorism. Out of concern with protecting liberties, local law enforcement in some places refused, at least initially, to carry out requests by the FBI to investigate members of their local communities. More than 400 local (and eight state) resolutions have also passed that include provisions opposing the PATRIOT Act and implementing local programs to protect individual rights.[63] This seems to be precisely what the Constitution anticipates in the federalism-based security apparatus it creates. Indeed, the point illustrates a broader theme. Though courts and commentators often talk about federalism's *division* of power between the nation and the states as the mechanism to protect constitutional interests, the national government's *dependency* on local personnel to carry out programs on the ground may be the best safeguard.[64]

## CONCLUSION

When it declared homeland security "too important for politics as usual to prevail,"[65] the 9/11 Commission was expressing an old idea. The Americans who ratified the federal Constitution understood that, in the system of government they had created, usual politics would leave some states with less security than they needed, and this would put the whole nation at risk. The Constitution's Protection Clause therefore takes the provision of security out of the ordinary operations of politics and imposes on the national government a constitutional duty to secure the states and their cities.

Alexander Hamilton was a New Yorker, but he was also an American. He knew that leaving his state to "sustain the whole weight" of protecting itself would not be "equitable as it respected New York," and in addition, that it would not be "safe as it respected the other States."[66] Hamilton would readily recognize today how a terrorist attack on Wall Street is also an attack on Main Street. Faced with a "danger [which] though in different degrees, is . . . common," Hamilton admonished, "the means of guarding against it ought in like manner to be the objects of common councils and of a common treasury."[67] The Security Constitution requires nothing less.

## Notes

1. Press Release, U.S. Conference of Mayors, "One Year Later: A Status Report on the Federal-Local Partnership on Homeland Security," September 9, 2002, http://www. usmayors.org/uscm/news/press_releases/documents/homelandstatus_090902.pdf.

2. Sara Kehaulani Goo, "Threat Level May Fall to Yellow," *Washington Post*, January 9, 2004 (final edition) (reporting the view of David Heyman (Center for Strategic and International Studies) that raising the alert status from yellow to orange entails $1 billion in additional security spending).

3. William K. Rashbaum, "Tougher Measures Appear to be Paying Off," *New York Times*, May 14, 2003 (final edition); see also Testimony of Raymond W. Kelly, Police Commissioner of the City of New York, *Eleventh Public Hearing of the National Comm'n on Terrorist Attacks upon the United States* 14, May 18–19, 2004, http://www.911commission.gov/hearings/hearing11/kelly_statement.pdf (reporting that New York City's annual counterterrorism costs are $200 million in personnel and overtime, and that necessary training and equipment cost an additional $261 million).

4. For fiscal year 2007, the Department of Homeland Security allocated nearly $1.7 billion under its Homeland Security Grant Program to states, territories, and urban areas to prepare for and respond to terrorist attacks and other disasters. Department of Homeland Security, FY 2007 Homeland Security Grant Program, http://www.dhs.gov/xlibrary/assets/grants_st-local_fy07.pdf

5. *The Federalist No. 24* (Alexander Hamilton) ed., Jacob E. Cooke (Hanover, NH: Wesleyan University Press, 1961), 155. All subsequent references to *The Federalist* are to the Cooke edition.

6. Ibid.

7. *The Federalist No. 34* (Alexander Hamilton), 12.

8. "Debates in the Convention of the Commonwealth of Massachusetts on the Adoption of the Federal Constitution," (January 18, 1788), in *The Debates in the Several State Conventions on the Adoption of the Federal Constitution*, ed., Jonathan Elliot, 2d ed. (Philadelphia, PA: J.B. Lippincott & Co., 1836), 2: 43 (hereinafter as *"Elliot's Debates"*).

9. *Annals of Congress 8 (1798):* 1961 (1798) (remarks of Rep. Otis), quoted in David B. Currie, *The Constitution in Congress: The Federalist Period, 1789–1801* (Chicago, IL: University of Chicago Press, 1997), 253 n.133.

10. See generally, David C. Hendrickson, *Peace Pact: The Lost World of the American Founding* (Lawrence, KS: University Press of Kansas, 2003).

11. Debates in the Convention of the State of New York (June 17, 1788), in *Elliot's Debates*, 2: 232.

12. See James Madison, *Notes of Debates in the Federal Convention of 1787*, ed., Adrienne Koch (Athens, OH: Ohio University Press, 1984) (1840), 29–30 (hereinafter as *"Notes of Debates"*).

13. Debates in the Convention of the State of New York (June 17, 1788), in *Elliot's Debates*, 2: 231–232, 2: 343–344, 2: 366.

14. Debates in the Convention of the State of Connecticut (January 4, 1788), in *Elliot's Debates*, 2: 186–190.

15. Debates in the Convention of the State of North Carolina (July 24, 1788), in *Elliot's Debates*, 4: 17.

16. Debates in the Convention of the Commonwealth of Massachusetts (January 18, 1788), in *Elliot's Debates*, 2: 42–43.

17. *The Federalist No. 4*, 21–22 (John Jay).

18. Ibid., 22.

19. *The Federalist No. 23*, 149, 150 (Alexander Hamilton).

20. *The Federalist No. 25*, 158 (Alexander Hamilton).

21. *The Federalist No. 41*, 275 (James Madison).

22. Ibid., 275–276.

23. *The Federalist No. 25*, 158–159 (Alexander Hamilton).

24. Ibid., 158.

25. Ibid., 159.

26. Ibid.

27. Ibid., 158.

28. A detailed account is found in Leonard L. Richards, *Shays's Rebellion: The American Revolution's Final Battle* (Philadelphia, PA: University of Pennsylvania Press, 2002).

29. Letter from James Madison to Edmund Randolph (April 8, 1787), in *The Papers of James Madison* (Robert A. Rutland et al. eds. Chicago, IL: University of Chicago Press, 1975): 9: 368, 9: 370–371.

30. Madison, *Notes of Debates*, 29.

31. Ibid., 32.

32. Ibid., 322.

33. Ibid., 395.

34. Ibid., 648.

35. To be accurate, Article I only gives Congress authority "[t]o establish an uniform Rule of Naturalization." In the early Republic, states monitored the arrival of foreigners in their ports. New York, for example, required masters of arriving ships to provide information on passengers and pay a tax on each of them, a measure aimed at deterring the indigent. In *New York v. Miln*, 36 U.S. 102 (1837), the Supreme Court upheld these requirements as an exercise of the state's police powers. In 1849 the Court retreated from this view, holding in *The Passenger Cases*, 48 U.S. 283 (1849), that state taxes on immigrants infringed Congress's exclusive Article I power to regulate commerce with foreign nations. In *Henderson v. Mayor of New York*, 92 U.S. 259 (1876), the Court extended the reasoning to invalidate all state laws regulating immigrants. The Court also held in *Chae Chan Ping v. United States*, 130 U.S. 581 (1889) (the Chinese Exclusion Case) that Congress as the national sovereign has exclusive power over the admission of foreigners.

36. The ten are: (1) "To regulate Commerce with foreign Nations, and among the several States, and with the Indian Tribes" (thereby preventing trade wars); (2) "To establish an uniform Rule of Naturalization"; (3) "To define and punish Piracies and Felonies committed on the high Seas, and Offences against the Law of Nations"; (4) "To declare War, grant letters of Marque and Reprisal, and make Rules concerning Captures on Land and Water"; (5) "To raise and support Armies"; (6) "To provide and maintain a Navy"; (7) "To make Rules for the Government and Regulation of the land and naval Forces"; (8) "[T]o exercise . . . Authority over all places purchased . . . for the Erection of Forts, Magazines, [and] Arsenals"; (9) the clauses empowering Congress "[t]o provide for calling forth the Militia"; and (10) "[to] provide for organizing, arming, and disciplining" them. An important limitation on Congress's army-financing power is that "no Appropriation of Money to that Use shall be for a longer Term than two Years. . . . " (U.S. Const. Art. I, sec. 8.)

37. This provision states: "The Privilege of the Writ of Habeas Corpus shall not be suspended, unless when in Cases of Rebellion or Invasion the public Safety may require it." See *Hamdi v. Rumsfeld*, 542 U.S. 507, 597–598 (2004) (discussing Congress's authority to suspend the writ).

38. U.S. Const. Art. I, sec. 8.

39. *Act of August 7, 1789*, 1st Cong., 1st sess., ch. 7, *U.S. Statutes at Large* 1 (1789): 49; *Act of September 29, 1789*, 1st Cong., 1st sess., ch. 23, *U.S. Statutes at Large* 1 (1789): 95.

40. *Act of September 29, 1789*, 1st Cong., 1st sess., ch. 25, secs. 1, 5, *U.S. Statutes at Large* 1 (1789): 95, 95–96.

41. Ibid., sec. 5, *U.S. Statutes at Large* 1 (1789): 96.

42. *Act of May 2, 1792*, 2d Cong., 1st sess., ch. 28, *U.S. Statutes at Large* 1 (1792): 264.

43. Ibid., sec. 1, *U.S. Statutes at Large* 1 (1792): 264.

44. Ibid.

45. Ibid., sec. 2, *U.S. Statutes at Large* 1 (1792): 264.

46. Ibid., sec. 3, *U.S. Statutes at Large* 1 (1792): 264.

47. Ibid., sec. 4, *U.S. Statutes at Large* 1 (1792): 264.

48. *Act of May 8, 1792*, 2d Cong., 1st sess., ch. 33, *U.S. Statutes at Large* 1 (1792): 271.

49. U.S. Const. Art. I, sec. 8.

50. *Act of May 8, 1792*, sec. 1, *U.S. Statutes at Large* 1 (1792): 271.

51. Ibid., sec. 1, *U.S. Statutes at Large* 1 (1792): 271.

52. *Act of May 28, 1798*, 5th Cong., 2d sess., ch. 47, sec. 11, *U.S. Statutes at Large* 1 (1798): 558, 560 (authorizing militia called into federal service to borrow arms and artillery from federal arsenals, with "proper receipts and security" and acceptance of responsibility for "the accidents of . . . service."); *Act of July 6, 1798*, 5th Cong., 2d sess., ch. 65, secs. 1–2, *U.S. Statutes at Large* 1 (1798): 576 (appropriating $400,000 for the purchase of 30,000 stands of arms, to be made available for sale to the states and their militia—with unsold arms available for borrowing by militiamen called into federal service); *Act of April 23, 1808*, 10th Cong., 1st sess., ch. 55, secs. 1–3, *U.S. Statutes at Large* 2 (1808): 490, 490–491 (appropriating $200,000 annually to purchase arms for distribution to the states in proportion to their militia enrollments).

53. For example, the *1798 Provisional Army Act* authorized the President, "in the event of a declaration of war against the United States, or of actual invasion of their territory, by a foreign power, or of imminent danger of such invasion," to raise an army of 10,000 men to serve for up to three years. (*Act of May 28, 1798*, 5th cong., 2d sess., ch. 47, sec. 1, *U.S. Statutes at Large* 1 (1798): 558.) The *1807 Insurrection Act* authorized the President to use regulars, as well as militia units, to respond to insurrections within states. (*Act of March 3, 1807*, 9th Cong., 2d sess., ch. 39, *U.S. Statutes at Large* 2 (1807): 443.)

54. See William Hogeland, *The Whiskey Rebellion: George Washington, Alexander Hamilton, and the Frontier Rebels Who Challenged America's Newfound Sovereignty* (New York: Scribner, 2006).

55. See Paul D. Newman, *Fries's Rebellion: The Enduring Struggle for the American Revolution* (Philadelphia, PA: University of Pennsylvania Press, 2004).

56. See "Fortifications: Copy of a Letter from the Secretary of War to the Secretary of the Treasury" (July 9, 1794), in *American State Papers: Military Affairs* (Buffalo, NY: William S. Hein & Co., Inc. 1993) (1861), 1: 105–106 (reporting initial disbursements of $104,025.52 for fortifying twenty-one coastal towns).

57. For example, following a series of aggressions by British ships in the early 1800s, residents of New York City demanded that the Congress do more to protect their harbor. When Congress made only modest allocations in the 1807 budget for harbor protection, the New York legislature issued a resolution exhorting the national government to meet its constitutional duty to protect the city. "Resolutions of the Legislature of the State of New York, Relative to the Defence of the City and Harbor of New York" (March 20, 1807), in *American State Papers: Military Affairs*, 1: 215. In 1808 Congress made available $1 million to fortify coastal towns (*Act of January 8, 1808*, 10th Cong., 1st sess., ch. 7, *U.S.*

*Statutes at Large* 2 (1808): 453), and out of additional fortification grants the next year in the amount of $1.2 million, $235,609 went to the New York City harbor. ("Report of the Secretary of War on the state of the fortification for the defence of the harbors of the United States," in *American State Papers: Military Affairs*, 1: 245, 1: 247.)

58. National Commission on Terrorist Attacks upon the United States, *The 9/11 Commission Report: Executive Summary* (Washington, DC: U.S. Government Printing Office, 2004), 9 ("[W]e can say with confidence . . . that none of the measures adopted by the U.S. government from 1998 to 2001 disturbed or even delayed the progress of the Al Qaeda plot. Across the government, there were failures of imagination, policy, capabilities, and management.").

59. *9/11 Commission Report* 396:

Recommendation: Homeland security assistance should be based strictly on an assessment of risks and vulnerabilities. . . . We understand the contention that every state and city needs to have some minimum infrastructure for emergency response. But federal homeland security assistance should not remain a program for general revenue sharing. It should supplement state and local resources based on the risks or vulnerabilities that merit additional support. Congress should not use this money as a pork barrel.

60. See Testimony of Michael R. Bloomberg, Mayor, City of New York, *Eleventh Public Hearing of the National Comm'n on Terrorist Attacks upon the United States*, May 19, 2004, 5, http://www.9-11commission.gov/hearings/hearing11/bloomberg_statement. pdf (criticizing funding formulas in which New York City received among the lowest per capita grants). Following years of criticism of federal allocations of homeland security funding, in 2005 the Department of Homeland Security ("DHS") announced it would allocate homeland security grants among states and cities based on an assessment of their vulnerability to attack. (See Shaun Waterman, "Security Grants to be Based on Risks; Population Size Less Influential," *Washington Times*, December 12, 2005.) In assessing risk, DHS relied upon input from governors, mayors, and local homeland security officials around the country. When the 2006 funding allocations were announced, New York City, which had received $207 million the previous year, was allocated only $124 million in funds. (See Audrey Hudson & Amy Doolittle, "Security Funds Shifted from New York, D.C. Area," *Washington Times*, June 1, 2006.) Federal law guarantees every state a minimum of 0.75 percent of State Homeland Security Grant Program funding. (*U.S. Code 42* (2002) sec. 3714 (c) (3).)

61. See *Printz v. United States*, 521 U.S. 898 (1997) (invalidating provisions of the *Brady Handgun Violence Prevention Act* because the Constitution prohibits Congress from requiring state law enforcement officials to enforce federal law, in this instance background checks); *New York v. United States*, 505 U.S. 144 (1992) (invalidating provisions of the federal Low-Level Radioactive Waste Policy Amendments Act because the Constitution prohibits Congress from commandeering state legislatures, in this case by passing a law to deal with radioactive waste within the jurisdiction of the state or to assume title to the waste).

62. Note, however, that the Constitution does not define "militia" and in passing the early militia laws Congress adopted and followed its own definition of the term. Congress, might, therefore, pass a modern statute specifying that the militia comprises local law enforcement and other first-responders. Alternatively, Congress might define the militia

broadly (to include every adult member of the population) but provide for calling forth that portion of the militia comprised of law enforcement and other first-responders.

63. See Susan N. Herman, "Introduction: National Authority and Local Autonomy in the War on Terror" (the Introduction to this book).

64. See Ann Althouse, "The Vigor of Anti-Commandeering Doctrine in Times of Terror," *Brooklyn Law Review* 69 (2004): 1231, 1274 (discussing how constitutional rights are protected when "[t]o carry out its programs, the national government...need[s] to inspire the confidence of the vast numbers of police and other personnel employed at the state, and, especially, local government level").

65. *9/11 Commission Report*, 396.

66. *The Federalist No. 25*, 158 (Alexander Hamilton).

67. Ibid.

# Index

# About the Contributors

ANN ALTHOUSE is Robert W. and Irma M. Arthur-Bascom Professor of Law, University of Wisconsin Law School.

VIKRAM DAVID AMAR is Professor of Law, University of California at Davis.

ERWIN CHEMERINSKY is Alston and Bird Professor of Law and Professor of Political Science, Duke School of Law and Duke University.

RONALD K. CHEN, formerly of Rutgers Law School, is now Public Advocate, State of New Jersey.

PAUL FINKELMAN is President William McKinley Distinguished Professor of Law and Public Policy and Senior Fellow, Government Law Center, Albany Law School.

SUSAN N. HERMAN is Centennial Professor of Law, Brooklyn Law School.

JASON MAZZONE is Associate Professor of Law, Brooklyn Law School.

ERNEST A. YOUNG holds the Charles Alan Wright Chair in Federal Courts Law, University of Texas Law School.